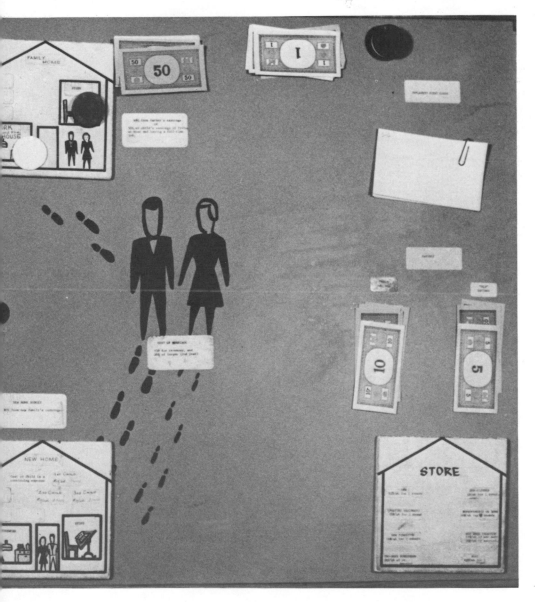

Adolescent Socialization in Cross-Cultural Perspective

Planning for Social Change

QUANTITATIVE STUDIES IN SOCIAL RELATIONS

Consulting Editor: Peter H. Rossi

UNIVERSITY OF MASSACHUSETTS
AMHERST, MASSACHUSETTS

In Preparation

Peter H. Rossi, James D. Wright, and Andy B. Anderson (Eds.), **HANDBOOK OF SURVEY RESEARCH**

Toby L. Parcel and Charles W. Mueller, **ASCRIPTION AND LABOR MARKETS:** *Race and Sex Differences in Earnings*

Published

Paul G. Schervish, **THE STRUCTURAL DETERMINANTS OF UNEMPLOYMENT:** *Vulnerability and Power in Market Relations*

Irving Tallman, Ramona Marotz-Baden, and Pablo Pindas, **ADOLESCENT SOCIALIZATION IN CROSS-CULTURAL PERSPECTIVE:** *Planning for Social Change*

Robert F. Boruch and Joe S. Cecil (Eds.), **SOLUTIONS TO ETHICAL AND LEGAL PROBLEMS IN SOCIAL RESEARCH**

J. Ronald Milavsky, Ronald C. Kessler, Horst H. Stipp, and William S. Rubens, **TELEVISION AND AGGRESSION:** *A Panel Study*

Ronald S. Burt, **TOWARD A STRUCTURAL THEORY OF ACTION:** *Network Models of Social Structure, Perception, and Action*

Peter H. Rossi, James D. Wright, and Eleanor Weber-Burdin, **NATURAL HAZARDS AND PUBLIC CHOICE:** *The Indifferent State and Local Politics of Hazard Mitigation*

Neil Fligstein, **GOING NORTH:** *Migration of Blacks and Whites from the South, 1900–1950*

Howard Schuman and Stanley Presser, **QUESTIONS AND ANSWERS IN ATTITUDE SURVEYS:** *Experiments on Question Form, Wording, and Context*

Michael E. Sobel, **LIFESTYLE AND SOCIAL STRUCTURE:** *Concepts, Definitions, Analyses*

William Spangar Peirce, **BUREAUCRATIC FAILURE AND PUBLIC EXPENDITURE**

Bruce Jacobs, **THE POLITICAL ECONOMY OF ORGANIZATIONAL CHANGE:** *Urban Institutional Response to the War on Poverty*

The list of titles in this series continues on the last page of this volume

Adolescent Socialization in Cross-Cultural Perspective

Planning for Social Change

IRVING TALLMAN

Department of Sociology
Washington State University
Pullman, Washington

RAMONA MAROTZ–BADEN

Department of Home Economics
Montana State University
Bozeman, Montana

PABLO PINDAS

Instituto Mexicano de Estudios Sociales, A.C.
Universidad Iberoamericana
Mexico City, Mexico

ACADEMIC PRESS 1983

A Subsidiary of Harcourt Brace Jovanovich, Publishers

New York   London
Paris   San Diego   San Francisco   São Paulo   Sydney   Tokyo   Toronto

ACADEMIC PRESS, INC.
111 Fifth Avenue, New York, New York 10003

United Kingdom Edition published by
ACADEMIC PRESS, INC. (LONDON) LTD.
24/28 Oval Road, London NW1 7DX

Library of Congress Cataloging in Publication Data

Tallman, Irving.
    Adolescent socialization in cross-cultural perspective.

    (Quantitative studies in social relations)
    Bibliography: p.
    Includes index.

    1. Socialization--Cross-cultural studies.
2. Youth--Mexico--Cross-cultural studies. 3. Youth--
United States--Cross-cultural studies. 4. Problem-solving
in children--Cross-cultural studies. 5. Social change--
Cross-cultural studies. I. Marotz-Baden, Ramona.
II. Pindas, Pablo. III. Title. IV. Series.
HQ783.T34 1983   303.3'2   83-2511
ISBN 0-12-683180-7

For Laura, Susan, Brett,
Pablo Alejandro, and Claudia del Rocio

Contents

Preface   xi
Acknowledgments   xv

1 Socialization in a World of Change   1

The Dilemma of Preparing for an Unknown Future   1
From Social Dilemma to Researchable Question   2
Basic Themes   6
Developing a Methodology   13
Basic Issues and Research Questions   17

2 Socialization, Problem Solving, and Social Structure   21

Socialization   21
Problem Solving: Processes and Outcomes   31
Social Structure   43
Conclusions   50

3 Socialization for Social Change: A Theory of Processes and Outcomes   53

The Scope of the Theory   54
The Basic Model   55
Parents, Their Child, and the Problem-Solving Process   56

Social Structure, Family Internal Structure, and Problem Solving   63
The Complete Model   71
The Social Context of Socialization for Social Change   72
Summary   78

4 Seeking the Answers   81

Introduction   81
The Research Sites   82
Planning for Cross-National Research   86
Instrument Development   87
Research Design   99
Summary   107

5 The Findings: Testing the Theory   111

The Community and the Family   111
Community Context and Parent–Child Socialization   120
Community Context and Children's Performance   132
Adolescent Problem Solving   140
Testing Alternative Explanations   147
Conclusions   148

6 Sex Differences   153

Sex Differences by Society and Class   154
Similarities in the Two Societies   174
Sex Differences and Socialization for Problem Solving   178
Conclusions   182

7 From Iron Cage to the Age of Narcissism   185

Evaluating the Theory   187
Revising the Theory   188
Coping Strategies in Mexico and in the United States   197
The Utility of SIMCAR   199
Socialization and Social Change in Mexico and
in the United States   208

Appendix 1:   Pre-Experimental Interview Schedule   219

Appendix 2:   Job Requirements   259

Appendix 3:   Family Unplanned Event Cards   261

Appendix 4:   Child's Unplanned Event Cards   265

Appendix 5:   Game Instructions and Rules: Mexican Version   273

Appendix 6:   Game Instructions and Rules:
              United States Version   279

Appendix 7:   Observations of Power and Support   287

Appendix 8:   Score Board   291

Appendix 9:   Post-Experimental Interview   295

References   297

Author Index   315

Subject Index   321

Preface

This book tells three stories, all related yet distinct. It tells about a theory of socialization, and how the theory was formed, developed, and changed. It describes a cross-national research project that employs new and innovative research methods for comparing people from vastly different cultures ranging from preindustrial to postindustrial. Finally, it tells about the dreams and plans of a group of families from the United States and Mexico, their attempts to implement their plans, and the consequences of these attempts for their adolescent children.

The theory begins with the premise that the better one learns how to solve problems in one's environment as an adolescent, the better one is able to cope with a rapidly changing, unpredictable society as one grows older. The specific task is to understand how such learning takes place. In undertaking this task we were confronted with the problem facing all attempts to develop socialization theories. That is, how can individuals be products of a society learning how to "fit in" and still be independent actors capable of changing the society of which they are a part? Increasingly, social psychologists have interpreted the relationship between the individual and the environment as one of mutual dependence and influence. How this mutual influence occurs, however, is not well understood and has been poorly studied. The theory developed in Chapters 2 and 3 proposes that the family provides an initial arena within which the needs of the individual and the requisites of the social structure are confronted. As a member of a family we begin the lifelong process of establishing an identity and thereby developing the duality of self by which we become both part of and distinct from society.

The family is seen as interpreting the social structure for its members as well as incorporating critical aspects of the social structure within its own structure. Therefore, social structure, as mediated through the family, plays a major role in effecting the identities people establish at a given time and the identities they wish to establish in the future.

Ours is a "story" about the theory because we go beyond the presentation of the theory's essential concepts, assumptions, propositions, and hypotheses. We trace what happens to the theory from its initial ideas to its eventual modifications. The modifications were necessary despite the fact that most of the hypotheses were supported by the data. But therein lies our tale.

Chapter 4 describes our approach to solving the methodological problems posed by attempting to test the theory through means of a cross-national study. In Chapter 7 we evaluate the results of that effort.

The research design called for a comparative study of families from blue- and white-collar communities from the Twin Cities of Minnesota in the United States and Zacapu in Michoacan, Mexico. A sample of rural peasant families from villages in Michoacan was also required. The data were gathered through interviews and observations of parent–adolescent interactions during a game simulation. The game was designed to simulate those aspects of the social structure that pertained directly and indirectly to planning a child's career beginning in late adolescence and extending over a 10-year period. The simulation enabled us to chart the career choices of family members over repeated game choices and, therefore, to identify different goal attainment strategies. It also enabled us to observe and to code the family members' interactions as they engaged in solving the problems posed by the game. Finally, we were able to simulate conditions of economic ease or hardship and to introduce the game equivalent of social change. In brief, we observed aspects of family interaction as they engaged in the socialization process as well as some of the performance outcomes of that process.

To our knowledge this is the first attempt to use a game simulation of this type in cross-national research. Consequently, we devote more space in Chapter 7 to analyzing issues relevant to the game simulation's validity than is common in research monographs.

The families described in this book differed in social status, occupational activities, income, parents' education, and the eductional and occupational opportunities available to their children. They also came from two very different countries. The United States was, at the time of the study, the most affluent and highly industrialized country in the world. Mexico was in the process of industrialization and modernization. However, these families shared in common an awareness that the world was rapidly changing and that the opportunities for adolescents entering adulthood would be different from those available to the parent generation. This awareness had a profound effect on the goals families set for their children and the behaviors adolescents employed to attain these goals. The data, presented in Chapters 5 and 6, support the frequently voiced claim that Americans are becoming personality oriented, "laid-back," and committed to the pursuit of pleasure. The Mexicans, on the other hand, especially the peasants, seemed committed to improving their economic situation through education, hard work, deferred gratification, and geographic mobility.

We also consider whether the adolescent's gender makes a difference in goals sought, skills learned, and identities desired. In one sense, we found what we expected. The ideology of *machismo* seemed to predominate among Mexicans, and the ideology of egalitarianism between the sexes was more prevalent in United States families. This ideology, however, did not have a profound influence on the actual career goals, power distribution, or sex-role segregation within the families. In fact, we found some dramatic reversals between sex-role ideology and actual behavior. For example, the females in the United States white-collar sample in many ways were less equal than any other group in the study.

In the final chapter we explore the implications of the data in view of current conditions in Mexico and the United States. We speculate as to how the adolescents in the study—now young adults—are dealing with the social changes occurring in the two countries. We also consider the implications of the data for predicting subsequent changes in both societies.

Acknowledgments

This project evolved within the framework of a research program conducted at the Minnesota Family Studies Center. We benefited greatly from a programmatic research grant from the National Institute of Mental Health. The grant, under the codirection of Reuben Hill, Murray Straus, Joan Aldous, and Irving Tallman, enabled us to plan projects sequentially with the intention of building a theory of family problem solving. If such a theory has, as yet, not been completed, the fault does not lie with the dedication of this group of scholars and the coterie of fine graduate students who committed themselves to the task, but rather with the complexities of the problem and the changing priorities of the investigators.

We gained much from the continued interest and involvement of Professors Hill, Straus, and Aldous. There existed in those days a "climate" that seemed charged with enthusiasm and excitement. We left our meetings with these three scholars always invigorated and with clearer insights as to how to approach our problems. We do not know what the elements are that make up such a "climate," but we believe much of it can be attributed to the special qualities of Hill, Straus, and Aldous and to the intellectual environment they created at the Minnesota Family Studies Center.

The development of the research reported in this book also benefited greatly from the summer-long seminars conducted at the Minnesota Center for the Comparative Studies in Technological Development and Social Change. The Center was headed by Robert Holt and funded by grants from the Ford Foundation. These seminars provided Tallman and, later, Marotz-Baden with the opportunity to exchange ideas and experiences with anthropologists, economists, political scientists, and engineers, all of whom had experience in cross-national and cross-cultural research. It was at these seminars that the idea of using simulations for comparative research was first considered. It was here, too, that the use of a game simulation as a means for modeling social structure and as a research methodology was initially proposed.

The Center also provided funds for Tallman and Marotz-Baden, along with other seminar members, to visit Mexico and the communities in Michoacan, which eventually became research sites.

It was also through the Center and the good offices of Reuben Hill and Robert Holt that Tallman and Marotz-Baden were introduced to the Instituto Mexicano de Estudios Sociales and to its director, Luis Leñero. The Instituto Mexicano de Estudios Sociales (IMES) became an indispensible vehicle in carrying out this project. At IMES, Pablo Pindas took major responsibility for planning the research in collaboration with Tallman and Marotz-Baden.

The Minnesota Center for Comparative Studies and IMES provided funds for two Mexican graduate students, Anna Roig and Guadalupe Zetina, to study at the University of Minnesota and work with the staff planning this research. Roig and Zetina, who also were on the IMES staff, were of invaluable assistance when we began gathering data in Mexico.

The research staff at the University of Minnesota participated in all phases of the study from conception to data analysis. Lance Wilson, Connie Bulbulian, Marilyn Ihinger-Tallman, and Rosalyn Cohen worked diligently planning and collecting data for the United States project. Their thorough understanding of the project combined with their abilities as interviewers, experimenters, and supervisors of other interviewers provided us with a highly competent and versatile group of colleagues. In Mexico, Anna Roig, Guadalupe Zetina, Ricardo Tirado, and Jorge Gutierrez worked closely with Marotz-Baden in performing the same functions as the United States staff.

Marilyn Sheean deserves special mention for her assistance in making the data ready for analyses and in organizing the thousands of pages of computer printout and hundreds of tables in forms that were readily accessible, readable, and easily understood.

Aid from our colleagues did not end when the research was completed. The writing of this volume benefited greatly from the advice and counsel of several scholars and friends. We are indebted to Bert Adams, Joan Aldous, Jeylan Mortimer, Charles Welch III, and Scott Long for their comments on the manuscript. Marilyn Ihinger-Tallman provided valuable assistance in identifying problems in organization and exposition. She also showed remarkable patience and durability in reading second and third drafts when one of the authors (Tallman) had reached the point where he could no longer stand rereading pages that had been rewritten so many times.

Reuben Hill's contribution to this volume was both subtle and profound. His questions, challenges, misgivings, and open disagreements provided a constant ballast for our tendency to soar into the stratosphere of imagination leaving the data far behind.

We must also acknowledge our special indebtedness to Roberta Simmons whose thoughtful and complete review of an earlier draft identified conceptual and research issues that we could not ignore. Roberta's comments resulted in our rethinking and rewriting large sections of the volume. She, therefore, is responsible for delaying publication of the book by several months. She also is responsible for the volume being much more thorough and exact than it would have been without her assistance.

If, despite the assistance of so many able scholars, this monograph is found wanting, it can only be attributed to the obstinance of the writers, who, when all was said and done, insisted on the last word. They must, consequently, bear responsibility for this book and its contents.

Margaret Davis, executive secretary for the sociology department at Washington State University, was indispensible to this project by keeping the department running despite the managerial ineptitude of Tallman who was serving as Chair at the time. Her good cheer and competence was communicated to the entire secretarial staff. Vicki Till, Anita Delgado, and Jan Miller typed various drafts of the monograph, managing always to find order in confusion.

We thank the Center for Political Economy and Natural Resources at Montana State University for the services of their editor, Marianne Keddington.

The research was supported by the National Institute of Mental Health grants 5 ROIMH 15521 and 1 ROIMH 26301 and The Midwest Universities Consortium for International Activities (MUCIA) #G-75.

Adolescent Socialization in Cross-Cultural Perspective

Planning for Social Change

1 Socialization in a World of Change

THE DILEMMA OF PREPARING FOR AN UNKNOWN FUTURE

In the winter of 1971–1972, Mexico and the United States were, as they are now, in the throes of fundamental change. Mexico was industrializing as rapidly as any country in the world. Its major cities were burgeoning in population and new industries; its middle class was growing in number of people and wealth. An increasing cadre of industrial workers were experiencing a standard of living never before attained in Latin America. Yet, in the midst of this change, the lives of the majority of Mexican peasants and lower-class workers were not significantly altered. The new wealth was being concentrated in relatively few hands. In Mexico in the 1960s, "The top 16 percent of the families received about half of the total income of the country (Stern & Kahl, 1968)." Based on 1960 census data, it was estimated that over 50% of the population lived in homes with only one room, 71% lived in homes without drainage, 68.4% lived without a water supply in the dwelling, and 64.6% did not have a radio or television (Gonzalez–Casanova, 1968). The inequities in the distribution of resources across classes and regions were viewed by many as evidence that the populist revolution of 1910 had failed in its goal of establishing a society that would benefit the peasant and the worker. Indeed, one of Mexico's most influential intellectuals, sociologist Pablo Gonzalez–Casanova (1968), devoted his considerable talents to a careful analysis of whether the time was ripe for another revolution in Mexico.

1

The United States in 1971–1972, at the apex of its power and affluence, was on the road toward losing the first major war in its history. It was a time of social and political turmoil; radical middle-class students were engaged in violent confrontations with police and their erstwhile brethren—manual workers, now termed *hard hats.* Intellectuals wrote of "The End of the American Era [Ashby & Stave, 1972]." Old values were being challenged and new uncertain values were being tested. The rate of change was viewed as one of the country's basic problems (Toffler, 1970). But in reality only a small percentage of the American population was directly involved in the turmoil. Despite much attention from the mass media, it was not clear whether Americans were changing too rapidly or whether there was a grow-ing resistance to change in the face of obvious worldwide social, political, and economic transformation.

The American rate of economic growth had slowed somewhat but pro-duction was sufficient to keep the vast majority of Americans consuming at a higher rate than ever before in the history of the human race. Daniel Bell (1968, 1973), popularizing the term *postindustrial societies,* pointed to the growing capacity of the highly industrialized nations to generate and in-tegrate knowledge and information at rates faster than human beings could possibly assimilate them. A small group of writers, generally ignored, pointed to the growing depletion of our finite resources (see Luten, 1978, and Catton, 1980, for historical reviews). There were serious doubts about how long the industrial countries could continue to develop at current rates (Daly, 1973).

For many sociologists, this was a period of assessing or reassessing theo-ries of social change. They were sensitive to the failure of their own and re-lated disciplines to anticipate the current state of affairs or to make knowl-edgeable forecasts of subsequent events. All that everyone seemed sure of was that rapid change was endemic and that all of us, whatever our present social conditions or the level of development of the societies in which we lived, should be preparing for a changing world. The question some were asking was, How do we undertake such preparation? It was this question, or more accurately, dilemma, that led to the study that is the subject of this book.

FROM SOCIAL DILEMMA TO RESEARCHABLE QUESTION

Daniel Bell (1968) posed the central problem as follows:

no longer would any child be able to live in the same kind of world—sociologically and intellectually—as his parents and grandparents had inhabited. For millennia—and this is still true in some sections of the globe, but they are shrinking—children retraced the steps of their parents, were initiated into stable ways and ritualized routines, had a common body of knowledge and morality, and maintained a basic familiarity with place and family. Today, not only does a child face a radical rupture with the past, but he must also be trained for an unknown future. And this task confronts the entire society as well (p. 149).

Bell's description highlights a key problem relevant to the rate and course of social change: How can an older generation prepare a younger generation for "an unknown future?" The question subsumes a number of related questions.

1. What behaviors and orientation best prepare people for a future that is unknown?
2. Can people who have learned (or failed to learn) to cope in one environment adequately prepare their offspring to cope in different environments?
3. What social conditions facilitate or hinder the process through which one generation learns from another ways to adapt to social change?
4. Is the current parental generation aware of ongoing social changes and the need to prepare their offspring for a world different from the one in which they currently live?

Most of this book is concerned with seeking answers to the first three questions. The fourth question can be dealt with immediately, at least for the parents who participated in the research to be reported here. The following statements are representative of the comments made by parents during interviews as they considered their children's future, and they serve as an informal introduction to the various groups of subjects of this research.

A peasant father from the Tarascan village of Tiríndaro, in the state of Michoacan, Mexico, talked about his plans for his 13-year-old son. "My wishes are that my children study some great field of study—so then they don't work in the country as I and my family have worked all this time. My hopes are that while I am living, I can do everything possible so that my children may go to school and study great things which aren't related to farming."

A Mestizo (mixed Indian and Spanish) peasant from another village spoke about his desire for his 12-year-old daughter to become a school teacher, "the environment that we are in, it is progress for us because it is easier for her (his daughter) to earn in life that way (as a teacher) than if she stays in the country."

A factory worker in the city of Zacapu in Michoacan, Mexico, discussed his desire for his son to be a factory worker. "A worker earns more than an office worker. His income is greater. But, of course, there is one problem. The office worker has an advantage. He doesn't have shifts, (yet) he lives a little . . . how should we say it . . . a little more falsely than a factory worker. He (the office worker) is troubled by more grievances and more economic problems and all those things."

A college educated employee of a bank in the same city talked of the things he wanted his daughter to realize. "Things like planning, organizing, distributing money, thinking if there will be money enough for one thing or another. Things like that." His wife adds, "For me, an intellectual woman (referring to the daughter) who knows more is better in a marriage. She understands her husband better. There is a comprehension and communication. More peace and love (says *peace* and *love* in English)."

A Minneapolis worker responded to an interviewer's question about his reasons for not emphasizing college for his son by saying that when he sees what is happening,

> More particularly in our immediate neighborhood, for people who are going to college, such as the big teacher wipe-out, and stuff like that, and . . . engineers with doctor's degrees pushing a cash register in a supermarket. The emphasis has been on high education, and I'm personally not knocking it, but it seems that there are too many people pushing pencils and there aren't enough people doing actual physical labor, and I think possibly right now we see that there is a big change in our nation's work force.

These statements, different as they are in language, style, and anticipated outcomes, share an essential theme: The world is changing for the parent as well as for the child. The parents' responses seemed to imply that what was important and relevant at this moment may not be important and relevant in the future. Thus, the concerns expressed by Daniel Bell and other social scientists were reflected by parents faced with critical daily decisions affecting their children's lives. "Social change," far from being an abstract concept, had meaning in the lives of parents concerned with their children's futures. Important too is the implication that these parents, regardless of background, were not committed to time-honored solutions to problems. For these people change implied learning and teaching new ways of coping with the environment. As we shall see very few of the families we will be describing, Mexican or North American, peasant, blue collar, or white collar can be considered "traditional" in the sense that they look to the past as a guide for the future.

In essence this study was designed to assess how families living with and being aware of social changes prepare their offspring to cope with a society that is changing in unknown ways. The process through which people are prepared to cope with society is generally referred to as socialization. We identify and measure those specific elements in the socialization process that pertain to coping with social change. The skills required to cope with social change are thought to be equivalent to the skills required for effective problem solving. Thus socialization for social change can be seen as equivalent to socialization for problem solving in a social setting. The study measures both the socialization process and socialization outcomes.

The families who participated in the study were selected to represent families living under different socioeconomic conditions in two countries, Mexico and the United States, countries which differed markedly in their level of economic development. A primary focus of this investigation was to determine how such conditions as material abundance or material scarcity, position in the social stratification system, and level of economic development influence the process and outcomes of socialization for problem solving.

These were the concrete purposes of the study. But the meaning of this research can be best understood if it is placed in a broader intellectual context. The research is relevant to at least four broad issues currently debated in the sociological literature.

First, achieving the concrete research goals necessitated developing a conceptual framework and a theoretical model based primarily on assumptions drawn from what has come to be known as the "exchange perspective." This perspective emphasizes the importance of relationships between people as the key element in human learning and action. Relationships are formed out of human efforts to attain maximum benefits from other people at the least possible costs. This research, then, is a test of an exchange based theory of socialization for social change.

Second, the study has implications for theories of social change and social development. Such theories have tended to emphasize different levels of analysis, stressing either the individual, the social structure, or the world configuration of societies. They have also differed on the priority they place on cultural variables (e.g., belief systems, ideologies, religions), as opposed to structural variables (e.g., stratification systems, distribution of occupations and roles, mobility opportunities, distribution of material resources). In this study the focus is on individual actors and the structural conditions that determine available options for action, thereby constraining and channeling behavior. The data gathered allow us to compare the relative behavioral affects of ideological versus structural variables. In Chapters 6 and 7 we consider the interplay between those variables and how they tend to influence each other. The research also provides an opportunity to expand on theoretical and empirical attempts to link the behaviors of individual actors to large-scale social events.

Third, the socialization process is explored within a single institution, the family. The family, of course, is not the only socializing agent in a society, though few would question the significance of its role in preparing the next generation to cope with the outside world. From the perspective of this research, the family is seen as mediating between society and the individual. As such, it reflects and interprets the society to family members. The relationships between family members are seen as the key to understanding how subsequent generations are prepared to cope with social change. Much of the data to be analyzed centers on the interactions that take place between parents and their child. From this perspective the research is an effort to contribute to knowledge about the mechanisms through which one generation transmits to the other not only information, values, and beliefs, but also ways of thinking about issues. In the broadest sense the study can be considered to contribute to knowledge about the family as a socializing agent.

Finally, the study employs a new methodology designed to meet the special problems posed by this research. The methodology has to be applicable to crossnational comparisons and must allow for observations of parent's and children's interactions while they plan for and cope with changing social conditions. To accomplish these ends, a mini-social structure was similated in the form of a game. The interpretation of the research findings depends in large part on the validity and meanings attached to the behaviors observed during the game simulation.

In subsequent chapters we describe in detail the conceptual framework, theory, research design, and methodology of the study. In this introductory chapter, we consider these components only in broad outline, identifying their essential elements and their underlying assumptions. We do not anticipate that these assumptions or the theory and methodology we constructed for this research will be universally accepted. As a consequence the data generated in this study may lend themselves to different interpretations than the ones we provide. An understanding of the sources of our ideas and possible biases may be helpful to the reader in making his or her own assessments. Some of the findings and conclusions we reach are contrary to conventional wisdom and are not in accord with other findings gathered at different times by different methods. It is possible, therefore, that our results may be viewed as controversial—all the more reason for making explicit the underlying premises upon which this work is based.

BASIC THEMES

Two themes predominate in this book. One pertains to the processes and outcomes of socialization, the other to social development and change. Socialization refers to a type of learning–teaching relationship in which novices learn ways of functioning in a social system. Social change refers to the transformation of a social system from a given state during one period of time to a different state during another period of time. Although the primary focus of this book is on how people learn to cope with social change, it also has implications for theories about how societies change. Efforts to link theories of socialization and social change are relatively rare, in large part because socialization involves the study of individuals in interaction and social change involves transformations in large scale or macro elements of societies. What follows is one conceptual approach to linking these two phenomena. In the concluding chapter of the book the issue is discussed in greater detail with the advantage of data and hindsight.

Social Change and Socialization

Despite at least a century and a half of consistent effort, social theorists have not succeeded in developing an integrated and parsimonious theory of social change that has attained any degree of consensus. This may be because of ideological overlay or philosophical predispositions, but part of the problem lies in the vast number of empirically identifiable sources of social change and part of the problem lies in the number of possible dimensions that should be included in any attempt to provide a comprehensive explanation. Social change can be precipitated by forces within as well as outside of the society; it can occur gradually or quickly; it can be evolutionary or revolutionary; it can be generated by the decisions or activities of an established elite or be the product of mass movements; it can be planned or the result of unintended consequences—the list of possible sources of change is almost interminable. It is probably for this reason that no adequate taxonomy of sources of social change exists.

The absence of a taxonomy contributes to the difficulties involved in theory development. At this level there is a continuing debate over the proper units of analysis required for explaining social change. Three levels are generally advocated, each successively larger in terms of the number of people involved and the scope of relationships included. The first focuses on the psychological and cultural characteristics of populations, emphasizing changing values, attitudes, cognitive styles, and culturally determined norms (see, for example, Hagen, 1961; Inkeles, 1969; Kahl, 1968; McClelland, 1961; Weiner, 1966). The second level emphasizes the institutional and structural arrangements within societies (Hoselitz, 1960; Smelser, 1966, 1968). From this perspective change is analyzed in terms of the growth or decline of the functions of social institutions such as the family, the polity, the economy, and the educational system, and changes in structural complexity and diversification within and between various institutions. Most recently there has been a growing emphasis on understanding social change within the context of world systems (Wallerstein, 1974). In general within this framework, change is analyzed in terms of the power and dependency of nations in an interdependent interlocking system (Chase–Dunn, 1975; Portes, 1976).

Despite heated debates about the merits of each of these perspectives, it is readily apparent that the three units of analysis are not mutually exclusive and that a theory of social change that integrates all three levels would be desirable (see Armer & Isaac, 1978, and Coleman, 1971, for discussions of the need for such integration). Whatever the precipitators of change— whether the product of the decisions of a small group of elites, the result of institutional or structural transformations within a society, or the consequences of shifts in international relationships—such change cannot be affected without altered behaviors on the part of people who make up the masses or nonelites of the society. Marx, despite his belief in the preeminence of historical and economic forces, recognized that the growth of capitalism depended upon a work force ready and willing to give up feudal ways. Furthermore, the next predicted change, revolution of the proletariate, would depend upon the growing class consciousness of the working class. Similarly, Weber (1930/1976, pp. 47–78) emphasized that the contribution of the "protestant ethic" to the growth of capitalism rested as much on providing a mass of laborers totally committed to a work ethic as it did on a capitalist class being ready to continually reinvest its profits. The actions and decisions of individuals in a given society, made on a daily basis and aggregated over thousands or millions of people, may not be sufficient to produce social change, but they are certainly necessary if changes are to take place.

These actions and decisions are the product of socialization and the progenitor of socialization for the next generation. Consider a peasant family in a country that is rapidly modernizing. A new institution is introduced into the community. The institution may be a school, a health service, an agricultural cooperative, a credit organization, or a modern factory. The family must make decisions concerning their relationship with and use of the institution. Should parents send their children to the new school or keep them home to work on the farm? Should the family farm be brought into the new cooperative to make use of the credit facilities or continue in the old mode and avoid indebtedness? Should family members seek employment in the factory and entail the risks of a breakdown of family ties and possible sudden unemployment? At a more subtle level, given these choices, how should the family invest its resources? Will they seek to maintain the farm and work in the factory only when the farm does not demand attention? Will they keep their children in school no matter what the economic cost, or will they remove them to work on the farm at times of economic difficulty? Whatever the decision, there also will be an implicit or explicit evaluation of the benefits or losses consequent to the decisions. Is the family better off? Are the children better prepared than they would have been if an alternative route had been selected? Through observation as well as direct participation in the decision process, children learn reasonable, appropriate, and desirable life goals. They also learn something of their chances of achieving such goals and the appropriate strategies for goal attainment. Such learning results from experiences that are part of a changing society—it also contributes to the course of social change.

Socialization for Social Change

As a practical matter, however, most socialization is not concerned with social change but with individual change. The study of socialization generally centers on a specific outcome or goal. Thus research attention is focused on socialization into designated occupations, sex roles, social positions, and so forth. Until recently, most theories of socialization sought to explain how people learned to fit into a particular group or social system. In short, they were theories of conformity (Wentworth, 1980, pp. 21–39; Wrong, 1961). The classic theorists in this field, George Herbert Mead (1934) and Charles Horton Cooley (1909), set as their task the understanding of special capabilities of humans to organize themselves into complex social collectivities and to communicate and transmit the essential elements of a social order from generation to generation. It was a formidable task and it generated a lengthy and useful body of theory and research. Yet change occurs and people must also learn to respond to changing social conditions. An adequate theory of socialization should be able to account for when and how people learn to adopt new behaviors as well as to conform to established norms. Socialization *for* social change, therefore, should be considered a subset of the more general phenomenon.

In this book the emphasis will be on testing a theory of socialization for social change, but implicit in this work is a framework for a general theory of socialization. The primary difference between the theory presented and the general theory is in the selection of specific variables. For example, socialization, as we define it, consists of two essential elements, one behavioral and the other situational. The behavioral element is also divided into two components—a process and an outcome. The socialization process is an ongoing, reciprocal system of interactions in which all individuals involved, regardless of their social roles, are both learners and teachers (Tallman & Ihinger–Tallman, 1977). Thus parent and child, professor and student, employer and employee, when they are engaging in socialization, are simultaneously learning and teaching. The issue, for the theoretician and researcher alike, is what exactly is being taught and learned? This, of course, depends on the particular outcomes of interest. The outcomes of most interest in this book are those behaviors that enable people to function effectively in a society whose opportunities and demands are changing. "Effective" functioning means the ability to adapt to environmental changes so that life chances for achieving desired goals are maximized. This ability depends on having access to appropriate information and the capacity to process that information so that barriers to achieving goals may be identified, alternative routes for overcoming the barriers may be evaluated, and courses of action may be decided upon. Since the specific barriers are not necessarily known beforehand and since the means for overcoming these barriers change over time, the ability also implies a pragmatic, flexible orientation and a readiness to take reasonable risks under conditions of uncertainty—in brief, the ability to *solve problems*. We conclude therefore that problem-solving experiences within a social environment represent the essential processes within which socialization takes place, and the ability to problem solve under conditions of social change is the key outcome variable. The exact nature of this process and the hypothesized outcomes are discussed in Chapters 2 and 3.

The decision to make problem solving a key aspect of this research was determined in part by prior research and interest in family problem solving (Straus, 1968, 1972; Straus & Tallman, 1971; Tallman, 1970; Tallman & Miller, 1974). It was also influenced by a body of research concerned with identifying the individual values, attitudes, and behavioral orientations associated with functioning in changing modern societies (Feldman & Hurn, 1966; Inkeles, 1966, 1969; Kahl, 1968; McClelland, 1961; Smith & Inkeles, 1966). Problem-solving behavior could, in fact, be subsumed under Inkeles's (1969) concept of "individual modernity," a behavioral set considered necessary for living in industrialized societies (see Straus, 1972, for a discussion of the relationship between the ideas of problem solving and modernity). Individual modernity, according to Inkeles, requires the following set of personal qualities: *(a)* openness to new experiences; *(b)* independence from traditional leaders like parents and priests; *(c)* abandonment of passivity and fatalism; *(d)* personal ambition for upward mobility; and *(e)* planfulness.[1]

---

[1] We differed in one essential way from those researchers and theorists who stressed the importance of individual modernity in understanding the course of social change. Problem solving was emphasized because social change implies an unpredictable future. Scholars emphasizing individual modernity claimed that a growing cultural homogeneity resulted from industrialization. Consequently, they argued, it was possible to designate the individual attributes necessary for functioning in the modern world (e.g., see Kahl, 1968, p. 3). This assumption, in our view, was not consistent with the available data (e.g., see Bell, 1968, 1973, for a discussion of rate of change in highly developed countries; Horowitz, 1966, pp. 335–363, for a discussion of variations and unevenness of development in third-world countries; Armer & Schnaiberg, 1975; Gusfield, 1967; and Portes, 1976).

The socialization process and outcome usually takes place within some social context (Gecas, 1981). At the broadest and most abstract level, the social context may be a social system, social environment, social structure, or social situation. At a more concrete level, it consists of specific institutions such as the family, the school, the neighborhood, the work place, and the community. Not only does socialization take place within a social context, but the learning involved is frequently contextual. Socialization often occurs indirectly by virtue of the individual's being part of a group and sharing the group's experiences and fate.

In brief, people learn how to act within societies through interactions that take place within social institutions—institutions that are themselves embedded within a larger social system. For this type of learning to take place, the institution must reflect or interpret essential aspects of the larger society. In this book we have selected one of these institutions—the family. Although no claim is made for the exclusivity of the family as a socializing agency, a case can be made for targeting the family as a good place to find the answers we are seeking. Socialization occurs in many social contexts, but it occurs with the most regularity and over the broadest range of behavior in the family. It is the one institution involved in the socialization of children that is common to all societies, regardless of their level of development (Levy, 1966).

Although, as illustrated earlier, parents seem aware of social change, it is not likely that in the essential daily tasks of work and raising children they think very much about how to prepare their children for such changes. In fact, it is most likely that parents' socialization activities take the form of assisting children to function within rather than outside of the family (Elder, 1968, p. 2). On those occasions when parents do consider their children's futures, they are likely to identify specific career goals and life-styles. Rarely do they consciously proceed to train their children to be effective problem solvers. Such socialization, when it occurs, takes place indirectly: Children learn feasible goals and strategies through observation, identification, and personal experience. Learning occurs by virtue of being members of a family facing and dealing with problems on a daily basis. Children cannot easily detach themselves from their families' successes or failures—their fates are intertwined. It is within the context of family functioning as an integral part of a changing social system that children learn the attitudes and skills for coping with their society.

The impact of family problem-solving experiences is probably greatest when children reach adolescence, a time when they project themselves into the world as social beings, seeking to integrate their sense of self with the perceived demands of family, peers, and society. According to Erik Erikson (1950), adolescents seek to structure cohesive, internally consistent identi-

out of a morass of conflicting demands. An important component in developing such identities is a sense of competence or personal efficacy (Bandura, 1977a, pp. 78–80, 1977b; Elder, 1968, p. 22; Smith, 1968). The maturational and social development that characterizes adolescents corresponds with a level of intellectual development that Piaget describes as enabling them to project into the future, to hypothesize, to plan, and to evaluate potential outcome (Flavell, 1963, p. 15). In brief, to learn to problem solve.

Adolescence is a time when tentative life plans are formulated (Elder, 1968, p. 25). Decisions that affect the future career of the child become salient not only for the child, but for the entire family. Should the child follow his or her parent's occupational path or seek new career routes? How much education or training is necessary? Are the costs worth the possible gains? Should the adolescent work part-time or devote all of his or her efforts to an education? If chances for getting ahead are better away from home in another community, should the adolescent leave family and friends? Should families deprive themselves of desired goods and services for the benefit of their children's futures?

How these questions are answered depends upon what life-styles people wish for themselves and their children. It has been argued, for example, that one source of resistance to modernization in the less developed countries is the priority given to familistic concerns among peasant populations (Rogers, 1969a; Maccoby, 1967).[2] Conversely, people in urban and industrialized countries are thought to have a greater commitment to individualism and to social and geographic mobility (Goode, 1963, p. 12).

Social goals are usually weighed against judgments of what is possible. Information about available opportunities in the community and the larger society, knowledge of the requisite skills and abilities required for specific jobs, and the accessibility of training must be evaluated against the adolescent's personal skills and attributes. Adolescents, independently and in concert with other family members, make decisions on a regular basis about how much time should be invested in study, work, and interaction with friends and family as well as how much money should be spent on education or other career-related activities rather than meeting current family needs and desires. These decisions are based on family members' prior experiences, their access to information about the future, their capacity to process available information, their confidence in the ability of their children, and the degree of optimism with which they look forward to future events. All of the preceding decision-determining factors are, from our perspective, affected to a significant extent by the level of development of the

[2] We will propose an alternative hypothesis in Chapter 3.

society and the families' position in the society's stratification system. This book assesses the correctness and usefulness of this perspective.

In sum, this research centers on families with adolescent children living under different social conditions. It explores whether and how social conditions such as social position and level of societal development are associated with families' and their adolescent children's life-style goals and problem-solving behaviors and adolescents' ability to problem solve under conditions of social change.

DEVELOPING A METHODOLOGY

There seems to be general agreement among students of socialization that the individual learns how to function in a society through interacting within that society. There is also growing support for the position that the individual is not a passive actor in this process. Despite variations in method and theory, most studies implicitly accept the principle proposed by Thomas and Znaniecki (1918, p. 14) that "The cause of a social or individual phenomenon is never another social or individual phenomenon alone, but always a combination of a social and individual phenomenon (quoted in Blumer, 1939, p. 9)." The principle is congruent with Bandura's (1977a, p. 194) concept of "reciprocal determinism." According to Bandura, "psychological functioning is a continuous reciprocal interaction between personal, behavioral, and environmental determinants." It is interesting that Bandura and Thomas and Znaniecki arrived at the same principles while using the methods of different disciplines and seeking to explain somewhat different phenomena. Bandura was concerned with explaining individual functioning; Thomas and Znaniecki were concerned with explaining social change as well as individual functioning. This melding of perspectives seems appropriate given the principle that neither social forces nor individual forces by themselves are sufficient to affect the course of events.

The methodological problem is how to isolate the essential social and behavioral elements, measure their interaction, and determine outcomes of that interaction in individual and social functioning. Students of socialization have generally focused on values and role performance as their indicators of the relevant social conditions. Thomas and Znaniecki, for example, were concerned with the value and role changes commensurate with the transition of people from rural nonindustrialized societies to highly industrialized urban areas. Others were concerned with cultural lags in which rapid social change resulted in anachronistic and ineffective roles (see Ogburn & Nimkoff, 1965). Still others focused on role implications of social catastrophies (e.g., Elder, 1974) or on the value and role implications of different rates of economic growth (e.g., McClelland, 1961).

Implicit in these studies is the notion that changing social conditions (however specified) produce changes in prior learned values and role expectations. Conversely such changes affect current social conditions. At a minimum, therefore, this type of research requires meeting the following four conditions:

1. Assessing the relevant social and individual variables in at least two time periods
2. Identifying those social conditions that affect socialization processes in period one and the socialization outcomes in period two
3. Identifying those key social conditions that have undergone change between periods one and two and the particular values and roles affected by that change
4. Evaluating the appropriateness of the socialization outcomes for period two and/or identifying the utility or lack of utility of the content of what was learned in period one for period two

Given these conditions, it is not surprising that much of the relevant research has tended to be retrospective or historical. These methods provide the investigator with information about current and past social conditions and the changes that have occurred, enabling the person to evaluate the appropriateness of learned values, role expectations, and role behaviors for such conditions. The investigator can then seek to reconstruct the socialization process that brought about the observed values and behaviors.

Erik Erikson's (1950) account of the social roles adapted by the young Sioux is an example of such an analysis. Using a case study method, Erikson described how the young Sioux male was socialized in the ways of his father to ride, hunt buffalo, and be a fearless warrior in an era when such roles were anachronistic in the dominant society. Beginning with a socialization outcome, Erikson sought to discover the process that produced the outcome. Erikson's work, however, is not restricted to documenting cases of maladaptive socialization. Using this method and his own perceptive talents, he has been able to identify critical linkages between life experiences and social conditions (see *Young Man Luther*, 1958).

Research reported by David McClelland (1961, pp. 107–158) used a content analysis of folk and children's stories to demonstrate the high incidence of achievement motivation in societies prior to periods of economic growth and the decrease of such motivation that accompanied economic decline. McClelland also provided data to illustrate the relationship between maternal pressure on children for independence and achievement and children's achievement motivation (1961, pp. 345–373). Differences in such socialization for achievement are reported cross-nationally, between social classes, and for ethnic and religious groups. The use of comparative data in these analyses adds an important dimension to understanding how social conditions are linked to socialization and the behavior of individual members of the society. By comparing societies and cultures, McClelland was able to illustrate the linkage between economic advancement in the society and the achievement motivation in the individual. (See also Bronfenbrenner, 1970, and Devereux, Bronfenbrenner, & Suci, 1962, for other examples of cross-national studies of socialization. See Lee, 1977, for a review of such studies.)

Glen Elder's study, *Children of the Great Depression* (1974), represents a somewhat different approach to the use of historical data. Elder sought to determine the effect of a major catastrophic event—the Great Depression—on family experiences and on the life careers of children who underwent such experiences. Like Erikson, he began his research knowing a considerable amount about the group he was studying: They were children of the depression who participated in World War II; they produced the baby boom of the 1950s; they raised the adolescents and young adults of the tumultuous 1960s. Elder analyzed data from a longitudinal study designed initially to examine the growth and development of children. Using level of economic deprivation as the precipitating social experience, he explored a wide range of dependent and intervening variables beginning with family adaptations to economic deprivation and including family organization and family interpersonal relationships. He also examined a large number of individual values, attitudes, and behaviors relevant to sex and family roles, status attainment, life-styles, and personality development. Elder's design can be envisioned as a funnel with the narrow end containing a single independent variable—the Great Depression—and gradually including an ever-widening array of intervening and dependent variables. The large end of the funnel includes a variety of personality characteristics, values, and indicators of status attainment. Although problem solving was not Elder's primary dependent variable, he nevertheless considered the relationship between deprivation and coping behavior; we shall have reason to refer to his findings in the latter portion of this book.

Our research faced the same methodological problems as the studies just mentioned. We also needed to devise a methodology that could measure social and individual variables at two points in time, to identify socialization processes in one time period and socialization outcomes in another and to assess these outcomes in the light of specific types of societal change. However, the question that was the springboard for this research, How does one generation prepare the next generation for an unknown future?, mitigated against a retrospective design. Perceptions and judgments of prior events are inevitably biased by knowledge of the present. This may not be a problem for some research purposes but it looms significant when we are seeking to understand how people deal with an unknown future. Behavior in the face of the unknown should be quite different from attempts to explain the known, retrospectively.

Our solution was to simulate a social structure and observe how parents and their early adolescent children planned the children's careers over a 10–year period. We then simulated social changes and observed how the children adapted to those changes. The simulation was carried out in the form of a game that parents played with their children and, subsequently, the children played alone. Participants in the game invested time and money in a variety of educational, recreational, religious, social, and occupational activities, some of which contributed directly to obtaining jobs, status, and money. The game simulation, described in Chapter 4, is a model of that part of society that differentially rewards people for investments of time, resources, and effort. It allows us to observe family socialization at one point in time and children's problem solving under conditions of social change at another point in time. At both points, the focus is on that aspect of the social system that provides payoffs in exchange for people's investments. This method was preferable to a longitudinal panel study because it eliminated the possibility of attrition—a problem of considerable concern in a comparative study in which out migration would be greater in some communities than in others. The simulation also allowed us to control possible confounding variables that could have had a vital effect on the results; for example, an increase in job opportunities in another community might remove a large number of fathers from the home, a national policy could change the availability of education to children, a natural disaster, such as a volcanic eruption could change the value orientations and life goals of families. In short, the very issue we sought to study, social change, could in a longitudinal study make it difficult, if not impossible, to test our hypotheses. Finally, the simulation allowed us to hold constant the conditions for measuring performance, thereby enabling us to test hypotheses pertaining to how family and structural conditions influenced a child's performance. For example, how much of the plight of the poor is attributable to the performance limitations of poor people and how much to lack of opportunities? The only way to adequately answer this type of question is to hold the opportunity structure constant for rich and poor alike.

There is another aspect of society, however, that is important for this research. Most behavioral scientists believe that people's life goals and life strategies for attaining goals are greatly influenced by the environment in which they grow and live. If this is true then it follows that socialization processes and outcomes will vary in different environments. In Chapter 3

we formulate hypotheses predicting a relationship between social environmental conditions, life goals, and socialization processes and outcomes. To
test these hypotheses we sampled families from different social strata in a
highly industrialized country, the United States, and in a developing, modernizing country, Mexico. This design possesses its own methodological
problems, not the least of which is the problem of comparing different cultures. The efforts to resolve this and other problems are discussed in Chapter 4.

BASIC ISSUES AND RESEARCH QUESTIONS

Parents do not rear their children in a social vacuum, unaffected by the
environment in which they live. There is general agreement that human
behavior is the product of the interaction between environmental conditions and individual attributes. Despite this agreement, however, there is
considerable debate as to how much each element influences socialization
outcomes. The debate is not mere hairsplitting; rather, it addresses basic assumptions about social reality. Its importance extends beyond explanations
of socialization processes and outcomes to theories of social change.

David Scudder (1982) has described the debate as centering on two fundamental philosophical issues. The first has been variously termed the
"subject–object," "mind–body," or "thought and being" problem. The second concerns the appropriate levels of analysis in the study of social phenomena. Although the two problems are not entirely independent, scholars
who take a particular position on one problem do not necessarily share the
same position on the other. In his discussion of the subject–object problem,
Scudder notes the predominance of two overarching theoretical orientations which he labels "cultural idealism" and "materialism." The cultural
idealist perspectives emphasize the primacy of ideas, beliefs, and values as
determinants of action. The materialist perspectives stress the ways material conditions constrain and channel behavior. The approach we have
taken generally falls under the materialist rubric. Social conditions are seen
as critical in influencing people's life goals, how they interpret and process
information, and how they develop goal attainment strategies. Yet, we
share with many cultural idealists an unwillingness to anthropomorphize
society. In our view, societies are abstractions incapable of volitional acts;
only people are actors. But, to paraphrase W. I. Thomas, having been
created and treated as real, societies have real consequences. Human decisions made by agents of social institutions have an affect on people who
may have played no part in the decision process. Wars, depression, short-
ages of resources, inflation, job opportunities, systems of stratification,

rules governing rewards and punishments affect the physical and social environment of everyone in a given population, regardless of their role in producing these conditions.

It is this environment that represents the reality with which people must learn to cope. It provides both the opportunity for attaining the goods and services we want and the constraints that limit the ways we can go about acquiring these things. The goals we establish for ourselves and the strategies utilized are, in the first instance, dependent upon our social position and the particular opportunities and constraints associated with that position. We, as actors, may proceed to change the way the stage is set but such change derives only from the original conditions with which we are confronted.

This concept of the relationship of the environment and the individual is not compatible with theories based on the primacy of ideas as determining the course of events. The difference has practical as well as theoretical consequences. In its basic sense a cultural–idealist perspective of change would stress the importance of changing people's minds in order to affect events. Those with a materialist perspective would argue that as social conditions change, people's minds change accordingly. To state the obvious that both are necessary is to obfuscate the central question of how change is induced. Will the course of social change be facilitated by introducing structural changes in a society or must such changes await basic alterations in people's attitudes and values? This research is based on the assumption that most often ideas are a consequence of prevailing social conditions and that changes in these conditions will, given reasonable lag time, result in changing attitudes and values.

In our earlier discussion of theories of social change, we indicated that the focus of our analysis would be on individual behavior. Such a focus is in sharp contrast with the orientation of some theorists strongly influenced by the Durkheimian tradition. "Macro theorists," Scudder (1982) points out, "contend that the whole is qualitatively different than the sum of the individuals involved and that social change must be explained by propositions that account for the structure of macro social relations (p. 4)." From this perspective individual actions are predetermined by laws pertaining to macro phenomena. Poulantzas (1969), for example, maintains that the individual is only the conduit through which structural behaviors are manifest. Therefore, efforts to develop linkages between individual and collective behaviors are by definition unnecessary. Similarly, Ekeh (1974) claims, "Social institutions, norms, and values grow out of the moral mandates of society (p. 185)." From this perspective society is no more an abstraction than is the human being. It is capable of acting under its own laws which are not necessarily linked to the laws determining individual behavior.

The individual perspective stresses the need to understand the basis for individual commitment to collective action. Such commitments focus on the ways in which the individual agrees to and accepts collective mechanisms of social control and develops a social identity (Homans, 1964; Tallman & Ihinger–Tallman, 1979). Those who hold this perspective argue that deductive theories are impossible at the macro level because macro theories cannot explain how social orders are formed (see Homans, 1964). Popper (1959) maintains that macro theories can only make projections on the basis of trend analysis rather than reach predictions derived from propositions.

Our position is not as absolute as Popper's. We seek to understand how individual actors influenced by identifiable social conditions socialize their children to cope with a future society. We recognize that the individuals involved in the socialization process are influenced and constrained by a variety of social institutions, but these institutions themselves are the product of human actions.[3] Thus we envision a dynamic interplay between social conditions, behavioral responses to such conditions, and subsequent social change. The central element in this formula is social behavior; social behavior, we suggest, is determined in large part by socialization. As we consider the correspondence between the data collected in 1972 and the social changes that have occurred since then, we can estimate the part parent–adolescent socialization in the 1970s may have played in fostering the social changes that have occurred in the 1980s. In a broader sense we shall seek to understand to what extent the study of socialization contributes to an explanation of the course of social events.

---

[3] It should be noted that we do not include in this conceptualization nonhuman constraints in the environment such as weather, wind, geographic topology, and available material resources. These conditions are eliminated only because their inclusion would expand the scope of this study far beyond its original purpose. We believe, however, that aspects of the physical environment play a role in influencing the socialization process.

2 Socialization, Problem Solving, and Social Structure

This investigation focuses on a specific type of socialization process and outcome. The process takes place between parents and their adolescent children as they engage in joint problem-solving activities. The outcome is the ability of the children to solve problems pertaining to obtaining career goals under changing social conditions. A basic assumption guiding the study is that the content, form, and quality of the socialization process and its outcome are largely affected by the social structural conditions in the communities where families live. In all, five concepts—socialization, problem solving, community, family, and social structure—form the cornerstones for our theory and research. In this chapter we attempt to explicate these concepts in order to (a) facilitate an understanding of their centrality for the theory of socialization for social change to be presented in Chapter 3; and (b) lay a foundation for explaining the steps taken in this research to interpret the concepts through observational measures and sampling techniques. We begin the analysis with the most pivotal concept, socialization, with special reference to adolescent socialization.

SOCIALIZATION

Adolescence can be considered as the transition period between childhood and adulthood (E. Campbell, 1969; Elder, 1968; Lewin, 1953). During this period the child's future as an independent, self-sufficient person becomes an impending reality. Elder (1968, p. 25) notes that this "developing vision of the future" includes the formation of life plans which involve establishing goals and the "means priorities" for attaining those goals. Adolescence is a time when present activities are likely to be interpreted in terms of their implications for the future. It is a time when a child "tries on" a variety of nonfamily roles and seeks to develop new competencies in educational, occupational, interpersonal, religious, recreational, and consumer social arenas. These new roles are accompanied by an increasing self-consciousness concerning the child's developing identity, an identity that is simultaneously linked with and separate from family, peers, and community (E. Campbell, 1969; Elder, 1968; Erikson, 1959).

Developing future plans, learning new roles and competencies, and forming identities are all part of a socialization process in which the parent–child relationship, past and present, is inextricably involved. The research evidence strongly suggests that despite fledgling efforts at independence and the growing influence of the peer group, the parent–adolescent relationship continues to have a significant influence on the child's development (see E. Campbell, 1969, pp. 827–833). To adequately understand the relevance of parent–adolescent socialization for our theory of socialization for change we need to first examine the elements that make up the socialization process and outcomes.

Defining the Concept

Despite a history of varying definitions and shifting emphasis, the concept of socialization seems to be universally applied to the problem of explaining how individuals and society interrelate. Its wide usage attests to its importance in sociological and social psychological thinking. Given such wide usage, it is somewhat surprising that there is so little agreement as to the concept's properties. (See Wentworth, 1980, pp. 13–40, for a chronological review of the various uses, meanings, and criticisms of *socialization*.) Much of the difficulty seems to lie in arriving at a definition of socialization that is sufficiently precise to be empirically useful while maintaining its appropriateness to the wide range of behaviors, events, and social conditions to which it is commonly applied (Gecas, 1981).

Confusion also results because the concept is applied differently, depending upon the theoretical perspective used. For example, the structural functionalist perspective has tended to focus on explaining how individuals are integrated into the social order (see Inkeles, 1968; Parsons & Bales, 1955); whereas the symbolic interaction perspective has emphasized how the social structure influences personality development, self-concepts, social identities, and so forth (see Gecas, 1981; Stryker, 1979). Structural functional explanations of how individuals fit into social groups have been criticized for contributing to an overly conforming view of society, ignoring the autonomous, creative, and self-assertive components of the individual (Di Renzo, 1977; Gecas, 1981; Wentworth, 1980; Wrong, 1961). Conversely, efforts to explain the development of autonomy and creativity in the individual do not contribute to an explanation of social order and intergenerational continuity. An adequate theory of the socialization of individuals requires explaining the development of both conformity and autonomy in persons as they take their place in social groups. Similarly, from the societal perspective an adequate theory should explain how socialization contributes to both social order and social change (see Inkeles, 1968; Pitts, 1961, pp. 685–701).

Underlying these general problems of application lie the more specific conceptual problems of identifying the elements that make up socialization processes and outcomes. For example, implicit in the term *socialization* is the notion that novices learn ideas and skills that enable them to function in social groups. But what precisely is being learned and taught? Is socialization different from any other type of teaching or learning that goes on in a society, or is all learning and teaching socialization? If socialization is distinguishable from other learning, what is its special content? If it has a special content, how is it transmitted? Also, since socialization pertains to individual behavior in social groups, what part do groups play in the learning process and its outcomes?

These questions are not new, nor is there a shortage of proferred answers; they have been the subject of considerable debate among students of socialization for over a century. To engage in the debate here would require a lengthy analysis that would detract from the purpose of this book.[1] Instead we shall describe our approach to solving the conceptual problems discussed earlier. The intent here is not to demonstrate the superiority of our perspective over others but only to indicate its appropriateness and adequacy for building a theory of socialization for change and for testing such a theory.

Our approach is an amalgam of three perspectives: symbolic interaction, social exchange, and social learning theory. We propose that the key to understanding the socialization process lies in understanding the processes of identification and identity formation. Forming an identity establishes an individual's bonds with specific social groups while specifying the person's uniqueness and capability for independent action. *Socialization*, as we shall define it, involves learning the roles and personal characteristics (both for

---

[1] For the interested reader, there are numerous excellent reviews of the various theoretical perspectives. See, for example, Clausen (1969), Di Renzo (1977), Mortimer and Simmons (1978), Wentworth (1980), and Gecas (1981).

oneself and for others) normatively attached to particular identities within a social group. The learning takes place at visceral, cognitive, and motor levels. One learns how people with given identities act and feel as well as think. Establishing an identity requires demonstrating the behavioral skills, values, attitudes, and feelings associated with that identity in a given social group. Identities, however, are not formed entirely through the volition or acts of the individual, nor are they merely the result of being labeled by others. Identities are the product of a consensus reached between the actor and those who are part of his or her environment. It is a consensus forged over time through subtle, often nonverbal interactions and negotiations.

The content of socialization, therefore, pertains to the skills and knowledge involved in negotiating identities. What is learned can be summarized under the following five categories:

1. The types of social positions, statuses, roles, and, consequently, social identities that actors hold or may hold within a given social context (see Stryker, 1980, pp. 53–65 for a more detailed discussion of this content)
2. The behavioral, affectual, and belief traits attributed to people with specified social identities in a given social context
3. The behavioral, affectual, and belief elements required to negotiate specific identities in a given social context
4. The expected reactions or reciprocal actions of others in response to a given action
5. The regularities (i.e., norms, commitments, loyalties, system related interdependencies) that govern the behavior of people within groups, thereby enabling groups to act as units (see Cartwright & Zander, 1968, pp. 485–502, for a discussion of such regularities; see also Swanson, 1974, for a discussion of the logic of group action)

By absorbing this content individuals learn the elements that make up their own identities as well as the identities of others in the social structure. They also learn the skills necessary to negotiate identities. Finally, they learn the types of interactions that are defined as legitimate and illegitimate within the group and the positive and negative sanctions that can be brought to bear as a consequence of the actions that are taken. Thus, adolescents begin to associate certain positions with privileges, power, and authority, and to anticipate the way power and authority will be used in given situations.

An identity locates a person in a social system (Stone, 1962). Being part of a social system, however, does not negate one's individuality. Identities have personal as well as social aspects (Goffman, 1963). The social aspects of identity refer to the broad social categories that are used to distinguish people and to establish behavioral expectations; they include gender, religion, occupation, nationality, status, and so forth. The personal aspects of identity refer to the unique ways people play out their roles and relate to others in their environment.

Still another aspect of identity that contributes to variation and individuality is its temporal quality. Identity involves past, present, and future (Gordon, 1968). Thus two people may hold the same social position at the same point in time but have quite different identities because of different pasts and the possibilities of different futures. Consider, for example, two 24-year-old male construction workers; one with a college degree in English literature with aspirations of becoming a novelist, the other a high school dropout with aspirations of maintaining a steady job to support his family. A major difference in the identities of the two workers lies in their pasts and anticipated futures.

Socialization content may be learned directly, as when conscious efforts are made in medical schools to convey the values, manners, and beliefs thought to be associated with the position of physician (Becker, Geer, Hughes, & Strauss, 1961). Most often, however, socialization takes place indirectly as an unintended, or at least, implicit consequence of an ongoing relationship. The relationship, in turn, takes place within a larger social context that places limits on information available to the actor and, therefore, determines the "reality" to which the individual is socialized. Thus, socialization is defined here as: A *process in which individuals living in a given social context learn, through interactions with each other, the particular identities extant within their social context and the ways to establish, maintain, and transform such identities.*

To understand the use to which we put this definition we need to explore the nature of the process as it is manifested in the parent–child relationship.

The Socialization Process

We begin with the assumptions that all human beings are satisfaction seekers, and that they will seek to maximize satisfactions and minimize the costs of obtaining them.[2] Later in this book, after we have explained our

---

[2] This assumption is relevant not only to the theory developed here, but to most exchange, decision, game, coalition, and problem-solving theories (see Heath, 1976, pp. 7–50). The assumption is also the basis for the criticism that the exchange perspective leads to tautological arguments in which "any action can be said to maximize one's gain (P.S. Cohen quoted in Emerson, 1976, p. 345)." This would be true if the assumption were allowed to stand alone. We use it as an orienting premise, which is not testable but which is an assumption in a theory that leads to testable predictions.

theory and research design and analyzed the findings, we will consider the utility of these assumptions. For the moment, they are presented as a guide to understanding our interpretation of the elements that make up the socialization process.

Socialization occurs in the course of a relationship. To focus on the individual or on a learning process is to focus on only part of a total equation. The process involves teaching as well as learning, and, like most relationships, it is a dynamic situation in which teaching and learning behaviors tend to be reciprocal (see Bronfenbrenner, 1979; Zigler & Child, 1973, pp. 23–31). We suggest that, despite the socially prescribed roles depicting parents as teachers and children as learners, these behaviors are less fixed than might be expected. A more reasonable description of the parent–child socialization process views parents and children alternately as teachers and learners. According to Harriet Rheingold (1969) this is true even for the parent-infant relationship. Rheingold acknowledges the obvious influence of the parent on the child but also notes, "The infant . . . may be thought of as socializer of his parents. He instructs them in the behavior they must display to insure his normal growth and development. He is an effective member of society to the extent that he fashions his caretakers into parents; he organizes a family out of separate individuals (p. 789)."

The parent–infant example provides the extreme case for the point we wish to make. Since the infant is almost totally dependent upon his or her parents for survival (a condition which gradually lessens as the child grows to adolescence, the significant period for our research), one might expect the parent's power over the child to be absolute. But, for a variety of social, political, economic, and biological reasons, the parent is also dependent upon the child. If the child behaves in ways desired by the parent, the parent feels gratified or is gratified from other sources (spouse, in-laws, friends, etc.). If the child does not behave in desired ways, the parent experiences distress, just as the child is distressed if the parent does not respond in a gratifying way. The parent must learn from the child how to get the child to behave in accord with parental desires, just as the child must learn how to get the parent to behave according to his or her desires.

Socialization occurs as an interactive process between people who have a relationship with each other and are dependent upon one another for the exchange of a broad range of goods and human services. This does not necessarily imply that the power relationship between parents and children is symmetrical. Parents control too many resources for this to be the case. We assume that as the child reaches adolescence the power relation is somewhat more in balance.

The problem faced by both parent and child is how to accommodate each other's desires. In extreme cases such accommodation may not take place, resulting in parent desertions, child runaways, high levels of parent–

child rancor, and child abuse. Despite great variations in patterns of ity and role definitions, however, most parents and children seen work out mutually satisfying relationships. The basic transaction t___ une form of parents providing for their children's sustenance, nurturance, and physical needs, and the child adopting the behavioral modes, values, and beliefs desired by the parents. If the parent's expectations are appropriate to their children's maturational development and capacities, then it is likely that the transactions will be mutually satisfying.

Identity Formation and the Identification Process

Parents are usually the initial interpreters of the external world for their children. Consequently, their interpretations become the first reality to which children learn to adapt. In addition, since conformity to parental expectations is usually rewarded, both parent and child find the child's behavior satisfying. As a result, the child is likely to repeat these behaviors and to eventually internalize them (Aronfreed, 1969; Scott, 1971). The process fosters a high degree of similarity between parents' and children's behavioral orientations, values, and beliefs (see E. Campbell, 1969, p. 827; Hill, 1970, pp. 42–47). The extent of such similarity tends to be ignored in the research literature, especially the literature on adolescents, perhaps because investigators have a greater interest in analyzing parent–child conflict. Generational conflicts do exist and theories of such conflict are valid and valuable (see Elder, 1968; Hill, 1970; Erikson, 1950, 1959, 1968). For the most part, however, these conflicts tend to be resolved in favor of continuing positive parent–child relationships. Parents and children, even adolescent children, tend to agree on highly valued issues such as those pertaining to life-styles and life goals (see Brittain, 1963; E. Campbell, 1969, pp. 827–828; Hill, 1970, pp. 43–47). These similarities provide a basis for identification with parents and the formation of an individual identity (Bandura, 1969).

Identification with parents usually begins early in life.[3] Nonfamily members in the community label children in terms of their family membership from birth. Such identification becomes much more salient, however, when children become aware of an external community. For most children it is only after they have interactions outside of the household, with peers, in schools, in neighborhoods, and so forth, that they notice that others hold different perspectives and world views. Thus, they gradually become aware

---

[3] The assumption that identification is a necessary element in the socialization process is the prevailing viewpoint of students of socialization (see Gecas's, 1981, summary). However, for those who define learning as solely a product of operant conditioning, identification, or any other concept that infers motivation, is not considered useful. (For a cogent defense of this position see Scott, 1971, pp. 146–154.)

of their differences from others while becoming more conscious of commonalities with their families. This process sensitizes the child to an outside world that is generally less supportive than the family, thereby strengthening the family bond and reinforcing the sense that family members share a common fate and must rely on each other.

Children learn in many ways that their fates are linked with that of their families. The celebration surrounding a sibling's success in school, a better life-style associated with a parent's business success, the discomfort associated with a family member's failure to be promoted, and the pain surrounding the disgrace or arrest of a family member all attest to the interdependence created by the family bond. The net effect is that in most cases one's self-concept probably cannot be completely separated from the family's collective experiences (see Turner, 1970, pp. 65–95, for a thorough discussion of the formation of identity bonds and their linkage to self-concept). This relationship between collective family experiences and self-concept becomes relevant in the next chapter when we consider how family problem-solving experiences affect children's socialization as problem solvers.

Family identity is not so completely determined by the larger society that the individual is helpless to alter or affect that identity. Despite formidable obstacles, it is possible for parents or children to break the family bond. For the most part the bond is a consequence of the attraction parents and children hold for each other and their joint family membership. This attraction is based on the capacity and readiness of each to gratify the other. In essence, the benefits of family identification generally outweigh the possible benefits of breaking family bonds. This seems to be true even during adolescence when the question of the child's forming an identity separate from parents and family takes on added importance (Douvan & Adelson, 1966; Elder, 1968; Erikson, 1962). The quest for an independent identity requires adding new, more autonomous roles without necessarily nullifying the earlier elements of identity that link the child to its family (Gottlieb & Ramsey, 1964, p. 33). Elder (1968, pp. 45–48) reviews a body of research that suggests that adolescents who perceive their parents as competent and rewarding models are more likely to develop autonomous orientations (see also Haan *et al.*, 1968, and Smith, 1968).

Thus far identification has been considered a bonding or belonging process. It is also a motive for learning. Not only does most socialization take place informally and indirectly, much goes on without ever directly involving the learner. If socialization depended entirely on direct experience, our lives would be much more precarious. As Bandura (1969) states:

"If social learning proceeded exclusively on the basis of rewarding and punishing consequences, most people would never survive the socialization process. Even in cases where nonsocial stimuli can be relied upon to elicit some approximation of the desired behavior, and errors do not result in perilous outcomes, people are customarily spared exceedingly tedious and often haphazard trial-and-error experimentation by emulating the behavior of socially competent models (p. 213)."

Such learning is also desirable from the perspective of the parent–child relationship because it avoids direct confrontations which force people into win–lose situations requiring the application of power—situations that produce tense and uncertain learning environments.[4]

Identificatory learning derives from a sense of commonality in a social system. It does not, however, imply mere imitation. By observing models one learns how *not* to behave as well as how to behave (Bandura, 1971). Furthermore, depending upon the diversity of behaviors available to the observers, this type of learning also contributes to the individual's capacity to develop new or creative responses (Bandura, 1977a, pp. 48–49; see also Swanson, 1974). In the next chapter we develop the proposition that such diversity depends to a large extent on diversity in the social structure (Stryker, 1980, p. 79).

The relationships between parents and children are part of larger more complex networks of social relationships. Such larger networks provide the context in which the individual learns about society and how to cope with it.

Contextual Effects

Although the parent–adolescent relationship is the central focus of this investigation, its contribution to socialization processes and outcomes is best understood when observed within a social context. All relationships are embedded in larger networks of patterned interactions called social structures. Through the interaction and identificatory process discussed above, we learn our relative positions within a network. These positions provide the opportunity to interact and engage in transactions with persons holding other social positions. Two attributes of these networks are particularly important for our purposes: (*a*) the networks are characterized by a division of labor in which specified tasks or roles are attached to particular positions; and (*b*) the networks do not link all positions with all other positions. Consequently, all people do not have the same opportunities for obtaining desired goods or services. These attributes contribute to heterogeneity and inequality within networks, two conditions which Blau (1974) suggests are endemic to all social structures.

---

[4] The identificatory process depicted here is portrayed in general terms as a learning principle. It varies, as we shall see, with social structure. Peasant children, for example, are probably exposed to far less diversity in potential models and viewpoints than United States urban children.

Locating one's particular position within a heterogeneous and unequal social structure is a key element in forming one's social identity both in the present and in the future. By identifying with a group and defining oneself as different from members of other groups, a person claims a particular social position with its accompanying roles, status, and life-style. The individual, in assuming an identity, thus takes responsibility for learning designated roles, assessing appropriate sources of information, and engaging in interactions with certain groups in the social structure. Identity thus links the individual to the environment and consequently influences future goals as well as the strategies available for attaining those goals.

In brief, social structural conditions channel people toward adopting and maintaining certain identities. Having identified their own positions, they become aware of differential statuses, power, resource control, and life-styles. They also become aware that, as part of their social identity, their life chances are different from others with different social identities.

Some of this learning is the result of direct tuition. A father tells his children in many ways, "You are a member of the Cruz family. We have a proud tradition in this village. The most important people will listen to you when they know you are a member of this family." Or, "We are not like the Sanchez family, they do not own land, they drink and they don't work hard—no one pays attention to them." Most of the time, however, such learning takes place through observation and vicarious experience. A peasant boy observes the deference his father pays to a potential employer, or someone with political influence. He also observes how such people treat his father, their virtual disregard of his presence and lack of concern for his opinions or well-being. Through this process much is learned about status, power, available opportunities, reasonable goals, and effective strategies. The observational process may also influence the child's sense of personal efficacy; his father's successes or failures may be felt as his own.[5]

Children also learn that their fate and the fates of those with whom they identify are not always subject to their own control; the building of a factory in a community, the closing of a school, changing the tax structure all im-

---

[5] It is, of course, conceivable that a child may not identify with his or her parents. This seems relatively uncommon (E. Campbell, 1969, p. 827) but, when it occurs, it is likely to occur because parents fail or are unable to provide an adequate model for their child. That is (a) there exist more attractive (i.e., more competent, potent, or rewarding) alternative models in the child's environment; (b) the parent can be discredited on the basis of values and norms accepted in the collectivity; and/or (c) the child is unambiguously rejected by the parent (see Bandura, 1969, pp. 248–249; and Bronfenbrenner, 1970, pp. 134–139 for a discussion of modeling). Alternative models are most likely to exist within social structures that provide for a diversity of roles and multiplicity of identities (see Stryker, 1980, pp. 65–84) for a discussion of social structure, roles, and identity). Relatively simple structures such as peasant villages therefore should be less likely to provide alternative identificatory models than complex structures such as those that exist in urban industrialized communities.

pinge on the lives of parents and children alike. Understandably, the awareness that events are controlled by external forces tends to be more pronounced among the poor and less privileged segments of a society (Gurin, Veroff, & Feld, 1960; McCloskey & Schaar, 1965). It is less clear, however, how external events affect the individual's self-concept (Rosenberg & Pearlin, 1978). Simmons, Rosenberg, and Rosenberg (1973) present data from a study of 2625 Baltimore schoolchildren indicating that the children who were in the early stages of adolescence (the age group of concern in our research) were more likely than younger children and somewhat more likely than older adolescents to have lower self-images. The investigators suggest that this decline in self-image may be due, in part, to the sudden changes produced by going to junior high school, an external event that decreases the child's sense of control and security. Bandura (1977a, 1977b) makes an important distinction between "efficacy expectations" alluding to an actor's sense that he or she can behave effectively in a given situation, and "outcome expectations," which may not be under the actor's control. For example, an adolescent may have a strong sense of self-efficacy concerning his or her ability as a student while also being aware that economic or social conditions are such that the skills learned in school may not be in demand and, therefore, unmarketable. The unanswered question, however, is what are the long-term direct and indirect effects of an unrewarding environment on the child's sense of efficacy and therefore on his or her life goals and subsequent actions. In this study we consider the consequences of external unplanned events on subsequent problem-solving behaviors. In general, the social context for the parent–child relationship is thought to account for how the social structure is interpreted as well as the forms of interactions that take place within the family. We propose that the social position of families within the social structure is a major source of influence on the goals that are sought for the child and the strategies designed to obtain those goals. Under conditions of social change problem-solving skills become important elements in determining these strategies. Therefore, problem-solving experiences involving family members seeking to attain goals within their social structure represents an important aspect of the child's socialization for social change. In the following section we describe essential components of this experience.

PROBLEM SOLVING: PROCESSES AND OUTCOMES

Engaging in problem-solving behavior requires the perception of a situation as a problem. The first step in explicating the problem-solving process, therefore, requires identifying the elements that make up a problem.

Defining a Problem

Four elements are proposed as integral to all problems:

1. There is a goal that is desired but not yet attained.
2. There are barriers to achieving the goal.
3. There is some level of uncertainty that the barriers can be overcome.
4. The means for overcoming the barriers, though not immediately apparent to the actors involved, are believed to be potentially attainable.

The presence of barriers and the uncertainty about the eventual solution are characteristics that differentiate problems from other means–ends situations. For example, an individual's attempt to attain a specific occupational goal, such as becoming a physician, is problematic because the person has to overcome barriers, such as achieving high grades in college, being accepted by an admission board, and so forth.

This emphasis on uncertainty is consonant with one conventional meaning of the term *problem*. Excluded from the definition, however, is the familiar use of the term as a detrimental or damaging event. In this latter usage, events may or may not be amenable to solutions and outcomes are not always in doubt. Thus, the death of a family member in our usage is not a problem, whereas the social and emotional reorganization of the family subsequent to the death is a problem. We define a problem, then, as any *situation involving an unachieved goal in which the means for overcoming barriers for achieving the goal though not immediately apparent are considered feasible and potentially attainable.*[6]

By *goal* is meant any desired or desirable anticipated outcome resulting from group or individual activity. *Barriers* is defined as those sets of personal, social, or material conditions that impede the group or individual from attaining the goal. *Means* signifies any set of material resources, verbal or motor skills, and cognitive competencies that, when appropriately utilized, enable people to attain their goals.

Career Planning and the Problem-Solving Process

Problem-solving behavior refers to those activities that are intended to overcome barriers for achieving a given goal, and the problem-solving process represents a sequential set of decisions and actions directed toward fa-

---

[6] This definition and the definition of *family* which follows later in this chapter are drawn from Tallman and Brent (1974). These definitions evolved from seminars, research, and theory development on family problem solving conducted at the University of Minnesota from 1968 to 1974. (See, for example, Tallman, 1970, and Tallman, Wilson, & Straus, 1974.) Klein and Hill (1979) use similar sources for their definitions of *problem solving* and *family*.

cilitating such behaviors. The particular set of decisions and actions depends upon the kind of problems an individual or group is seeking to solve. The problem of interest in this book involves the family's efforts to establish life-style goals for the adolescent and to realize those goals as the adolescent progresses toward adulthood. For purposes of brevity we shall refer to this problem as "career planning."

Two types of goals, terminal and instrumental, are relevant to career-planning problems. Terminal goals are broad, overarching expectations that establish the general parameters of the desired life-style; they represent the endpoint of a given problem-solving endeavor. Instrumental goals are desired achievements considered to be a facilitating step toward the terminal goal. Instrumental goals are more specific and generally are more amenable to change and modification than terminal goals. Consider a family that sets as its terminal goal that their adolescent son will become a wealthy adult. Suppose that when the adolescent is 13, the family members believed that becoming an engineer would enhance the boy's opportunities for becoming wealthy. However, when the boy reaches the age of 18, the initial assessment that a career in engineering leads to wealth might be challenged by subsequent evidence. It may seem that engineers rarely attain more than middle-level salaried positions, or that the chances for their son to become an engineer are poor, or that there will be too many engineers on the labor market by the time the boy completes his education and training. If the terminal goal of wealth is paramount, the family may select an alternative career in banking, business, politics, or some other perceived route to financial success. Thus the terminal goals that represent long-range fundamental values persists, whereas instrumental goals (becoming an engineer, banker, and so forth) are subject to change to keep them in the service of the terminal goal. Such flexibility seems necessary if effective problem solving is to take place.

The preceding example illustrates an important characteristic of career-planning problems. In this type of problem, both the goals and the barriers to achieving such goals are located within the social structure. It follows that much of the information needed to guide decision making must emanate from and be concerned with the social structure. Thus the sources of information the family members use in making decisions are often external to the family. This suggests that some of the members of the family, usually those who are working or studying away from home, will have greater access to such information than other members of the family. Later in this chapter we consider how access, as well as the amount and type of information available within a given social structure, affect actors' abilities to process, integrate, and utilize information. For the moment however, our concern is not with information-processing ability, but with how information about the social structure influences the decision-making process.

Making a decision involves choosing a particular course of action from two or more alternatives (Simmons *et al.*, 1977, pp. 235–236; Bachrach & Baratz, 1970, p. 39; Tversky & Kahneman, 1981). We can assume that actors will choose the course of action that they perceive provides them with the best chance of obtaining their instrumental goals and, in the long run, their terminal goal. A key question is how much information about any given alternative or the number of available alternatives will decision makers seek prior to making a choice? It is a question which has plagued students of decision making for many years. In our opinion, no universally satisfactory answer has been provided (see Simon, 1976; Janis & Mann, 1977; Simmons *et al.*, 1977). The available evidence does not point to any clear-cut pattern of information search and decision making. Simmons and her colleagues (1977, pp. 241–250) report that persons who decide to donate their kidney for a transplant operation do so almost instantaneously, without deliberation and without any conscious search for information. At the other extreme, Leik and Tallman (1977) suggest that, under certain crises conditions, actors may postpone making a decision for seemingly interminable periods of time, preferring to wait for additional information which they hope will provide a definitive answer to their choice dilemma.

How do actors decide when they have enough information to make a decision? The most prevalent answer to this question assumes that actors will seek to maximize or optimize their desired outcomes (see Camilleri & Berger, 1967). It is also assumed that an effort will be made to choose an alternative that provides the best possible outcome. It follows from these assumptions that seeking to maximize outcomes requires an extensive information search and evaluation. The probabilities of success for all possible courses of action must be weighed against the costs involved with each alternative, and the consequences of failure must be weighed against the reward potential. Recent critics have argued that the optimizing strategy is empirically unlikely and theoretically unreasonable. These critics maintain that actors do not have access to complete information about alternatives or the number of available alternatives; moreover "determining all of the potential and unfavorable consequences of all the feasible courses of action would require the decision maker to process so much information that impossible demands would be made on his resources and mental capabilities [Janis & Mann, 1977, p. 22]." Finally, it is argued that the optimizing strategy does not take into account competing goals and values, making it difficult to maximize one value at the cost of another. For example, actors may deliberately seek to moderate rather than maximize their goal of income or wealth if that goal is perceived to be at the cost of family well-being (see Janis & Mann, 1977, p. 23–24). Based on criticisms such as these, Herbert Simon (1976, p. xxix) has suggested that decision makers will generally not seek to maximize their outcome but rather will look for courses of action that will meet a minimal set of requirements. These requirements establish a "good enough" or "satisficing" criteria for outcomes. He reports that most business decisions follow this satisficing format.

The problem, of course, is how to determine what constitutes a "good enough" outcome? In some situations it may be very close to the maximizing or optimizing solution, whereas in others it may be achieved with minimal concern about the possibility that better outcomes exist. The available evidence provides no definitive answer to this question. Certain criteria seem to be emerging, however. Some problems require quick decisions, others allow for more deliberation; some problems are solved with less information than others, either because the information available will not help solve the problem or because there is little available information. In general we suggest the following five criteria are relevant in estimating the amount of information to be sought prior to making a decision: (a) the *time frame* within which the problem must be solved; (b) the number of *alternative choices* that are available; (c) the perceived *alterability of decisions*; (d) the *task requirements* necessary for overcoming the barriers to goal attainment; and (e) the degree of *control over possible outcomes* available to actors.

Career planning for adolescents covers a relatively long time frame with no clear-cut deadline required for finally evaluating the success or failure of the outcome. This is especially true if outcome is measured in terms of attaining the terminal goal. The problem-solving process involves a developmental sequence in which a variety of skills must be learned in seeking intermediate instrumental goals (see Newell & Simon, 1972, pp. 847–848; and Tallman *et al.*, 1974, pp. 18–20, for a discussion of time parameters as distinguishing characteristics of problems).

The number of career routes perceived as being available are greater in some social structures than in others but in any case, it is not likely that families would seek to examine all possible routes. More likely the family will accept the first route that fits the adolescent's talents and family values and proceed to test its utility for the child. Many of the choices made during adolescence, especially early adolescence, are tentative and reversible. It is a time when learning from experience is not as costly as it might be when the child is an adult away from the family or responsible for his or her own family. Here the satisficing principle seems eminently reasonable since a lengthy search would be costly and once completed would probably not offer much additional assurance that the outcome would be successful.

The relatively long time frame, the lack of a specific deadline, and the number of alternative routes combined with the fact that most career-planning intermediate decisions are not irrevocable, suggests that continued monitoring and processing of information will occur with periodic evaluations over a period of years. This is especially likely since the stakes are relatively high. In career decisions there is no neutral point. Every adolescent will end up with one career or another.

The fact that career planning is imbedded in the social structure implies that problem solving requires learning appropriate procedural, analytical, and regulatory rules. Social structures are maintained by systems of norms that regulate social interactions. In the career-planning problem, both instrumental and terminal goals are achieved by attaining specified social positions. The means through which these positions are attained requires knowledge of the normative system. Adolescents seeking a given adult position must follow established procedures, such as obtaining the required education or training, undergoing proper prerequisite experiences and apprenticeships, mastering appropriate skills, and displaying these skills in appropriate forms and places. Learning the skills and determining the timing and relevant forms for their display requires the utilization of rules of analysis. Finally, knowledge of regulatory rules helps the person avoid breaking (or being caught at breaking) the rules governing proper conduct in competition for designated positions.

Information pertaining to rules relevant to a given social position is most likely acquired from sources outside of the family. The need for external information from a variety of sources implies that career-planning problems are best solved when various family members cooperate in sharing available information. Family members not only provide necessary information, advice, and support, but also play a critical role in skill training. Thus it is not likely that an adolescent could effectively solve the problems involved in attaining career goals without the coordinated efforts of other family members. It would seem that the task requirements for a career-planning problem fall somewhere between what Kelley and Thibaut (1969) and Steiner (1972) label "conjunctive" and "disjunctive" problems. Conjunctive problems require all, or most, members of a group to make coordinated contributions to the problem solution, whereas disjunctive problems can be solved by the efforts of one person. Accordingly, conjunctive problems require effective group organization to mobilize appropriate actions from all group members. Disjunctive problems, on the other hand, need the best ideas possible, and such ideas can come from any single group member. A group solving disjunctive problems, therefore, should encourage the free flow of communication from group members (Maier & Solem, 1952; Tallman *et al.*, 1974, pp. 26–27). The problem under consideration here may be termed *quasi-conjunctive*. Reaching an appropriate solution is likely to require the contribution of more than one and less than all family members. It is conceivable that an adolescent might solve his or her career problems independently of family assistance, but it is highly unlikely. The quasi-conjunctive nature of the problem suggests that a family organization, which coordinates and channels information, and a climate that allows for free flowing discussion can provide the most effective problem-solving environment.

No matter how competent a career plan may be, the planners have only partial control over the outcome. As we noted in our discussion of socialization, an important component of learning to function in social structures is the developing awareness that events occur in which the actor is not directly involved but which, nonetheless, influence his or her life chances. Since the actors in a social structure generally share a common culture, they are also likely to share many of the same values. We can assume, therefore, that competition exists for the most highly valued positions. In addition, the relative scarcity or abundance of a given position as well as the requisite criteria demanded for holding the position will vary with social, political, and economic conditions. Given these conditions, career planning takes the form of a strategy in which actors make estimates about changing social conditions and the nature of the competition, and plan courses of action accordingly. Strategies involve tentative plans of action and anticipation of the actions and reactions of others. Strategic planning is therefore always contingent planning in which various forms of negotiation, bargaining, coalitions, and cooperation are employed (see Tallman *et al.*, 1974, pp. 31–34).

As noted earlier, during early adolescence, career-planning choices are more easily altered if or when they prove unsatisfactory. When the adolescent approaches adulthood, commitments to courses of action have more lasting implications and consequences. We assume, therefore, that over the adolescent years, family members will seek to gradually reduce their level of uncertainty concerning the outcome of choosing a particular career route. Two sources of information are particularly relevant in this process; one internal to the family, the other external. Internally, the family seeks to draw on its members' skills and knowledge in assisting the adolescent to learn appropriate role performances. Most important, however, is an assessment of the adolescent's skills and performance abilities to play designated social roles. Externally, the family seeks information regarding changing rules and opportunities in the social structure. However, such information will only be partially effective in reducing the family's uncertainty about outcomes. Most families do not have access to adequate information about current social and economic trends. Moreover, even if such information were available it is not clear that it would assist in reducing the family members' level of uncertainty about conditions 8–10 years in the future. The forces operating outside of the family's control are so numerous and complex that successful prediction is extremely difficult not only by family members but by governments, scientists, and other "experts." In the face of this uncertainty, families are likely to make their choices on the basis of their assessment of the adolescent's ability, the continued monitoring process that occurs, and the experience of family members, kin, and acquaintances (see Ornstein, 1976). Given rapid social change the key ability that may affect the adolescent's future career is not the specific skills learned but the more general ability to solve problems in the face of changing conditions.

In broad outline we suggest that family decision making relevant to career-planning problems will be concerned with the following six questions:

1. Is the situation a problem?
2. Do the actors wish to do anything about it?
3. If yes to 2, which alternative course of action should be chosen?
4. Is the alternative course of action acceptable?
5. If yes to 4, and subsequent to the action, is the outcome satisfactory?
6. Should the problem-solving effort be continued or terminated? (See Newell & Simon, 1972, pp. 88–104, for a detailed discussion of such decision processes.)

The decisions relevant to questions 1 and 2 depend, in part, on the values actors place on specific outcomes. Given our assumptions about human motives, we infer that the more highly valued a potential goal, the more motivated actors are to seek the goal. The search for alternative means—question 3—involves the motivation to search out information and the ability to process that information. Questions 5 and 6 refer to the evaluation of the success and failure of problem-solving activities and estimation of the probability of future success. Thus three processes—goal formation, information processing, and evaluation—constitute the essential minimal elements in problem-solving behavior. Each of these elements will now be discussed.

Goal Formation

The instrumental and terminal goals pertaining to life-styles are key elements in the effort to locate the adolescent in the social structure. Consequently, they are integral to the adolescent's developing identity. For example, if a child is identified as a member of a poor family and is a good student, planning to go to college and medical school in order to become a pediatrician, that child is located in the social structure. Furthermore, the child is located in the past, present, and future, and the roles associated with the present and future positions are designated and evaluated (see Gordon, 1968, for a discussion of time tenses and self concept; also see Stryker, 1980, pp. 130–134).

The value (defined here as preferential ordering) placed on given life-style goals reflects more than a simple assessment of the potential gratification to be obtained from some end state (e.g., money means one can buy things); it also reflects how the actor wants to be viewed by others in his or her environment (e.g., a wealthy person with status).

How can we explain the formation of these values? Rokeach (1973) provides a clue about how such preferential orderings take place. He reports two values that best distinguish those who are poor from those who are rich. They are "emphasis on being clean" and "having a comfortable life." The poor ranked these values highest and the rich ranked them lowest.

> The low ranking of clean by the rich may be interpreted to mean that the affluent take cleanliness for granted, rather than they do not care about it. Its high ranking by the poor suggests . . . that those who must live under squalid conditions regard cleanliness as a very salient condition indeed. . . . As with clean, the poor may value a *comfortable life* highly because they lack it and the affluent considerably less because they possess it (p. 62).

We interpret Rokeach's statement as implying that the principle of "diminishing marginal utility" is applicable to the formation of human values.[7] This principle states that the "additional utility derived from consuming successive units of a product will *eventually* decline as the utilization rate increases (Gwartney, 1977, p. 74)." It follows that the more one possesses of a product, service or amenity, the less scarce it will be and the less it will be valued.

This research focuses on goods, services, and amenities that are generally considered essential to human survival—and are amenable to social change. The three most prevalent indicators of social change reported in the literature are income distribution, rates of industrialization, and lifestyle. These indicators involve decisions in two primary domains: One includes material rewards such as money, jobs, and property; the other includes rewards associated with interpersonal relationships such as affection, feelings of closeness, and respect.[8] These two domains represent the primary life-style goals in this research.

[7] Rokeach (1973) maintains that this is only one means among many of forming values. For the values of importance in this book it is the primary basis for value formation.

[8] Gurr (1970, pp. 26–27) proposed three categories of values, or, more accurately, value domains, as generic to most of the problems people face. These were welfare values, power values, and interpersonal values. In this book, we are concerned with the first and third of these categories. See also Tallman (1976, pp. 59–60).

Although we can reasonably assume that most people would like to maximize rewards in both domains, sociologists from Toennies to Parsons have argued that maximizing one is often done at the cost of the other. A number of investigators have demonstrated that commitment to social relationships, such as familism, is at the cost of material advancement (Kahl, 1968; Rogers, 1969a; Stuckert, 1963). McClelland (1961, pp. 165–166) reports data indicating a negative association between "need affiliation" (defined as an orientation toward "establishing, maintaining or restoring a positive affective relationship with another person (p. 160))" and economic growth. These findings do not deny that people seek to maintain both material attainments and interpersonal satisfactions; they suggest only that, in many circumstances, such dual payoffs are not possible. (See Blood & Blood, 1978, pp. 287–331, for a discussion of the personal dilemmas posed by this problem.) The question is which domain would be most valued when a choice must be made?

Applying the principle of diminishing marginal utility to the question leads to the prediction that people prefer the domain that is perceived as most scarce. Thus, families who live in a "modernizing" country like Mexico should be more likely to value material rewards over satisfactions deriving from interpersonal relationships. Conversely, families living in countries with material abundance like the United States should be more likely to stress interpersonal satisfactions.

Information Processing

Once goals are established and barriers toward attaining them are identified, the next steps in the problem-solving process are to decide on a course of action and to make probability estimates for successfully attaining the goal through that course of action. These decisions, as noted earlier, require an information search.

Information contributes to the problem-solving process through its content, quantity, and diversity. The content provides actors with knowledge enabling them to consider, estimate, and compare the consequences of taking alternative courses of action when confronted with a problem. Quantity affects the actor's ability to process information. If there is too much information the actor's processing capacity is overloaded; if there is too little, there is nothing to process. Diversity influences the actor's ability to integrate the information. If information is too disparate, the actor is unable to gather the data into any meaningful whole.

The discussion that follows is consonant with the views of Piaget (Inhelder & Piaget, 1958), Mead (1934), Schooler (1972), Swanson (1974), and, most recently, Kohn and Schooler (1978); it draws most heavily, however, on theory and research reported by Schroder, Driver, and Streufert (1967). Schroder and his colleagues propose two interdependent cognitive properties relevant to processing information. The first is the number of parts or dimensions individuals or groups are capable of discerning in an observed phenomenon. For example, a piece of pie may be viewed as food to be eaten, as containing a certain number of calories, and as having certain economic value. The second cognitive property is the number of rules used to process a given bit of information. For example, the piece of pie may be viewed in terms of how much food is sufficient for satiety, in a more complex sense of chemical combinations or of nutritive density, in the normative sense of justifying whether or not to eat this particular type of food, or whether the time to eat this food is appropriate and so forth. According to Schroder *et al.*, the greater the number of dimensions perceived, the more likely a large number of integrative rules will be applied in processing any bit of information. It should follow that the amount and diversity of information available in the environment will affect the group or individual's level of information processing.[9]

Schroder *et al.* (1967) hypothesize a U-shape relationship between diversity in the environment and level of information processing:

> Overly simple environments, which fail to present sufficiently diverse and/or numerous dimensional units of information, fail to stimulate the processes of integration—that is, simple structures are sufficient for coping with such environments. Overly complex environments, which provide excessively diverse and/or numerous dimensional units of information, reduce the generation of integratively complex rules for processing information and also reduce the levels of differentiation and integration involved (p. 31).

They suggest, therefore, that there is some optimal level of environmental diversity at which persons reach a maximum level of information processing. In applying these principles to our research, we found ourselves unable to establish an empirical basis for determining such an optimal level. Thus, we assumed that a linear relationship existed between environmental diver-

---

[9] Information processing abilities should not be misconstrued as intelligence. We make no assumptions about the differences in intelligence of persons living under varying social structures, nor do we believe that our theory suggests that such differences exist. It is possible for persons living in simple social structures to be highly intelligent and not be able to process information at a complex level of integration. The functioning of a digital computer is illustrative of this point. By some standards a computer may be considered as having high intelligence since it has almost perfect recall of a large amount of data and can solve complex problems very quickly. Nevertheless, the computer operates as a simple information processing structure. Without external instructions it is neither able to move to higher levels of abstraction nor to formulate new rules. Correspondingly, humans socialized into thinking in only one mode may not be able to utilize another mode without training, even if they are highly intelligent.

sity and level of information processing, while acknowledging the possibility that the United States, as a postindustrial society, may contain environments characterized by information overload (Tallman, 1972; Toffler, 1970). In brief, we assumed that an increase in amount and diversity of available information is associated with an increase in persons' abilities to interpret such information in multiple ways and to collate the information according to multiple sets of rules.

Intervening between the environmental conditions and the group or individual's levels of information processing are a series of behavioral operations that determine how new information will be identified and utilized. Schroder *et al.* (1967, pp. 16–17) suggests that in simple environments individual and group information processing will have the following cognitive form: *(a)* thinking in categorical, or black and white terms; *(b)* minimizing conflict; *(c)* anchoring behavior in external conditions, that is, not conceiving of the self as an agent for affecting change; and *(d)* failing to consider change as a potential aspect of existence. These behaviors result in low levels of information integration and processing. As information in the environment grows in amount and diversity, there is a corresponding increase in the group's or individual's capacity to think in abstract terms, tolerate conflicting viewpoints, be self-reliant, and self-consciously serve as an instrument of change.

As these behaviors change, people's abilities to assimilate and integrate information along multiple dimensions and to apply multiple rules in information processing should also change. According to Schroder *et al.*, the difference between moderately high and very high levels of information processing can be described as the difference between empirical and theoretical outlooks. At the moderately high level, a number of classes of empirical relationships are possible; at the high level, it is possible to generate or apply general laws that systematize a large and differentiated body of information. The ability to apply general laws and to generalize beyond empirical phenomena makes it possible to generate new ideas and alternative solutions to existing problems. People with such capabilities should not only be able to utilize available choices extant in the social structure but should also be able to process new and changing information.

Following Schroder *et al.*, we propose that the level of information processing and integration in career-planning problems depends upon the following three cognitive styles or capacities: *(a)* the level of cognitive abstractness; *(b)* tolerance for opposing opinions; and *(c)* tolerance of ambiguity (e.g., the willingness to avoid premature closure). Implicit in these cognitive styles is *(d)* an equalitarian orientation that seeks open channels of communication and critically evaluates information regardless of its sources. Research with small problem-solving groups suggests that these four conditions combine to produce effective group problem solving (Kelley & Thibaut, 1969; Tallman, 1970; Tallman *et al.*, 1974).

The Evaluating Process

Equalitarian groups which allow for a free flow of discussion and information appear most able to arrive at new or novel solutions to problems (Klein & Hill, 1979; Tallman & Miller, 1974). Such creativity is required in solving career-planning problems but the new solutions cannot be implemented without knowledge of the rules extant in the social structure (Dunnette, Campbell, & Jaasted, 1963; Taylor, Berry, & Block, 1958). A structure that allows for the expression of a diversity of conflicting views—views that are subject to evaluation and criticism—is necessary (Hoffman, 1965). Problem-solving effectiveness requires a readiness to base judgments on evidence; this implies a mind set that does not seek immediate or premature closure. Such a mind set has been found to positively affect problem-solving outcomes (Hoffman, 1965; Hoffman & Maier, 1961). The optimum problem-solving group structure requires a cognitive style that attempts to differentiate useful from peripheral or nonrelevant information while being able to generalize from the available useful information. Studies reporting a relationship between "elaborative" language in parents and problem-solving skills in children provide indirect support for this hypothesis (Bee, 1971; Bernstein, 1961; Hess & Shipman, 1965).

In brief, equalitarianism, abstract thinking, tolerance of ambiguity, and tolerance of conflict have all been shown to be associated with problem-solving effectiveness. It should follow that if these attributes are present in the parent–child relationship they should facilitate the child's socialization as an effective problem solver. Furthermore, we would expect that the social context within which the parent-child relationship occurs would either facilitate or inhibit the development of these attributes. The contexts most relevant for our purposes are the family and the community.

SOCIAL STRUCTURE

Social context, as we have used it, is synonymous with environment, setting, milieu, and society. It refers to the entire set of conditions that constrain, orientate, and channel behaviors that take place in a given relationship. The social context is so pervasive that some have claimed, *"all* socialization is contextual (Gecas, 1981, p. 157). " In the sense that socialization, like all forms of behavior, takes place within social contexts, the statement is unquestionably true. However, the relevant questions here are *(a)* can socialization that takes place in one context be generalized to other contexts? *(b)* if so, are some social contexts or settings more amenable to fostering socialization than others? and, *(c)* if yes, what contextual conditions are most likely to affect the quality and content of the socialization process?

Within specified conditions, the first question can be answered affirmatively. Although some socialization may be situation specific, much learning is transferable at least to similar situations (Aronfreed, 1969; Bandura, 1977b; Gewirtz, 1969). Some socialization contexts, specifically those that maintain long-standing relationships of relatively high intensity, are likely to be more influential in the socialization process than contexts in which relationships are casual and of limited duration (Gecas, 1981). It would appear, then, that the family and community are especially effective contexts for studying socialization. Thus, the primary issue in this section derives from the third question, identifying those contextual elements that are most likely to influence the socialization process. These elements are best communicated by the concept of social structure.

Sheldon Stryker (1980) makes the point succinctly, "If the social person is shaped by interaction, it is social structure that shapes the possibilities for interaction and so, ultimately, the person (p. 66)." The social structure establishes the conditions under which social interaction takes place and, therefore, places constraints on where, how, and with whom the socialization process occurs. In considering socialization for problem solving within social structures, it is important to note that the structure contains the conditions that produce both the problem and the means for overcoming the problem. In fact, the primary conceptual and measurement difficulty posed by the concept of social structure is its ubiquity. We will try to overcome this difficulty by breaking the social structure into its component parts. In so doing we will seek to identify those aspects of the social structure that contribute to problems, those that contribute to solutions, and those that influence the socialization for problem-solving process.

Defining the Social Structure

The social structure is a network of social relationships. Actors in different positions in the network have the opportunity to interact with persons in other positions, but not all positions in the network have access to all other positions. People in some positions may have direct access to other positions, but return access is either not allowed or circuitous. The president of a company can, by picking up the phone, have immediate access to any employee; the same is not true for an employee of the company. The principle holds for presidents of countries and citizens or for any other hierarchical structure. In brief, people have unequal access to each other. For some, the opportunities to engage in transactions for the exchange of goods and services do not exist; for others, the cost of seeking such transactions is extremely high; for those in more privileged positions, the opportunities for transactions are relatively greater and the costs lower.

The distribution of populations into various social positions is not random. Certain positions are restricted to those who fall within designated social categories. Age, sex, nationality, education, religion, and income are among the most common determinants of social position. Some of these categories, such as age, education, and income, are inherently hierarchical; others, like sex, religion, or place of birth, though not intrinsically gradated are nonetheless frequently used to determine people's rights to hold particular positions. This differentiation occurs in large part because different behavioral expectations (e.g., roles) are associated with given social positions. Thus, the social structure not only establishes the conditions for determining who interacts with whom, it also influences the *content* of such interaction. The doctor–patient, employer–employee, and parent–child relationship all have associated with them different behavioral expectations.

In brief, the social structure, regardless of the size or the type of social organization it supports, consists of differentiated relationships. This differentiation has two elements; it is heterogeneous and hierarchical and, therefore, unequal (see Blau, 1974). Heterogeneity facilitates the identification process by fostering an awareness of similarities and differences. Inequality affects aspirations, goals, and motivation to solve the problems extant in the structure.

People are born into ongoing social structures, thereby inheriting a given social position with its accompanying role expectations. They may, over time, be able to change positions to some degree, but, in the aggregate, their initial position plays a significant role in determining their ultimate place in the social structure (Blau & Duncan, 1967). There is, then, in any actor's efforts to solve problems in the social structure, an interplay between inherited factors and available opportunities. We term these the *ascribed structure* and the *opportunity structure*.

The *ascribed structure* refers to those aspects of social position that predetermine, through no fault of or credit to the individual, the individual's social identity. This includes the child's position within the family and the family's position within the community. The ascribed structure, by affecting the individual's access to information, educational opportunities, and social and economic resources, influences the actor's ability to process and integrate information.

The *opportunity structure* refers to the objective life chances available to actors at a given time period. An essential component of the opportunity structure is the set of social conditions that affect an actor's chances for attaining a given goal. Ideally, the opportunity structure should be the same for all people. We say this not so much from an ideological perspective, as from the perspective of researchers. Only if the opportunity structure is held constant can we adequately assess the impact of the ascribed structure. Unfortunately, the available correlational evidence suggests that, other things being equal, people of different class and ethnic and racial backgrounds have different chances of attaining designated social positions and statuses (Blau & Duncan, 1967). Those born into privileged positions have a greater chance of ending their work careers in privileged positions. One of the questions we confront in this study is whether this fact can be attributed to the greater problem-solving abilities of the privileged group.

Community Social Structure

A community is a collectivity organized to carry out the essential economic, social, political, and educational purposes of daily life within a limited geographical locality (see Hawley, 1960, pp. 251–252; Olsen, 1978, pp. 62–63). The boundaries of the community provide the basis for defining people as members and nonmembers and is, therefore, a primary source of individual and family identification. Accordingly, Bensman and Rosenberg (1976) describe the community as follows:

> Persons and groups define themselves and are defined as belonging to a particular community—a specific group that occupies a specific place at a given time. This territorial identification is the foundation of loyalties, pride, mutual aid, friendships, feelings of inferiority and superiority to outsiders, rivalries, competition, and warfare; it is the very basis of social relationships (p. 119).

It follows that communities are characterized by a high degree of member interdependence. The level and intensity of that interdependence, however, varies with size of the community and the diversity of its activities. These variables, as we shall see later, are linked both to social development and to problem solving.

Community structures can be analyzed internally, in terms of their system of stratification, and comparatively, in terms of their level of industrial development, degree of relative affluence, availability of education, and so forth. Four structural variables, social position, access to information, number of possible roles, and diversity of roles, are relevant for both internal and comparative analysis. All of these variables have implications for socialization for problem solving.

Within any given community structure those persons born into the lower social positions are likely to have less access to information and fewer roles available to them than persons born into social positions that provide higher status, greater resources and greater educational opportunities. This is best documented in the area of occupational choices (Blau & Duncan, 1967, p. 170; Ornstein, 1976; Parnes, Miljus, Spitz, & Associates, 1970). Students of social development report similar differences in number of role choices between social structures. Smelser (1964), for example, states that role differentiation increases as societies modernize, "structural differentiation is a process whereby 'one social role or organization ... differentiates into two or more roles or organizations which function more effectively in the new historical circumstances' (p. 261)." Role differentiation leads to a diversity of choices. According to Apter (1971), "development refers to the expansion of choice opportunities, alternative modes of action available to a given population in any society (p. 10)."

Corresponding with an increase in the number of available roles within social structures is an increase in the diversity of activities associated with given social roles. Compare, for example, the range of tasks required of a Mexican peasant and of an industrialized farmer in the United States. The peasant is expected to know little about changing commodity prices, soil chemistry, interest rates, and so forth. Indeed, such knowledge and activities can be as dysfunctional for the peasant as it is necessary for the industrialized farmer because they do not appreciably increase the farmer's yield. Similar comparisons can be made about the range of activities of an automotive engineer and a worker on an automobile assembly line.

Such diversity is not limited entirely to occupational roles. For example, the middle-class wife's "traditional" role in an industrialized social structure may include such diverse activities as childrearing, nursing, participating in local politics, providing transportation, gourmet cooking, managing the household, gardening, shopping, balancing budgets, managing social affairs, interior decorating, interpersonal counseling, and having expertise in the arts of conversation and companionship. This diversity is neither necessary nor desirable in simple social structures where greater energy is required for providing the family with basic necessities. Foster (1967) describes the wife's role in a Michoacan peasant village as follows: "Women do the cooking, shop for food, wash clothes, keep house, tend the children, feed chickens and pigs, take a hot noon meal to their farmer husbands working away from home, or assume a major responsibility in making pottery (p. 61)." It is not so much the number of activities that contribute to the difference between the peasant wife's role and the United States white collar wife's role as it is the diversity of activities, the range of skills, and the knowledge involved in carrying out the role. In brief, progression up the social ladder within a social structure or along an industrialization continuum seems to result in both an increase in the number of role choices and an increase in the complexity of the tasks associated with roles.

The same correspondence between social position and social development exists when access to information is considered. There is agreement among investigators that people in lower social positions have less access to information (Piker, 1968; Schatzman & Strauss, 1955) than people in higher strata. These differences exist not only for access to media such as television, radio, newspapers, and magazines, but also for access to educational facilities, private sources of information, special contacts, and so forth (Freedman & Sears, 1965; Wade & Schramm, 1969). Information, then, may be considered as a reasonably scarce resource (Piker, 1968, pp. 101–145).

A similar pattern occurs with social development. Apter (1971) describes modernizing societies as "derivative" and industrialized societies as "innovative." In essence he argues that modernizing societies are primarily oriented toward the utilization of available knowledge, whereas industrialized societies are committed to the generation of more and new knowledge. The introduction of new knowledge tends to destabilize modernizing societies. Apter (1971, p. 36) maintains that transistor radios and other means of obtaining knowledge about different life-styles are major sources of information giving rise to feelings of deprivation (see also Rogers, 1969b; Lerner, 1958). Such knowledge is consequently not only a source of conflict but also a source of pressure for continuing change in the direction of more rapid economic development. According to Apter, " 'The moving edge' of development is where information is generated at the fastest rate and applied with the greatest consequences (1971, p. 18)."

The effects of social position, social development, and derivative or innovative knowledge are most clearly manifest in the community setting. The community provides the experiential nexus used by people to form their conceptions of the formal, impersonal world that exists outside of primary relationships, the world that is generally perceived as "reality." Of course, forces outside of the community affect this "reality." Employment or educational opportunities attract people to other localities. Governmental authorities or large corporations may determine events that directly affect entire communities. Nevertheless, most of these conditions are experienced *within* the community. Community influence is greatest among the young who have not obtained sufficient independence from family or community institutions to consider alternatives to the reality with which they are confronted. The community, claim Bensman and Rosenberg (1976), "is still the first territorial institution a child is aware of and to which he first orients his behavior. Concepts of the state and of the nation are relatively difficult for children to understand; they master these only after establishing their identity as members of a community (p. 119)." But, as we have noted, this identity depends largely upon the family's social position. The child's experiences in the community are filtered, sifted, evaluated, and interpreted in the more intimate, safer climate of the family.

The Family

The family is the institution within the community that is primarily responsible for the socialization of subsequent generations. Although not all socialization is carried out within families, they provide the original arena within which both personal and social identities are forged.

Virtually all the families in our research are organized as nuclear families. The nuclear family exhibits relatively less variation in its basic structure across societies than other family forms, such as the extended, stem, or clan family. Moreover, the nuclear family is unquestionably the most common form of family structure extant. It consists of one man, one woman, and their children. The nuclear family is a small group of interacting individuals whose interests are so interdependent that the outcome of the group's actions affects each member's well-being. It differs from other cooperative small groups in that it is "kinship structured" (Reiss, 1980, p. 34). The family is organized on the basis of strong normative bonds which foster emotional ties among its members; these bonds may be biological, cultural, or affinal (in most societies they are usually all three), but whatever their basis, they imply the strongest type of socially sanctioned mutual commitment possible in a society. According to Kuhn (1974), this implies, "that at least some goals and processes are decided for the family as a unit rather than being a fortuitous outcome of the separate members seeking their separate goals (p. 416)."

The family also differs from other social groups and organizations in that its life course is generally coterminous with the life course of at least one of the original parents; that is, the nuclear family ceases to exist when both of the original parents have died.[10] Moreover, the incumbents in the various family positions are not entirely replaceable. Although incumbents in the role of husband and wife can be replaced, those who hold the biological roles of parents, children, or siblings will maintain those roles throughout their lives. Thus, the family has biologically linked maturational characteristics that are not inherent in other social groups.

The family shares in common with other natural groups a history and a future; both conditions influence the nature of its organization and the

[10] See Footnote 6.

types of decisions it makes. It also shares with many natural groups a multi-purpose character; that is, its functions are varied and dependent upon changing contingencies in the environment. Thus, the various rights, duties, and skills required in particular roles are likely to change with given situations over time (Vincent, 1966). Despite this variety, however, we assume that family activities evolve around two essential domains—one concerned with material benefits, the other with interpersonal affection.

Age and sex are the primary criteria for differentiating positions within the family structure. The age dimension distinguishes parents from children; it also may be a factor in establishing the positions of siblings, both in relation to each other and to their parents. In virtually all societies sex is a criterion for establishing role expectations. The families' internal division of labor between mothers and fathers, sons and daughters, and brothers and sisters has tended to be determined by sex and the way the family earns its living (Barry, Child, & Bacon, 1957; D'Andrade, 1966; Lee, 1977). This division of labor is linked to the distribution of prestige and authority within the family, and as such is relevant to patterns of decision making.

The internal family structure provides the mechanism for mediating between the social structure and the individual family members. We propose that this is done in two ways. First, the family interprets the social structure to its members in terms of current conditions and available opportunities. In this sense the family plays an essential role in establishing life goals and estimating life chances for its members. Second, aspects of the social structure are replicated by the family structure. Specifically, the degree of role diversity within the community social structure has consequences in the way the family structures its patterned interactions. These two sets of structural conditions are, as we shall see in the next chapter, proposed as essential for determining the course of socialization for problem solving.

CONCLUSIONS

We have explicated five concepts that provide the underpinnings for a theory of socialization for social change. Two of the concepts, socialization and problem solving, refer to behavioral processes that are amenable to direct observations. The other three concepts, social structure, community, and family, refer to networks of patterned relationships. These networks provide a set of conditions that influence the course of social interaction. The social structure may be envisioned as a stage setting that places actors in particular positions on the stage and in relation to certain props. The setting thus channels communication and access to resources. The only way the actors can attain the goals they want is through the transactions they can conduct with the other actors on the stage. It follows that an actor's initial position on stage places him or her at a relative advantage or disadvantage in relation to the other actors. It also follows that the problems faced by actors differ depending upon their position. We refer to these starting positions as the "ascribed structure."

The actor's script, however, is not completely written; there is room to maneuver, to plan, to negotiate with other actors. This freer aspect of social structure we call the "opportunity" structure. Problem solving occurs within the opportunity structure.

Socialization occurs in a learning–teaching relationship, based on the exchange of goods and services that foster positive relationships and mutual identification. Identification with models perceived as similar or attractive facilitates the process of identity formation, and learning by observation enables actors to incorporate role expectations for one's own as well as others' identities. The content of what is taught and learned, the particular goods and services exchanged, and the models that are chosen depend on social structural conditions. Socialization for problem solving within the social structure is conceptualized as learning how to attain desired identities under conditions of social change. In the next chapter we examine how the social structure not only constrains choices and behavioral alternatives in problem solving, but how it influences what people want from society and the strategies they develop for attaining these wants.

Reduced to a bare minimum, the problem-solving process involves deciding on goals, searching for and processing information relevant to the means for attaining these goals, and evaluating the effectiveness of the goal-seeking efforts. In the next chapter we develop propositions that link the stages in this process to structural conditions within the community and the family. The theory is designed to explain how these structural variables affect the problem-solving process as it is carried out in an ongoing relationship between a mother, father, and young adolescent son or daughter. The key outcome to be predicted is the child's problem-solving ability under conditions of social change.

3 Socialization for Social Change: A Theory of Processes and Outcomes

How can one generation prepare the next to function effectively in a world whose future is unknown? The answer to this question, like the answer to most questions concerning social functioning, requires an understanding of the relationships that exist between society, the institutions that teach us about society, and the individual human being. At the empirical level, these relationships are so complex, variable, and fluid that they defy complete categorization, description, and, consequently, explanation. The first task, therefore, is to reduce this complexity to a set of identifiable and measurable relationships. This was begun in the previous chapter by explicating the five concepts that form the basic elements of our theoretical answer to the question. Implicit in the explication of these concepts are five premises:

1. Functioning effectively (i.e., successfully achieving desired goals) within a society under conditions of uncertainty requires the ability to problem solve. Therefore, preparation for an unknown future involves teaching and learning how to solve problems.
2. Within the context of family problem-solving activities, the parent–child relationship provides an experiential nexus that makes it possible for children to learn (a) to evaluate and commit themselves to specific life-style goals; and (b) to develop the problem-solving skills requisite for attaining such goals under conditions of social change.

3. This special kind of learning, called socialization, usually occurs indirectly as children identify with their families in seeking to attain desired goals within their community social structure.
4. Through the socialization process, children form a social identity, learning an array of expected behaviors associated with social positions and roles, while learning how to process information, generate ideas, and evaluate the consequences of action.
5. Variations in the socialization process and its outcomes are largely attributable to social structural conditions manifest in the community and mediated through the family.

THE SCOPE OF THE THEORY

These premises point to two critical scope conditions for the theory.[1] First, the theory relies entirely on structural conditions for explaining variations in the socialization process and for specifying particular outcomes of the process. Clearly cultural, genetic, personality, historical, and ecological factors also influence the socialization process and its outcomes. In our view, however, the structural explanation offered the most heuristic potential of any of the possible explanatory variables for building a theory linking microphenomena, such as parent–child relationships, to macro phenomena, such as social change. Second, the theory directs attention to the parent–child relationship as it occurs around the single activity of problem solving and within the specific social setting of the family. As noted earlier, socialization occurs in many settings including those created by peer groups, schools, and jobs. Even within the family, not all socialization involves parents and children. For example, siblings play a significant role in mutual socialization, and the marital relationship is an ongoing socialization process (Hill & Aldous, 1969).[2] There is little question, however, that the family is usually the initial and most pervasive setting within which socialization takes place.

In this study, the parent–child relationship is restricted to three persons: a mother, a father, and a 12- to 15-year-old son or daughter. The inclusion of both a mother and father with either a son or a daughter provides the op-

[1] Scope conditions are used here to "define and constrain domains of applicability (B. Cohen, 1980, p. 82)." In general our use of conditional statements in this theory chapter is intended to follow the principles proposed by Bernard P. Cohen (1980) in his essay "The Conditional Nature of Scientific Knowledge" in *Theoretical Methods in Sociology*, edited by Lee Freese (Pittsburgh: University of Pittsburgh Press, 1980, pp. 71–110).
[2] The question of sibling socialization is poorly understood and rarely studied. There is the suggestion that siblings may play a powerful socializing role but the evidence is sparce (see Bossard & Boll, 1960, pp. 39–49; Ihinger, 1975; Schvaneveldt & Ihinger, 1979).

portunity for considering sex-linked behaviors and the parents' influences on same- or opposite-sex children. It should be noted, however, that the exclusion of single-parent–child relationships limits the theory's generalizability to so-called intact families.

Children aged 12–15 years were chosen because they were old enough to develop an awareness of their own identities and were able to articulate, anticipate, and negotiate a changing identity. Such children have also reached a maturational level that allows them to think abstractly—an important problem-solving component (see Elder, 1968, pp. 38–40, for a review of the literature on adolescent intellectual development). At the same time, most children at this age are still sufficiently dependent on their parents so that their growing desire for autonomy and independence is not yet a governing motive. Adolescents who are slightly older may be less concerned with family problem solving and more concerned with expressing their identities as separate from their parents. In our view, therefore, children from 12 to 15 are at the most propitious age for studying their problem-solving socialization as it relates to functioning in the social structure.

THE BASIC MODEL

The broad outlines of the theory can be expressed in the form of a causal model in which structural conditions within a community, as mediated through the family, affect the socialization process that occurs between parents and their children while they engage in problem-solving activities. The result of this sequence influences children's abilities to solve problems in their social structure. Figure 3.1 illustrates these essential relationships.

The model as depicted in Figure 3.1 blocks out the skeletal elements of the theory and provides the direction of the relationships between these elements. The next step is to fill in the blocks with specific variables and establish the principles linking the variables to each other. Since social structures do not act but only provide conditions under which individual or col-

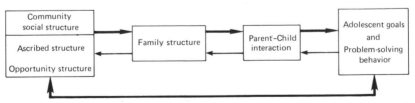

Figure 3.1. *This is a general model depicting hypothesized direction of influences linking community social structure, family, and parent–child interaction to adolescent socialization for problem solving. The heavy arrows show directions predicted by theory. The narrow arrows show reciprocal relations not predicted by theory.*

lective actions are probable or improbable, we need first to establish the types of actions our model seeks to explain—that is, those particular actions that occur in the relationship between parents and their children as they engage in problem solving.

PARENTS, THEIR CHILD, AND THE PROBLEM-SOLVING PROCESS

The premises presented at the beginning of this chapter imply that socialization for problem solving occurs indirectly as parents and their children engage in problem-solving activities. The socialization process involving the adolescent child within the family, however, requires stipulating two antecedent conditions:[3]

1. Prior socialization experiences have generally resulted in mutually satisfying outcomes for parents and the adolescent child.
2. The adolescent child has identified him or herself as a family member.

As we indicated in the previous chapter, these conditions hold for the vast majority of adolescents.

In Chapter 2 we proposed that problem solving activities involve, minimally, three steps: (a) defining the situation as a problem; (b) evaluating alternative courses of action; and (c) evaluating the outcomes of a given course of action and (on the basis of the evaluation) returning to the second step or terminating the problem-solving effort. In the discussion that follows we will develop propositions pertaining to the influence of each of these behavioral processes on socialization for problem solving.

Defining the Situation as a Problem

Previously we suggested that the more highly valued a potential goal, the more motivated actors would be to attain the goal. Since defining a situation as a problem implies a commitment to take action, it seems likely that the more motivated actors are to attain a given goal the more willing they will be to define the situation relevant to attaining the goal as problematic.

[3] Antecedent conditions according to Cohen (1980, pp. 78–79) provide the "if" statement in an "If . . . then" proposition. More significantly they provide guidelines for using a predictive statement. Accordingly, our statement could read, If children and parents have had prior satisfactory exchanges and if the adolescent child identifies him or herself (and is identified) as a member of the family then socialization for problem solving will occur as the parents and child engage in the problem-solving process.

The following propositions, therefore, derive from our definition of the problem-solving process and our assumptions concerning human motives.

Proposition 1: The more highly actors value a particular goal, the more likely they will be to consider the attainment of the goal as a problem.

Proposition 2: The more likely actors are to identify a situation as a problem, the more likely they are to seek to solve the problem. Thus,

Proposition 3: The more highly actors value a particular goal, the more likely they are to seek to solve problems associated with attaining the goal.

If propositions 1, 2, and 3 are true, one means of determining the situations in which parents and their children will engage in problem solving is to determine the basis on which families value certain goals more highly than others. Earlier, we applied the principle of diminishing marginal utility to the valuation of goals. Applying this principle, the following proposition can be derived:

Proposition 4: Holding the satisfying potential (utility) of a goal constant, the more scarce the goods and/or services associated with the goal are perceived to be, the more highly the goal will be valued.[4]

Thus far we have not distinguished between individual or group problem-solving behavior. Although the problem-solving process can occur both individually or in groups, when it occurs in groups, the assumption is that a consensus about goals has been reached. However, at any point in time group members may not share the same goals. If there is not consensus, the group may not be able to coordinate its problem-solving activities. The issue becomes particularly complex when we consider the family.

Unlike many other social groups, the family has multiple goals which may vie for prominence at given times (Aldous, 1971; Weick, 1971). Families may, therefore, not always be sure of how much consensus they have with regard to a specific goal. The research and theory generated by David

[4] The reason for the condition of holding utility constant is discussed in Chapter 2. Restated briefly, we propose that the value of goods depends not only on scarcity but on its satisfying potential. Thus, the value of some goods and services will never reach zero regardless of abundance, and other resources may never be valued highly regardless of scarcity. In brief, the relationship between values and scarcity is not completely linear. Proposition 4, however, is concerned with a truncated distribution of goods, all valued equal in satisfying potential—that is, most people would want them if they were available. Under these conditions we predict a positive linear relationship between scarcity and value.

Reiss and his colleagues (D. Reiss, 1971a, 1971b, 1971c) suggest that families tend to develop consensus around basic perspectives, and, along with these perspectives, they develop common styles of thinking and reacting to external events. These perspectives and styles are so integrated that they rarely require open discussion. Reiss's findings indicate that when families have not developed a consensus on major perspectives—that is, when they are self-consciously involved in consensus concerns—they perceive the external world as haphazard and threatening (Reiss, 1971c). These data support Tallman's (1971, pp. 338–342) claim that families that do not develop consensus on key issues will not be free to deal effectively with external environmentally induced problems. We therefore considered consensus within the family as another antecedent condition of career planning.

Different families may have the same valuation of a given success goal yet they may differ in their readiness to commit themselves to solving the problems necessary for attaining the goal. There are two reasons for this. First, the barriers to achieving the goals are more formidable for families in some social positions than for others. It is often more difficult, for example, for a black family to purchase a home in a quiet suburb with a good school district than it would be for an upper-middle-class white family. Second, families (or individuals) may differ in their estimates of probable success—a difference that may be based on prior experience. We infer that actors will be more willing to take necessary risks to solve a problem if they consider their chances of success as good than if they consider their chances as poor. Therefore:

> *Proposition 5:* Holding valuation of a given goal constant, those who perceive their chances of attaining a goal as good are more likely to engage in problem-solving activities than those who perceive their chances as poor.

At first glance it may appear that proposition 5 contradicts the first four propositions. If, as indicated in proposition 4, the value of a good or service is largely determined by its scarcity, then from propositions 1, 2, and 3 we can infer that the more scarce the good, the more likely actors are to engage in problem-solving activities. But proposition 5 holds that problem-solving activities are enhanced if actors think their chances of attaining the goal is good. Do the two predictions contradict each other? We do not believe they do, although there is need for further specification. It is possible for an actor to perceive himself or herself as being in a good position to attain a goal that is generally considered scarce within the social structure. This can occur under three conditions:

1. The actor perceives himself or herself as holding the necessary attributes (e.g., ability, energy, motivation) to have a competitive advantage in attaining the valued goal.
2. The actor conceives his or her position in the social structure as providing a competitive advantage in attaining the valued goal. This can occur because the position enables the actor to control resources that can be used in exchange for the valued good or because the actor has access to information or training that improves chances of successfully accomplishing a goal.
3. Actors perceive future opportunities as better than current opportunities. Thus, the perceived scarcity of a particular goal may contribute to its being highly valued while the perception that opportunities are changing may give the actors hope that the goal will eventually be attainable. This condition is particularly relevant to the parent–child relationship because it can enable the parents and child to anticipate opportunities for the child that are not presently available and were not available to the parents.

The general principle asserted by proposition 5 is that only if actors perceive their chances of attaining a goal within some acceptable positive range will they seek to solve problems involving attaining highly valued goals. Condition 3 is of particular relevance in this study.

It is conceivable that parents living under a given set of circumstances perceive the future opportunities available to their children as substantially different from the opportunities currently available to family members. According to the principle implicit in proposition 5, these estimates of future changes in life opportunities should influence the child's readiness to engage in problem solving. Therefore:

Proposition 6: The more likely parents are to perceive their child's future life chances in positive terms, the more likely the child will be to engage or seek out problem-solving situations.

Information Search and Processing

This phase of the problem-solving process involves the search for alternative courses of action that eventuates in choosing a set of actions or strategies that the decision maker believes will lead to the attainment of a desired goal. Such a choice requires estimating the consequences of future acts. These estimates are based on actors' past and present experiences and their ability to process new information. The anticipation of future change affects actors' motivations to engage in problem solving for a specific goal (proposition 6). At this point, however, we consider motivation as a constant and focus attention on the abilities that must be learned to process information effectively.

As reported in the previous chapter, two cognitive properties—the number of dimensions discerned in a given bit of information and the number of rules employed to integrate the information—are positively associated with the ability to process complex bodies of information. These two properties, in combination, are also associated with the capacity to think in abstract terms, to tolerate the conflict of ideas, to tolerate ambiguity, and to maintain an orientation that assesses the usefulness of an idea independently of the status of the person who presented it. It follows that when these characteristics are manifested in the parent–child relationship they should lead to high levels of information processing and, therefore, to more effective problem solving. This should be especially true for career-planning problems which, as noted in the previous chapter, require the utilization of ideas from other family members, knowledge emanating from sources outside the family, continuous monitoring of information, and flexible strategies. We propose therefore that when the parent–child relationship focuses on the career-planning problem, the child develops the information processing skills and cognitive flexibility that contribute to his or her being an effective problem solver in a wide range of social situations. Our focus here, however, is more specifically on problem solving with the career-planning problem.

The following propositions state the predicted relationship between the designated parent–child interaction patterns and the child's problem-solving skills resulting from efforts to engage in career planning:

Proposition 7: Holding motivation constant, the more open the flow of information between father, mother, and child, the greater the child's capacity to process information.

Proposition 8: The greater the abilities of family members to tolerate opposing ideas and differing viewpoints, the greater the child's capacity to process information.

Proposition 9: The greater the ability of the members of the parent–child relationship to tolerate ambiguity (i.e., to postpone closure on an issue when information is inadequate), the greater the child's capacity to process information.

Proposition 10: The greater the ability of family members to use abstract as opposed to concrete concepts, the greater the child's capacity to process information.

Finally, three variables are thought to contribute additively to the child's abilities to process information and subsequently to solve problems effectively. Hence:

Proposition 11:   Equalitarianism, tolerance of conflicting viewpoints, and tolerance of ambiguity within the parent–child relationship each have an independent and positive relationship with the child's level of information processing.

Evaluation of Outcomes

Most careful observers of group interaction have reported that evaluation of behavioral outcomes occurs almost simultaneously with ongoing action (A. Strauss, 1978). Evaluation is part of the ongoing process that utilizes continuous and often subtle feedback to monitor and modify subsequent actions. The cumulative effect of such feedback is to set actors on a particular trajectory that determines subsequent courses of action. Our interest in these cumulative effects lies in their relevance to actors' and groups' expectancy of success or failure in subsequent problem-solving efforts. The available data suggest that individuals or groups who experience prior problem-solving success are more likely to anticipate success in subsequent actions.[5] Oosterbaan–Bulbulian (1975) concludes in her review of the research literature on the effect of success–failure outcomes on group performance that, "Performance outcome was found to be related to expectancy of success which, in turn, was positively related to subsequent performance (p. 64)." In sum, the net effect of success–failure experiences is that actors find themselves on a predictable course from which it becomes increasingly difficult to extricate themselves. The following quotation from Brewster Smith (1968) aptly summarizes this conclusion.

> In social life, there is much bitter truth of the biblical maxim, "to him who hath shall be given, from him who hath not shall be taken away even that which he hath." Launched on the right trajectory, the person is likely to accumulate successes that strengthen the

[5] There is a great deal of literature in this area and there are a large number of qualifications to the general principle. There is evidence, for example, that persons with expectations for failure will seek to turn successful situations into failures and some will attribute success to variable conditions such as luck rather than ability (Aronson & Carlsmith, 1962; Weiner, Heckhauser, Meyer, & Cook, 1972). Attributing success to variable conditions clearly does not lead to subsequent expectations of success. These adaptations in our view result from socialization that leads actors to expect failure, and thus is subsequent to the socialization period of interest in this book. The question is clearly open and we shall return to it in Chapter 6 when we seek a post datum explanation for some surprising sex differences.

effectiveness of his orientation toward the world, while at the same time he acquires the knowledge and skills that make his further successes more probable. His environmental involvements generally lead to gratification and to increased confidence and favorable development. Off to a bad start, on the other hand, he soon encounters failures that make him hesitant to try. What to others are challenges appear to him as threats; he becomes preoccupied with defense of his small claims on life at the expense of energies to invest in constructive coping. And he falls increasingly behind his fellows in acquiring the knowledge and skills that are needed for success on those occasions when he does try (p. 277).

We suggest that a major launching pad determining the child's trajectory is the parent–child relationship as it exists within the family experiences of success and failure. The success or failure of family problem-solving activities need not be directly attributable to the child's performances. Rather, through the process of identification and the sense of shared fate with other family members, the family's collective experience is sufficient to orient the child toward anticipatory success or failure in a given problem-solving endeavor. Thus an adolescent engaged in career planning may use the experience of other family members as a basis for estimating his or her own chances of attaining instrumental goals. If the family experiences are perceived as consistent over repeated circumstances involving a number of instrumental goals, the adolescent's estimates of attaining terminal goals should also be affected. For example, if family members have a history of doing poorly in school and consequently of being unable to attain high status occupations, an adolescent member of the family may estimate his own chances as poor for attaining a good education and a high status occupation. The net effect is a reluctance to engage in problem-solving behavior in a specific problem area. Given our definition of problems, such behavior involves taking risks with regard to the specific problem. Thus:

Proposition 12:   When confronted with new problematic situations, parents and children who have had continued prior success in their problem-solving activities will be more willing to engage in risk-taking behavior than those who have experienced persistent failure.

Summary of Proposed Factors Affecting Socialization for Problem Solving

Three essential parent–child experiences are proposed as particularly salient in socialization for problem solving in the area of career planning. First, parents' interpretations of appropriate life goals and their children's chances for attaining those goals are considered critical in determining which situations will be defined as problematic. Second, the cognitive style involved in the search and processing of information determines the level of complexity applied in integrating information for use in problem solving. Third, prior problem-solving experiences affect parents' and/or children's readiness to undertake the risks involved in problem-solving activities. Variations in these three types of experiences are thought to determine the instrumental and terminal goals the child will establish and, therefore, the problems he or she will seek to solve, as well as his or her effectiveness. The following proposition summarizes the predicted effects on socialization outcomes:

> *Proposition 13:* The effectiveness of an adolescent's problem solving in a given problem area is influenced by (*a*) parents' valuation of social goals and interpretation of life chances; (*b*) the cognitive styles employed by parents and child while engaged in problem solving; and (*c*) the family's prior problem-solving experiences in the given problem area.

Particular social structural conditions in a community, as mediated through the family, are proposed as influencing each of the variables identified in proposition 13. We turn now to an examination of these conditions.

SOCIAL STRUCTURE, FAMILY INTERNAL STRUCTURE, AND PROBLEM SOLVING[6]

It seems patently obvious that the family's position in the social structure has a direct effect on the problems family members must solve. A Mexican peasant family earning less than $1000 a year must give a greater priority to feeding, sheltering, educating, and supporting its members than a middle-class United States family earning $30,000 per year. Not only do some families have more money to buy goods and services, but those who are better off also tend to have more opportunities and choices. Greater opportunities and choices exist for people who are literate and have marketable skills than for those who are illiterate and inadequately trained for the job market. Moreover, the level of industrial development in the larger society affects the number of choices available in a community structure.

---

[6] We use the phrase *family internal structure* to differentiate our use from the more common use of *family structure* as implying kinship organization. The distinction is particularly important because of the research linking this latter conception with social structure (see, for example, Blumberg & Winch, 1972; Goode, 1963; the review by Lee, 1977, pp. 151–160; Winch & Blumberg, 1968). The distinction should help to avoid confusion between our conception of structural complexity and that used by Winch and Blumberg and Lee.

These differences in opportunities affect more than occupations, they hold for education, leadership, and even entertainment and recreation. Thus position in the social structure influences the way family members interpret the opportunity structure and some of the ways family members interact with each other. Both of these influences are directly related to socialization for problem solving.

Interpreting the Opportunity Structure

Do these differences affect what people want out of life? The preponderance of evidence indicates that the answer is yes (see, for example, Hyman, 1953; Kerckhoff, 1972; Kohn, 1969; Rokeach, 1973; Stodtbeck, 1958). But at least one ambiguous point remains. There is considerable disagreement over whether persons in the lower social strata have the same success goals for their children as do those in the higher strata (Della Fave, 1974; Goodwin, 1976; Hyman, 1953; Rodman, 1963). Although the preponderance of evidence suggests that parents in different social classes do not differ in their aspirations for their children (Rodman & Voyandoff, 1969; Turner, 1964), there is some indication that such a conclusion is highly speculative (R. Bell, 1965; Haller & Miller, 1963; Hyman, 1953). One study reports that lower-class youth have unrealistically high aspirations for themselves (Della Fave, 1974).[7] Rosen (1959), Rodman (1963), and Rosenberg and Simmons (1972) have all shown that although members of the lower class seem to have aspirations similar to those of the middle class, the range of acceptable outcomes is greater for lower-class persons and families.

The comparative nature of values offers another approach to clarifying the basis upon which success goals are determined. If we accept the common definition of value as a preferential ordering, a reasonable way to assess how highly a given goal is valued may be to compare the preferences for one goal with preferences for other goals (Rokeach, 1973). This procedure seems particularly useful when considering the two types of terminal goals we propose as most relevant to problem solving within a social structure: material well-being and interpersonal satisfaction. Taken independently, both goals are likely to be highly valued. The important question, however, from the perspective of determining value hierarchies, is which goal would be sacrificed for the other, if both goals are not attainable?

Applying proposition 4 to this question leads to the prediction that in social structures where material goods are abundant, parents and their children will be more likely to prefer interpersonal satisfactions; and in struc-

---

[7] The question remains open, however, and we hope our research contributes to this body of literature (see Marotz–Baden & Tallman, 1978).

tures where material goods are scarce, such goods will be more highly valued, even at the cost of interpersonal satisfactions.

Parents, of course, may advocate other life goals: a religious or moral life, hedonism, the scholarly life, the significance of a given profession, and so forth. But, as noted in Chapter 2, the goals we have emphasized seem to prevail in most societies and are consonant with the most common indicators of macro social development and social change. They have also been described as fundamental value domains relevant to future expectations in virtually all societies.[8]

According to propositions 1, 2, and 3, the more highly valued a goal, the more likely it is that situations involving the attainment of the goal will be defined as a problem and therefore the subject of problem-solving activities. It follows therefore that the goals of material attainment and/or interpersonal satisfaction will influence the strategies used in adolescent career planning.

In fact, there is evidence indicating that family achievement goals establish guidelines and rationales for specific types of planning and action (Elder, 1974, pp. 35–36; Rosen, 1962; Strodtbeck, 1958). The work of Sarnoff (1966) and Ronen (1978) is particularly relevant. They compare two different value orientations that approximate our distinctions between material and interpersonal goals—"values of aggrandizement" and "values of realization." Values of aggrandizement emphasize the acquisition of wealth, prestige, and power. In most societies the strategies associated with attaining such rewards, if not acquired by inheritance, entail deferring immediate gratification for purposes of savings and reinvestment. Education is seen as instrumental for utilitarian reasons such as developing marketable skills or attaining knowledge that can be applied to practical ends. Values of "realization" emphasize individual growth and development rather than material rewards. With this value orientation, deferred gratification should be less important than experiences that provide insights, understanding, and personal and interpersonal satisfaction. Similarly, education and work are sought as intrinsic satisfiers rather than as investments for future rewards.

Parental goals for children appear to be positively related to the goals and behavioral strategies children adopt only if the goals are sensible in the light of available opportunities (Gecas, 1980; TenHouten, Lei, Kendall, & Gordon, 1971). As Elder (1968) notes, "Instead of generating achievement motivation and a sense of competence, high parental aspirations may produce rebellion or withdrawal through fantasy when not accompanied by training in mastery and self-reliance, when the goals far exceed the adolescent's

[8] See Footnote 8, Chapter 2.

ability or when opportunities are not available (p. 89)." Thus, propositions 5 and 6, which state that parents' optimistic assessments of children's life chances are associated with motivation to engage in problem-solving activities, should hold only to the extent that parents' perceptions of their children's opportunities are grounded in objective information. The important point suggested in proposition 6 is that parent's estimates of the *future* for their child may have an effect on motivation for problem solving. Future estimates are determined in part by social conditions.

In recent generations, virtually all societies have been undergoing rapid change. If such change is in the direction of increased industrial development, it is conceivable that parents may anticipate, even expect, that their children's economic opportunities will be better than their own. This can occur, however, only if parents are aware of the social changes happening in their society. Such awareness depends upon access to accurate information.

Access to Information

Even if people were all equally motivated, some would be better problem solvers than others. Effective problem solving, at both the family and individual levels requires the abilities to obtain, process, and integrate relevant information. These abilities serve to direct and guide problem-solving behavior by identifying the alternative means available for overcoming barriers impeding goal attainment. In Chapter 2, we pointed out that the available data suggest social class differences in access to information. These differences exist for both the amount and the diversity of information available.

Social Structure and Family Interpretations of Opportunities: Four Theorems

By definition, we conclude that the social position of the family within the community social structure determines family members' control over material resources and access to key sources of information (see Chapter 2). Therefore, applying propositions 1, 2, 3, and 4, and assuming the antecedent conditions of prior socialization effectiveness, identification with family, and family consensus on goals, we derive the following four theorems pertaining to structural conditions and families' interpretation of available career opportunities for their children.

> *Theorem 1:* Families faced with choices between obtaining material goods or seeking interpersonal satisfactions will be more

likely to define the attaining of interpersonal satisfactions as a problem if they hold relatively privileged positions in their community's social structure (e.g., high socioeconomic status), and they will be more likely to define the attainment of material goods as a problem if they hold less privileged positions in their community's social structure (e.g., low socioeconomic status).

Using the same antecedent conditions and applying the same propositions, the second theorem considers problem identification from a developmental perspective.

Theorem 2: Holding social position constant, families living within communities whose level of industrial development provides a high degree of material abundance will be more likely to define the attaining of interpersonal satisfactions as a problem, whereas families living under conditions of relative material deprivation will be more likely to define the attaining of material goods as a problem.

Closely associated with defining a situation as a problem is the perceived difficulty in resolving the problem. The more difficult or costly the problem-solving activity is perceived to be, the less likely actors will be to commit themselves to making the effort. Data suggest that this condition is most common among people in the lower social strata. Hence:

Theorem 3: Family members who hold lower socioeconomic positions in a community social structure will be less motivated to engage in career-planning problem-solving activities within their social structure than family members who hold higher positions within the structure.

However, when projections of opportunities for children are taken into consideration, future conditions, particularly the rate and direction of social change, become part of the equation. Thus, assuming that the parents' projections are reasonable:

Theorem 4: Children whose families reside in communities in which the social structure is changing in the direction of desired family goals will be more motivated to engage in problem-solving activities involving the social structure than children whose families reside in communities where change is less apparent or the change is in undesired directions.

Being able to obtain, process, and integrate relevant information is learned, in large part, by engaging in problem solving within the family—an experience that is directly affected by the family's interaction styles and patterns. In the following section we consider the relationship between community social structure and family interaction styles and patterns.

Family Interaction Patterns

A number of studies have demonstrated linkages between social structure and family structure (Aberle & Naegele, 1952; Bernstein, 1960; Rainwater, 1966; Straus, 1968; Strodtbeck, 1958). The most direct evidence linking family structure to social structure, however, comes from studies that focus on the influence of the father's occupation on childrearing practices (Kohn, 1969; McKinley, 1964; Miller & Swanson, 1960; Mortimer, 1976; Pearlin & Kohn, 1966). These studies suggest that the work-related experiences of the father (e.g., the number of available choices, the amount of information he assimilates and generates, the level of concreteness at which he works) have corollaries in family behavior and parent–child relationships. For example, Kohn (1969) reported that closeness of supervision on the job

> is associated with the constricted orientation. Closely supervised men tend not only to value conformity for their children, but also to emphasize extrinsic benefits that jobs provide rather than opportunities for intrinsic accomplishment—to have standards of morality keyed to the letter rather than the spirit of the law, to be distrustful, to be resistant to innovation and change, to lack self-confidence, and to be anxious (pp. 166–167).

Moreover, he found that

> *the complexity of organization of work* also is associated with self-directedness of men's orientation. Specifically, men who work at complexly organized jobs, in addition to valuing self-direction for children, tend to emphasize intrinsic aspects of the job, to be open-minded and tolerant of non-conformity, to have moral standards that demand more than conformity to the letter of the law, to be receptive to change, and not to be self-deprecatory (p. 167).

Interpolating these findings within our framework suggests that the level of information integration required on the job has its corollary in the home. Referring to our discussion in Chapter 2, most manual workers can be considered to be operating in "modernizing" structures in that they are not expected to generate new information but rather they are expected to apply the information given to them by superiors. White-collar workers, at least at the upper echelon, tend to use knowledge described as typifying "industrialized" structures; that is, they generate knowledge for prediction and future planning. The cognitive abilities associated with these types of information integration are thought to carry over into the family.

The same correspondence between community and family social structure can occur with regard to diversity of roles and information. Extrapolating from Schroder *et al.* (1967), we predict that families that have access to diverse kinds of information and a broader range of role choices provide a context that allows for a free flow of communication, tolerance for the conflict of ideas, tolerance for ambiguity, and the communication of abstract ideas. Conversely, families that live in relatively simple community social structures are likely to restrict the flow of information, to require conformity of ideas, to lack tolerance of ambiguity (thereby seeking premature closure on decisions without being able to assimilate new information), and to tend to communicate in concrete terms.

In summary, two principles provide the links between community social structure and internal family structure:

1. The level of complexity or diversity in the social structure is positively associated with complexity or diversity in the internal family structure.
2. Such diversity is positively associated with the cognitive styles that facilitate high levels of information processing and integration. Applying these principles results in the following propositions:

Proposition 14: The greater the amounts of available information and diversity in role choices within a given community social structure, the more likely that families residing within such structures will allow for a free and equal flow of information when engaging in joint career-planning activities.

Proposition 15: The greater the amount of available information and diversity of role choices within a community social structure, the more likely that families residing within such a structure will provide an atmosphere that tolerates the expression of conflicting ideas among family members while engaging in career-planning activities.

Proposition 16: The greater the amount of available information and diversity of role choices within a community social structure, the more likely that families residing within such a structure will establish an atmosphere that avoids premature closure in searching for information and, correspondingly, tolerates ambiguity while information is being sought.

Proposition 17: The greater the amount of available information and di-

versity of role choices within a community social structure, the more likely members of families residing in
such communities will tend to synthesize and abstract
such information in their communication with other
family members.

When these propositions are combined with proposition 11, we have the
basis for establishing the chain of relationships between community social
structure, family internal structure, parent–child interaction, and the
child's problem-solving performance.

Theorem 5: The greater the amount of available information and diversity of role choices within a community social structure, the
greater the equalitarianism, tolerance of conflicting viewpoints, tolerance of ambiguity, and use of abstract concepts
within the parent–child relationship.

Therefore (from theorem 5 and proposition 11):

Theorem 6: The greater the amount of available information and diversity of role choices within a community structure, the more
highly developed the level of information processing of
families living within that structure.

Family Problem-Solving Experience

Propositions 1, 2, 3, 4, and 12 suggest that, given the specified antecedent conditions, prior family problem experience will affect family members' willingness to define a situation as a problem and to take necessary
risks in an effort to solve the problem. Therefore:

Theorem 7: When confronted with new situations involving obstacles
to attaining career goals, adolescents in families whose
members have experienced repeated problem-solving success in similar situations will be more likely to define the
situation as a problem and will be more willing to take reasonable risks in attempting to solve the problem than will
children whose family members have experienced repeated
failures in such situations. More generally, the greater the
problem-solving success in previous similar situations, the
greater the readiness to define a new situation as a problem
and to take the risks necessary to solve the problem.

Finally, applying proposition 13 with theorems 5, 6, and 7, we derive:

Theorem 8:   The greater the amount of available information and the more diverse the role choices available to families within a community structure, and the greater the families' histories of problem-solving success, the more effective will be the problem-solving activities of adolescents who are members of such families, when seeking to solve problems related to career planning.

THE COMPLETE MODEL

We now have a completed explanatory model with the essential variables and the proposed relationships between the variables (see Figure 3.2).

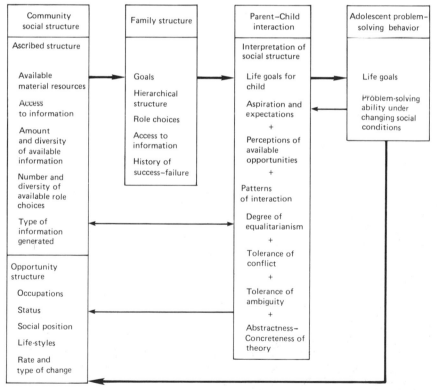

Figure 3.2. *This is an explanatory model indicating the relationship of community and family structure variables on parent–child socialization for problem solving. The heavy arrows show relations predicted by the theory. The narrow arrows show expected reciprocal relationships not considered in this theory.*

The first two blocks in Figure 3.2 identify the specific contextual conditions that channel or constrain parent–child interactions and, subsequently, affect the adolescent child's life goals and problem-solving skills. The behaviors amenable to direct observation are in the third and fourth blocks of the figure.

The variables identified in the third block indicate an additive relationship between adolescent problem-solving ability and the following eight variables: (a) parents' level of aspirations; (b) parents' expectations for their children; (c) parents' optimism or pessimism; (d) degree of family equalitarianism; (e) tolerance of conflict within families; (f) tolerance of ambiguity within families; (g) level of abstraction; and (h) family willingness to take reasonable risks.

The first two blocks provide the conditions that, we hypothesize, affect variations in these behaviors. In the next section of this chapter, we consider these conditions and behaviors in more concrete terms. Specifically, we discuss the five kinds of community social structures that are represented in this study and their hypothesized influence on family structure and parent–child interaction.

THE SOCIAL CONTEXT OF SOCIALIZATION FOR SOCIAL CHANGE

In the previous sections of this chapter, we have provided the essential principles for our explanation for how people learn, set career goals, and solve problems in a changing world. In this section we will illustrate how variations in community social structure influence adolescents' problem solving by affecting the family structure and, consequently, the parent–child relationship. We begin this phase of our analysis with the simplest social structure—the preindustrial peasant village.

Preindustrial Village Structure

A chief characteristic of most preindustrial peasant villages is poverty. In most developing societies, these villages represent a lagging part of a changing economy (see Pi–Sunyer, 1972, pp. 99–100, for a discussion of Mexican peasants' lives). A distinguishing factor of peasant social structures as compared to social structures in more industrialized communities is the fact that the family unit is also the production unit (Diaz & Potter, 1967; Firth, 1969). These units are characterized by a relatively limited number of role relations. The village economy depends upon a few long-standing occupations. Consequently life-styles change only slightly from generation to generation. The social structure has only a few fixed rules, because relationships within the structure are relatively stable and predictable. (See Rogers's, 1969b, discussion of traditional villages, especially pp. 338–340; see also Foster's, 1967, p. 59, breakdown of occupations in a Michoacan village similar to the ones we studied; Nelson, 1971.) Socialization of the young, therefore, should be relatively unambiguous. In this kind of a social structure the sudden introduction of new information cannot be processed with the few established rules or dimensions, consequently much information may not be perceived, may be rejected, or may be simply ignored (proposition 16; Rogers, 1969b, pp. 229–231).

The level of poverty that characterizes most peasant life should, according to theorem 1, result in peasants placing a higher value on material well-being than on familism or other forms of interpersonal well-being. This hypothesis runs contrary to some prevailing notions and seemingly contradicts a considerable body of ethnographic data. In fact, most social scientists tend to agree that the peasant village social structure is centered on the family and kin structure (Doob, 1969; Firth, 1969; Foster, 1967; Nelson, 1971). The issue, however, is not the centrality of families in peasant life but the underlying reason for this centrality. Our position is that loyalty and commitment to family exists primarily for economic purposes rather than interpersonal satisfactions (see Miller, 1973; Young & Young, 1966). Thus if forced to choose between family and economic gain, we predict most peasants would choose the latter (see Rosenfeld, 1958). The alternative position (and perhaps the prevailing position) is that familism results in a nonmaterialistic orientation or, at the very least, inhibits peasants' improving their material lot. Rogers (1969a), for example, maintains that the familism orientation that characterizes peasant life requires sharing the products of individual effort with the family, resulting in low levels of aspirations. Furthermore, he argues that reliance on older family members results in an unwillingness to take risks or to favor innovations. Others maintain that familistic values are negatively related to their measures of "modernity" (Smith & Inkeles, 1966).

Evidence is not overwhelmingly supportive of either of the preceding positions (see Straus, 1972, for a review of the contradictory findings). A critical test of whether peasants would choose familistic over materialistic goals could only be undertaken if peasants were provided a choice between the two alternatives without one alternative confounding the other. Such a test would require that those choosing familism would do so at the cost of material gain and those choosing material advancement would do so at the cost of interfamily relationships. We designed such a test and describe it in the next chapter.

Through access to the mass media, peasant parents are becoming increasingly aware of more affluent life-styles and the rate of rapid change in the larger society. It is reasonable to expect that parents would want their children to enjoy this better life and might have fairly high aspirations for their children. However, because they are pragmatic and realistic, their expectations for their children are likely to be lower than those of members of the society living in a more advantageous social strata.

From theorem 5, we hypothesize that peasant families living in simple social structures will tend to be more patriarchically structured than families living in more complex structures. They should also be more likely to evidence concrete as opposed to abstract thinking and low tolerance for ambiguity, and to allow less conflict over ideas and opinions than families living in more complex structures. As a consequence, we predict that children who live in such family structures will be less able to integrate and process new information and, therefore, will be less competent problem solvers (theorem 6).

These predictions are in accord with those made by investigators who consider peasants to be less able than persons in other social strata to utilize innovations or to risk resources in order to improve their material position. Rather than ascribe this inability to culturally determined orientations, we attribute it to the structural conditions under which these people live. The primary difference between our theory and other explanations (a difference we sought to test) is the stipulation that specific social contextual and family interaction patterns explain differences between social strata in career planning and problem solving.

Modernizing Social Structures

For people functioning in simple social structures, life is clear and unambiguous, although hard. At the same time, the visibility of more affluent life-styles increases the pressure for change. Given our basic assumptions, we infer that the desire for a better life is pervasive; if new information is introduced with clearly beneficial consequences, it will gradually be incorporated into people's thought processes. For example, if chemical fertilizers are introduced to improve the crop yield and to create a surplus for marketing, new rules and additional knowledge will become necessary if people are to deal effectively with these innovations. Rudimentary knowledge of soil chemistry, availability of storage facilities, marketing expertise, the ability to use the existing monetary system to finance equipment purchases all become vital. Experts are called upon and occupational roles are differentiated. Concomitantly, the structure of the village becomes more complex; people are no longer merely villagers or strangers; instead, the categories expand into bankers or salespeople or engineers. As the kinds of roles increase, the ambiguity of stimuli also increase. It takes time to process cues when applying different integrative rules to multiple stimuli. There is a growing awareness that available rules are not always applicable and that new rules need to be generated. The proliferation of roles also increases the proliferation of interest groups with a resulting increase in social conflict (see Eisenstadt, 1966, Chapter 2; Marriott, 1964).

As the social structure increases in complexity, there should be a concomitant increase in the level of integration in information processing (proposition 17). As noted earlier, in modernizing social structures, knowledge is essentially derivative. Thus, family members must discover the established information and the rules for processing that information. Given the primacy of material values in modernizing countries, we expected that families living in modernizing structures would seek to incorporate the rules applied in industrial societies for material advancement and that there would then be an emphasis on deferred gratification, the importance of work, the accumulation of resources for reinvestment, and so forth.

Mexican manual workers and their families approximate this level of development. The line between manual workers and peasants, however, is tenuous and arbitrary. Though not among the most rapidly developing groups in Mexico, peasants, particularly those in central Mexico, do not live under conditions that could be characterized as completely "traditional." Although their daily lives have not changed markedly from past generations, within most villages someone owns an automobile or a truck. Almost every family has a transistor radio and there tends to be at least one or two television sets in a village. Many of the villagers have been to the United States, working as *Braceros* (Cone, 1976, Chapter 13), and others have been to Mexico City or have visited or lived in regional cities.

The vast majority of the manual laborers and service workers in cities have peasant origins. In his description of the Michoacan town of Zamora, Pi–Sunyer (1972) concluded that "the *pobres* (poor) or Zamora ... have much more in common with the *campesinos* (peasants) of the little mestizo ranchos (hamlets) than with the bourgeoisie of the town (pp. 33–34)." Miller's (1973) study of a new small town in Mexico, however, reveals a growing emphasis on the norms of production and achievement among ex-villagers who became the town's workers.

Because of greater opportunities in urban areas, we expected manual workers to be somewhat more optimistic than peasants about their children's life chances. We also believed that because of that optimism, worker's families, when compared to peasant families, would be more likely to stress the value of deferred gratification, to emphasize hard work, and to advocate the benefits of saving money. We hypothesized that, since blue collar families lived in a somewhat more complex social structure, such families would be less authoritarian than peasant families; they would have somewhat more tolerance of ambiguity, and they would be more tolerant of conflicts over ideas (theorem 5). Consequently, we anticipated that although the working-class children in the Mexican sample would share the same life-style goals, they would be more able than their peasant cousins to cope with social changes.

Blue-collar families in highly industrialized societies like the United States pose a different problem. In 1972, when we did our research, the Caucasian blue-collar worker in the United States was probably as economically well off as any group of workers in modern history. This affluence was relatively recent and, therefore, the members of this group had a firmer commitment to the life-style orientations that they believed led to their current affluence. Although blue-collar workers did not have the array of choices available to white-collar workers, and though their work required derivative rather than innovative knowledge, the number of role choices available and the complexity of the social structure suggested that the United States blue-collar families would be more equalitarian and more tolerant of conflict and ambiguity than their Mexican counterparts (theorem 5). We anticipated, then, the children of Twin Cities blue-collar families would value materialistic life-styles but would prove to be better problem solvers than the children of Mexican peasants and workers (theorem 6).

Industrial Social Structures

As structural differentiation continues to develop, career planning tends to approximate more complicated games of strategy. When problems requiring strategic solutions are involved, the actor must be able to anticipate and respond to contingent actions from others in the social structure. If this situation is complicated by conditions of rapid change, established rules for processing information may be inadequate and new rules may need to be generated.

Although the white-collar families in modernizing countries like Mexico functioned within a national society that is in the throes of development, the immediate experiences faced by such families are similar to those facing families living in industrialized structures. With increasing industrialization, the traditional occupational roles for educated persons in Mexico are rapidly expanding. No longer are these roles limited to those of doctor or lawyer; there is a growing need for engineers, planners, civil servants, computer experts, educators, and bureaucrats. In 1972, Mexico was trying to increase its productive capacity through industrialization based on borrowing expertise from industrialized countries. Like other modernizing countries it depended upon derivative knowledge for its development. Thus, the white-collar Mexican family was existing in a paradoxical situation: Their social position placed them in an industrial context while the society as a whole was operating in a modernizing world.

Given this combination of modernizing and industrial structural conditions, we expected white-collar Mexican families to display a more complex division of labor within the family than the other Mexican families or the United States blue-collar families. We also expected that such families would be more equalitarian, would exhibit greater tolerance of differences in ideas, and would be more tolerant of ambiguous situations. They should also have been relatively optimistic concerning their offsprings' life chances. Yet, because such families existed in a modernizing country characterized by scarcity of material goods, we expected them to place a high valuation on material well-being. The children of such families, we hypothesized, would be more effective problem solvers than any group thus far described.

"Postindustrial" Social Structures

If the Mexican white-collar families bridged the gap between modernizing and industrial structures, the United States white-collar families in 1972 seemed to amalgamate experiences that incorporated both industrialized and postindustrialized social structures. The postindustrial society, according to Bell (1968, 1973), is characterized by an exponential rate of growth in specialized, technical, and sophisticated information. It is a society in which pockets of experts, called professionals, develop an idiomatic language that fosters the precision of their communication but limits their audiences to professionals like themselves. The result is a complex, integrated social structure with a great diversity of social positions and social roles. In such a society information processing is highly developed and highly specialized. The number of different occupations is consequently very large. Members of such societies, especially those in privileged positions, appear to have an almost infinite number of career choices.

In 1972, and even today, postindustrial societies like the United States are characterized by an abundance of material goods. We predicted, therefore, based on the theory developed in this chapter that United States white-collar families would be less likely to value material attainment at the cost of interpersonal satisfactions. Thus we expected the terminal career goals of United States white-collar adolescents to emphasize such outcomes as happy family life over being wealthy or having a well-paying job.

The complexity of the social structure and the high levels of information processing that characterized their social structure led us to hypothesize that the United States white-collar families would be egalitarian and have high levels of tolerance for ambiguity and conflict. Consequently we also expected that United States white-collar adolescents would prove to be the best problem solvers in the study. We are wiser now—but that story must wait for Chapter 5.

SUMMARY

We have presented our a priori answers to the questions, How do children learn to cope with a changing society? and How do the social structures of the communities and the family combine to affect this learning process?

Socialization patterns within the family are considered to be affected by the social structure in which the child and his or her parents live. The family, through the parent–child relationship, mediates between the child and the social structure. Through the mediation process the child learns the skills to apply when dealing with a changing society. This mediation process takes two forms: (*a*) the interpretation of the social structure to the child; and (*b*) experiences and decisions that take place as parents and their child collectively engage in planning and problem solving.

It was hypothesized that the life-style goals families project for their offspring are largely determined by the scarcity of material resources. In some ways these predictions are contrary to the collective wisdom pertaining to social development. Rather than viewing familism in developing countries as a deterrent to continued development, familistic orientations are considered to be of secondary importance to material attainment. In fact, it is suggested that the affluent white-collar Americans rather than the Mexicans are the most likely group to have a major commitment to the family and to other sources of interpersonal satisfaction.

Although we did not predict class differences within societies on life-style goals, we did predict such differences for parental aspirations and expectations and parents' perceptions of their children's opportunities. We expected peasant and working-class parents to have reasonably high aspirations but lower expectations and perceptions of opportunity for their children than middle-class parents.

The number, distribution, and diversity of role choices plus the amount and diversity of information within the social structure were hypothesized to be positively associated with the level of information processing and information integration within the family. The variables, in turn, were thought to produce effective problem solvers. Briefly, we hypothesized that the more complex and diverse the social structure, the greater the necessity for families to be egalitarian and to tolerate ambiguity and conflict. These family attributes were then linked to developing problem-solving skills.

Finally, it was hypothesized that family members' experiences of success or failure in attaining instrumental or terminal career goals will affect children's problem-solving orientations. Children who experienced an atmosphere of failure were predicted to be more tentative and less innovative in

Table 3.1

Hypotheses Pertaining to the Relationship between Structural Complexity and Success Goals, Family Structure, and Children's Problem-Solving Ability

Structural complexity (least to most)	Goals	Family structure		Child's problem-solving ability
		Interpretive	Reconstructive	
Mexican peasant villagers	Materialistic	Moderately high aspirations—moderately low expectations Poor life chances for offspring	Rigid hierarchical structure (patriarchal) Concrete black and white thinking Low tolerance of ambiguity Low tolerance of conflict	Poor
Mexican manual workers	Materialistic	Moderately high aspirations—moderate expectations Moderate life chances for offspring	Somewhat rigid hierarchical structure (patriarchal) Moderately concrete (black and white) thinking Some tolerance of ambiguity Some tolerance of conflict	Poor–Moderate
United States blue-collar	Materialistic	High aspirations—moderate expectations Moderate life chances for offspring	Moderately rigid hierarchical structure (patriarchal) Moderate concrete thinking Moderate tolerance of ambiguity Moderate tolerance of conflict	Moderate
Mexican white collar	Materialistic	High aspirations—moderate expectations Good life chances for offspring	Moderately rigid hierarchical structure Abstract thinking Moderately high tolerance of ambiguity Moderately high tolerance of conflict	Good
United States white collar	Familistic	High aspirations—moderate expectations Good life chances for offspring	Equalitarian family structure Abstract thinking Tolerance of ambiguity High tolerance of conflict	Good

their own problem-solving activities than those whose families had a history of relative success.

The theoretical explanation was applied to families and children living under five social structural conditions—preindustrial peasants, blue-collar workers and white-collar workers living in a modernizing community structure, and blue-collar and white-collar workers living in a highly industrialized structure. Table 3.1 provides the hypotheses that derive from this application.

These hypotheses represent our best thinking prior to conducting the research. We were not so naive that we expected the results to support all of our hypotheses. Our theory was neither precise nor complete enough to suggest such an outcome. We did hope, however, that our research would provide an adequate test for the major theorems in the theory and thereby would provide a basis for assessing the theory's essential utility.

4 | Seeking the Answers

INTRODUCTION

To meet the requirements of the theoretical model, we needed to compare three different units of analyses—the community social structure, the parent–child relationship (within the family structure), and the individual child. Providing an adequate indicator of the social structure was particularly problematic. The theory required measures of both the "ascribed" structure and the "opportunity" structure. We needed to assess variation in the ascribed social structure while holding constant the opportunity structure. It was also necessary to develop a means for observing family patterns of interaction, to measure the affects of success and failure in the family's efforts to achieve its goals, and to observe the child's ability to problem solve under conditions of social change. These measurements had to be made in two time periods so that we could differentiate between socialization processes and outcomes. Finally, our methods had to be applicable to different social strata and cultures.

This chapter describes our efforts to deal with these research problems. In broad outline, we developed a game simulation to measure parent–adolescent socialization in both hypothetical and real time. We asked parents and their adolescent child to plan a child's career over a hypothetical 10-year period. This provided a means for estimating the life goals families set for their children and how they plan to attain those goals. The real time

81

period was limited to the 1–1.5 hours the parents and child participated in the game simulation together and to the additional hour during which the child played the game alone. During the initial game, observers recorded game choices and coded family interactions, allowing us to measure socialization for problem solving. The child's performance during the game that was played alone provided a means for assessing the outcome of such socialization.

Variation in the ascribed structure was produced by sampling families living under different levels of social development and holding different social positions in given stratification systems. The opportunity structure was held constant by means of the game simulation which provided equal opportunities to families who were sampled from different social strata and from communities representing different levels of social–industrial development. In the parent–child game, we introduced conditions of success or failure, and in the child's game we simulated conditions of social change. Data from the family game were the bases for drawing inferences about the family's internal structure. We determined the values, goals, and expectations of families through interviews prior to the family's participation in the game simulation. The child's problem-solving performance was determined by measuring his or her choices and achievements while playing the game.

These are the bare bones of our methodology. The details and dimensions necessary for understanding what we did, why we did it, and the constraints under which we did it follow.

THE RESEARCH SITES

The natural history of a research project rarely follows the logical steps outlined in methodology texts. Our decision to use the Twin Cities as a research site, for example, derived from the fact that most of the research staff were employed by the University of Minnesota and the funds for the project were administered by the University of Minnesota Family Study Center. The decision to use Mexico as our modernizing country was influenced in large part by prior and long-standing relations between social science faculty at the University of Minnesota and a group of sociologists at the Instituto Méxicano de Estudios Sociales (Mexican Institute of Social Research), or IMES, in Mexico City. Under the direction of Luis Leñero, IMES had conducted a number of significant studies of Mexican families and had participated in several collaborative studies with University of Minnesota social scientists.

Despite these extraneous influences, the choice of Mexico and the

United States can be justified on theoretical grounds. These countries were comparable in stressing equalitarian values and emphasizing the value of earned (or achieved) status. Both societies also tended to emphasize money as a legitimate reward for successful achievement. They differed, however, in the three ways that our theory suggested would influence life goals and the strategies people would employ to achieve those goals. First, the United States was considerably more affluent than Mexico. Second, the number and types of possible occupational roles were much greater in the United States than in Mexico. Finally, at the time of the study, in 1972, Mexico was one of the most rapidly developing countries in the world. Although the urban middle class enjoyed the greatest benefits from this economic growth, change was visible in many segments of the population and there was an increasing awareness of mobility opportunities, even among peasants. This, we thought, would have a direct effect on parents' perceptions of job opportunities for their children.

In a series of conferences sponsored by the Minnesota Center for Comparative Studies in Technological Development and Social Change, conducted in both the Twin Cities and Mexico City in the latter part of 1970, a cooperative program of research was agreed upon between IMES and the Center. It was agreed that the focal point of this research would be the state of Michoacan and the city of Zacapu, an industrialized town of 32,000 people. In addition to Zacapu, four rural villages were selected for study. The villages consisted almost entirely of peasant families. The limited number of occupational roles available to villagers, and an economy that wavered between a subsistence and a minimal cash orientation, suggested that these villages approximated the preindustrial peasant communities described in the previous chapter.

Michoacan was part of a region slated for governmental assistance through "Plan Lerma," an agency concerned with fostering self-development through technical assistance. Plan Lerma introduced fertilizer to some farms, helped develop cooperatives for marketing pottery and other handicrafts, established schools for training adolescent girls to serve as public health aides, and so forth. As a result, some peasant villages had been the recipients of considerable governmental attention, whereas others remained relatively untouched. Plan Lerma was also a major reason for the interest of IMES in the area.

The state of Michoacan and the city of Zacapu offered several advantages for this project. First, a number of nearby towns had been sites of ethnographic studies over the past 40 years, and considerable data describing the area had already been reported. This provided background material which allowed us to put the research in cultural and historical perspective. Also, unlike other cities in Michoacan, Zacapu was primarily an industrial rather than a commercial center. Even a cursory glance at the city with its neon signs, bustling streets, television antennas, retail stores, small factories, large Celenese plant, and streets filled with trucks suggested that it differed dramatically from the closest neighboring city, Patzcuaro. Patzcuaro, the local center of colonial Spanish rule, remained a farming community and a tourist center for marketing peasant goods.

The four villages are located in and around an old lake bed that had become a fertile agricultural resource. Three of the villages, Tirindaro, Naranja, and Tarejero, were inhabited primarily by Tarascan Indians; the other village, Tariacuri, was mestizo (a mixture of Indian and Spanish). Tirindaro and Naranja are located on the highway to Patzcuaro on the flatlands at the southern edge of the old lake bed. Tariacuri and Tarejero occupy the hillsides of what once were islands in the lake. Tarejero had a population of 1970, Tirindaro, 2591, Naranja, 1942, and Tariacuri, 2001. Most of the people in these villages earned their incomes from farming the lakebed—mainly corn. Only Tirindaro and Tarejero had secondary schools. (For a more detailed description of the villages and Zacapu, see Cone, 1976.)

The Twin Cities metropolitan area in 1972 had a population of slightly less than 2 million people representing about half the population of the state of Minnesota. In many ways the area cannot be considered typical of United States metropolitan communities. The central cities of Minneapolis and St. Paul maintained a much larger proportion of its middle-class population in the 1950s and 1960s, when many United States cities lost these populations to the suburbs. The proportion of black, Native American, Chicano, and other minorities of non-European background was less than 3% of the population.

At the same time, the Twin Cities community, like most United States metropolitan areas, had a considerable degree of ethnic and religious heterogeneity. St. Paul was predominantly Catholic with strong Irish and German influences. Minneapolis was predominantly Lutheran; and since the Civil War, people of Scandinavian origin were a major economic, political, and social force in the community. Despite these influences, most religious groups are represented in the Twin Cities area, and there are sizable numbers of people with French, Polish, Ukranian, and New England Yankee backgrounds.

The industrial and occupational composition of the community is also heterogeneous. The Twin Cities began as shipping, trading, and commercial centers for the upper Northwest and they still carry out those functions. In the latter half of the nineteenth century, the cities also became centers for the flour milling and lumber industries. Since that time the economy has become increasingly more diversified; most recently the area has established a large number of electronic and computer firms. In 1972, when our study was conducted, unemployment in the Twin Cities was low and the income levels for both blue- and white-collar workers were at an all-time high.

In each research site, we sampled families with 12–15-year-old sons or daughters. Our family unit consisted of a father, mother, and one son or daughter. Thus, the study was restricted to "intact" families (i.e., both parents were present) with at least one early adolescent child.

In Zacapu and the Twin Cities, we sampled both blue- and white-collar families. The determination of whether a family was blue- or white-collar was based on the father's occupation. In Zacapu, with the full cooperation of the municipality's superintendent of secondary education, all students of public primary and secondary schools between the ages of 11 and 14 were asked to fill out a form listing the names and addresses of their parents, their father's occupation, and their own names and ages. Samples of equal numbers of blue- and white-collar parents of boys and girls were drawn. First-year social science students from Ibero Americana University in Mexico City were trained to administer the structured interview schedule. They personally contacted all families in the sample, arranged for appointments, and interviewed separately each husband and wife. The total completed interview sample consisted of 179 blue-collar fathers and mothers and 154 white-collar fathers and mothers in Zacapu. The refusal rate was under 5%.

In the villages virtually all families who had appropriately aged children were interviewed. These families were identified in the same way as was done in Zacapu. However, as fewer children were in school, the lists were augmented by interviews with key informants. Since the villages averaged between 1500 and 2000 inhabitants, such identification was not particularly difficult. In total, we interviewed 111 families, and all agreed to participate in the interviews. The reasons for this cooperation were complex, but in retrospect we believe that the peasant families may have been somewhat coerced by the middle-class Mexico City students who conducted the interviews. Also, we found that the Michoacanos, both in Zacapu and in the villages, rarely refused any request directly. In general, however, the Mexican families seemed genuinely pleased to see our interviewers and participated with interest and enthusiasm.

The sampling procedures in the Twin Cities were more complex and less adequate. The high degree of religious and ethnic homogeneity in the Michoacan population made it difficult to make comparisons with the more varied Twin Cities population. In an attempt to control some of this variability, census data were used to select representative blue- and white-collar districts within the cities. Then we contacted the Lutheran and Catholic churches in these areas, since they represented the dominant religions. These churches provided lists of children between the ages of 11 and

15, their parents' names and addresses, and their fathers' occupations. We sent letters to the parents explaining the project and followed up with telephone calls to schedule interviews. Slightly less than ⅔ of our United States sample was drawn from these sources. The sample was completed by using names provided by the Twin Cities YWCA, the Boy Scouts, and city directories of white-collar and blue-collar suburbs on the urban fringe. Husbands and wives were interviewed separately by trained graduate and undergraduate research assistants from the University of Minnesota. The total United States sample consisted of 142 blue-collar parents and 156 white-collar parents. The refusal rate was 36%.

PLANNING FOR CROSS-NATIONAL RESEARCH

Drawing appropriate samples for comparisons is only one of the problems with which we had to be concerned in undertaking comparative and cross-national research. In this section we discuss the problems we anticipated and our efforts to overcome them. Later we consider how successful these efforts were and some of the problems we did not foresee.

The difference between cross-national research and research within a given culture is not so much a difference in kind as in degree. Errors in design and measurement can occur more easily and can produce more devastating effects in cross-cultural research (see Frey, 1970, p. 80, and Straus, 1968). Armer (1973), in his review of the literature on comparative research, concluded that most of the critiques of research in the field can be classified under two essential areas of concern, problems of *cultural appropriateness* and problems of *conceptual equivalence*. Appropriateness refers to how applicable the entire research process is to each culture under study. According to Armer:

> The primary methodological implications of foreign settings is that theoretical problems and concepts, strategies for gaining access and cooperation, sampling methods, measuring techniques and instruments, data collection, and analysis procedures and other aspects of the research process which are appropriate for research in one's own culture, will often not be appropriate and valid for research in foreign cultures. Indeed, it should be assumed that research methods may have to be adapted or newly devised for each culture (p. 3).

Culturally appropriate research requires that the investigator have a reasonable understanding of the kinds of interpretations subjects will make of the stimuli presented to them as well as how these interpretations may differ with different forms of presentations. Without such an understanding, the inferences drawn from subjects' responses are likely to be invalid. Achieving such appropriateness requires that the stimuli presented to subjects be placed in a culturally relevant context so that the responses elicited will pertain to the concerns of the investigation.

Because stimuli must be culturally appropriate, it is frequently not possible to provide respondents in different cultures with exactly the same stimuli (Blood & Hill, 1970; Frey, 1970; Przeworski & Teune, 1970; Straus, 1969). Blood and Hill (1970) illustrate the problem in their discussion of attempts to replicate the Blood and Wolfe (1960) marital power instrument in foreign countries. The essential problem was that certain decision-making issues in Blood and Wolfe's Detroit sample were not salient in Japan, Greece, France, and Belgium. Housing and life insurance, important decision-making issues for husbands and wives in the United States, were not relevant in Japan and Greece. In France, deciding which doctor to go to was not so much a matter of marital power as of family status. These difficulties do not imply that the concept of marital power was not relevant for each of the countries, but rather that the choices provided as indicators of such power in the United States were not always appropriate for other countries studied. Cross-cultural comparisons require that the items (or stimuli) used are *conceptually* equivalent, not that they are identical (Frey, 1970; Miller, Slomczynski, & Schoenberg, 1981; Straus, 1968).

How do investigators assure themselves and others that their measures are conceptually equivalent? There is no cookbook approach to this problem. Frey (1970) suggests that the key test of conceptual equivalence lies in the validity of the measures. But Frey, Armer, and others also point out that more than instrumentation is involved in obtaining comparable data. They submit that a complete solution to the problem of obtaining both cultural appropriateness and conceptual equivalence is never fully achievable.

The problems of cultural appropriateness and conceptual equivalence are relevant to all aspects of the research endeavor. They were, therefore, of central concern in the development of the research instruments.

INSTRUMENT DEVELOPMENT

The development of the interview schedule and the game simulation proceeded simultaneously in both countries. Because the design called for the interview to precede the game simulation, we shall begin with a discussion of the interview.

Development of the Survey Interview

The interview was designed to elicit data on parental occupations, expectations, and aspirations for their children, as well as values pertaining to time orientation, role expectations, and commitment to deferred gratification. In addition, demographic information was collected to allow us to identify migration patterns, intergenerational social mobility, family size, occupations, education, and social class. (See Appendix 1 for the complete interview schedule in English and in Spanish.)

To determine parental aspirations, expectations, and perceptions of opportunities for sons or daughters, we used a ranking system of pictures depicting a variety of occupations. A series of 40 drawings representing 20 different occupations for women and 20 for men were developed in each country. The costuming and physical characteristics of the persons depicted in the drawings were appropriate for the two societies. After pretesting and modifying the original drawings, 10 pictures were decided upon for each of the four subgroups (United States boys and girls and Mexican boys and girls). The occupations chosen for each country could be hierarchically ranked on the basis of skill and/or prestige. Pictures for boys in both Mexico and the United States depicted the following occupations: physician, clergyman (in Mexico, the picture clearly represented a priest; in the United States, the illustration was such that the distinction between priest and minister was not discernible), teacher, politician, storekeeper, skilled worker, farmer, soldier,[1] mason, and laborer. For girls, the occupations were doctor, politician, nun, teacher, nurse, clerk (in the United States) or small store owner (in Mexico), secretary, farmer, maid, and wife and mother. Parents, interviewed separately but at the same session, were shown the pictures at three different times during the course of the interview. First, they were asked to compare each picture with every other picture and to select the occupation that they would most prefer for their child if it were a perfect world and if their child could have any occupation he or she wished. These responses provided the data for rank ordering parents' aspirations. The pictures were again shown to parents, and they were asked to determine whether in the present world they thought a person had a good, bad, or moderate chance of attaining the particular jobs being depicted. This gave us an estimate of parents' perception of opportunities for their children in their current social structure. The parents were asked a third time to rank order the pictures in terms of the occupation they thought their child had the best chance of obtaining. This provided us with the rank ordering of parental expectations.

There was relatively little difficulty in using this technique in the pretests conducted in the United States. In Mexico some initial resistance was encountered. The staff claimed that parents refused to participate in rank ordering the pictures. After a number of conferences with both per-

[1] The occupation of soldier was included because some consultants thought that the military was a means of upward mobility for the poor Mexicans. Nevertheless, Mexican parents generally ranked soldiering low.

sons in Mexico and persons in the United States who had experience in cross-national research, we were convinced that the technique was workable. We thus encouraged the staff to persevere, and subsequent pretests demonstrated that the procedure was possible in Mexico.

The interview schedule was originally written in English then translated into Spanish. Ramona Marotz–Baden, Pablo Pindas, and Guadalupe Zetina, a graduate assistant, rewrote questions that were culturally biased. Finally, the schedule was translated back into English to check comparability of meanings.

The IMES staff was disturbed by the number of Likert-type scales in the original interview schedule. This type of scale forces the subject to select from five to seven levels on a continuum using descriptive statements such as *like very much, like somewhat,* and so forth, to *dislike very much.* In previous studies the IMES staff found that five-point scales were cumbersome, confusing, and difficult. One of the problems was the greater wordiness of the Spanish language. It was difficult to find concise gradations that could be made in Spanish without requiring a large number of words. The Mexican staff believed that the time it would take to explain how respondents could score a Likert scale would be excessive. In fact, although the pretests of the interview took less than an hour in the United States, the same interview in Spanish took almost two hours. Most scales were therefore reduced to three levels in both countries.

The Kluckhohn–Strodtbeck (1961) time orientation scale was used as our indicator of future orientation. The Spanish translation of the scale had been used with Spanish-Americans in the southwestern part of the United States and with Mexicans in the Yucatan. However, the Mexican staff felt that the language in a number of the items was inappropriate for Mexico and made the appropriate alterations. Language was also changed in some instances because the Spanish-American dialect differs significantly from the Mexican. Other scales utilized were the Reissman Social Mobility Scale (1959) and Tharp's Marital Role Expectation Scale (1963). In addition, we developed a measure of distributive justice beliefs. This set of questions was divided into two sections, one pertaining to appropriate beneficiaries of an individual's efforts and the other posing specific exchange relationships and varying the statuses of the hypothetical persons involved. For example, one of the questions posed was, "Imagine you own a farm and you want to hire one person to help you. Two people who are equally good workers apply. One is a relative who is not very poor. The other is a stranger who is very poor. To whom would you give the job?" The respondents were then asked to give the reasons for their answers.

At the end of the interview, the game simulation was described to the parents and they were asked whether they would wish to participate if they were selected. All the Mexican parents agreed to participate, and only 5% of the Twin Cities parents declined.

SIMCAR: The Game Simulation

The simulation we developed, which we called SIMCAR (SIMulation of CAReer patterns), falls somewhere between the survey and the laboratory experiment in its realism, representativeness, level of complexity, capacity to control confounding variables, and ability to manipulate independent variables.

SIMCAR: Underlying Principles[2]

The term *game simulation* depicts the two essential elements of this technique. It is a simulation or simplified model of certain aspects of social life in game form.

The use of simulation games as a research technique is largely based on two assumptions: Games of one form or another are found in all cultures; and the rules by which games are played can be linked to elements in the social structure. Coleman (1970) states that the game is similar to life situations in the following formal characteristics:

> *a)* The players have goals toward which they act, although these goals may be changed by the course of the game; *b)* their actions are governed by a set of rules that specify which actions are prescribed, which are permitted, and which are proscribed; (and) *c)* there is another set of rules, which may be either stated in advance or discovered only in the course of play, that specify the consequences of each action in aiding or inhibiting each player's movement toward his goal (p. 3).

In essence, he claims that the structure of games—that is, the implicit rules by which they are played—is isomorphic with essential elements in the social structure.

Games differ from life situations in two important aspects. First, they have specified beginnings and predictable, foreseeable ends. The outcome may be problematic for any given individual, but the type of outcome and the time span for achieving goals are known. Second, even though virtually everybody has an implicit knowledge of the underlying structure of game playing, there are cultural differences in the types of games played and the individuals designated as appropriate game players. These differences need

---

[2]The description that follows is drawn, in part, from "SIMCAR: A Game Simulation Method for Cross-National Family Research" by Tallman, Wilson, and Straus (1974).

consideration in assessing the utility of game simulation as a research methodology.

SIMCAR attempted to replicate aspects of the life situation of participants. To the extent that players became involved in the significance of the decisions they made, the simulation ceased to be a game in the frivolous sense of the term. In our research, most parents in the United States and in Mexico considered SIMCAR as an opportunity to plan career contingencies with their children. In fact, the most prevalent criticism of the game was that it was not sufficiently realistic. For example, several Twin Cities white-collar families became angry when they found that they had not saved enough money in previous rounds to put their children into college, stating this would never happen because they would be able to borrow the money. Others complained that no opportunities for graduate school were provided or that specific occupations were not included. Such reactions suggest that the significance of the game to the participants transcended the usual notion of play.

Assumptions Underlying the Construction of SIMCAR

Although simulations replicate aspects of social reality, they are nonetheless simplifications of such reality. Moreover, the designer of the simulation has complete knowledge of the rules, payoffs, and alternatives available to the participants—a condition never possible in reality. In effect, simulations are a model of the designer's conception of social reality.

We set out to simulate those aspects of social structure related to lifestyle opportunities and career advancement. The minimal rewards in the social structures of both countries were honor, prestige, power, money (and the things money can buy), interpersonal support, and affection. We assumed that, of the various rewards available, the most universally desirable were material goods. In both industrial and industrializing countries this takes the form of money. In any society, some people may seek to maximize nonmonetary values, but, for the society as a whole, money appears to have a ubiquitous influence. Values like prestige, power, and positive interpersonal relations appear to be positively correlated with income. We concluded, therefore, that in both Mexico and the United States success would be associated with the acquisition of money. Even if other values such as family well-being were considered more important than money, money should still be considered as necessary to maintain the family.

Thus SIMCAR was constructed on the basis of an economic-consumption model. That is, the way to make the most points in the game was to choose alternatives that maximized financial return. Alternative routes were provided, but they did not yield maximum points. Doing well in the game implicitly emphasized the values of deferred gratification and occupational career orientations.

Our intent was to achieve conceptual equivalence between the Michoacan and Twin Cities samples by having families participate in an activity that was salient in both societies: planning the future of a child within the context of a money oriented social structure. We also hoped to maximize cultural appropriateness by providing choices and career patterns that were familiar to the residents of each of the communities we studied. The game simulation allowed us to vary the choices in each community while maintaining conceptual equivalence among these choices. The underlying structure of the game in the villages, Zacapu, and the Twin Cities established choice and decision patterns, operating rules, and status differentials that were the same across cultures, whereas the specific choices were between familiar items in each of the communities studied.

Description of SIMCAR

SIMCAR is a greatly modified version of the simulation game CAREER, developed by Boocock (1968) for educational purposes. The SIMCAR modification simulates occupational, educational, marriage, religious, and consumption decisions typically made by and for children in late adolescence and early adulthood.

Five alternative occupational routes were provided in each of the three communities. Two routes, agriculture and machine (or factory) work, were more common to men; two others, home economics and dress manufacturing in the United States and nursing and dress manufacturing in Mexico, were more common to women; one route, office work, was common to both men and women. Families and children were free to choose any of the five routes they wished (or, for that matter, to shift from one route to another).

The routes were divided into four hierarchical levels, each requiring certain educational and work experience prerequisites. Money earned in the game was proportionate to the occupational level achieved. The occupational routes and their requisites were presented in the form of tiles on the playing board and were described by the experimenter so that families could plan a career pattern for the child even before the first round of the game. (See Appendix 2 for the routes and the education and work experience requirements for obtaining a given hierarchical level.)

The game was played on a board upon which were placed tiles depicting the various activities and the amount of time and money required for each.[3]

---

[3] Time requirements were depicted by one color and money requirements by another. Although part of the Mexican sample could not read, all could identify numbers as well as add and subtract. Furthermore, at least one member of the family, the child, was literate.

The tiles were 5 × 5 inches and contained illustrations of the activities they represented. For example, the agricultural career route in the United States and in Zacapu was depicted by a farmer on a tractor and in the villages by a farmer with a hoe. Items that could be purchased in the store were illustrated on another tile, and so forth. The tiles were sufficiently large so that the participants could place the money and time chips on them. The United States and Mexican boards are pictured on the end papers of the book. Figure 4.1 provides an enlarged replication of one tile.

The SIMCAR phase of the study was divided into two parts. With few exceptions (to be described later), in the first part the parents and child played the game together. In the second part, the child played the game alone while the parents were interviewed in another room.

In both the family and child-alone games, the simulation was introduced as a game played covering 10 years of a child's life, starting with the last year of high school or its cultural equivalent. The object of the game was to obtain as many points as possible; the points could be redeemed for money at the game's conclusion. Participants were told that it would be advisable to plan their investments of time and money over the length of the game. Points were won through selection of activities (all of which required investments of time, money, or both), such as going to school, working, playing

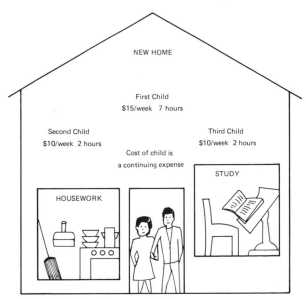

Figure 4.1. *This is an enlargement of tile for new home option (subsequent to marriage). The new home budget equals 80% of the new family's earnings. The cost of marriage equals $10 for ceremony plus 20% of the income (second year).*

sports, marrying, having children, choosing various leisure time activities, and purchasing items. Points were given at the end of each round based on the investments made, providing feedback as to the utility of the players' choices.[4] The best strategy for maximizing points would be to study or work as much as possible, save money, and spend it in the final round when investments in marriage, children, and store purchases did not entail subsequent costs. Although the choices were not identical for all samples, they all represented the same categories—education, work, religion, leisure, consumption, family, and friends. Thus, comparisons of the priorities in investments were possible between the Twin Cities, Zacapu, and village samples.

Players decided how much time and money to invest in each of the choices. In the first round, they had $20 and 60 hours to invest.[5] The money available varied in subsequent rounds depending on the education, job, and consumption decisions made. The hours, however, remained constant; that is, players had 60 hours to invest in each round. When the family played, the child was assumed to be 16 years old at the start of the game. Each round represented 2 years in the life of the child and a total of 6 rounds were played.[6] The child's game began at age 18 and went for 10 rounds, with each round representing 1 year in the child's life.[7]

Prior to each round, an "unplanned event card" was picked from the top of the deck of such cards and read to the players. These cards were equivalent to external conditions over which families had no control. Cards re-

[4] The point allocation system is presented in Appendix 5 and 6.

[5] The family was actually given $100, but $80 was taken for household expenses. Throughout this discussion, the United States form of the game will be discussed in the text and the Mexican equivalents will be presented in footnotes. With regard to the money allocations, the greater range of incomes in Mexico beween white-collar, blue-collar, and village families necessitated different allocations of funds for each group. In the first round, white-collar families started with 1000 pesos, blue-collar families, 500 pesos, and village families, 100 pesos. The costs of all investment choices were made proportional to incomes and points earned were equivalent in all groups including the United States. Hours remained constant across cultures. Money was represented by play money appropriately designated for the United States and Mexico. Hours were represented by poker chips.

[6] Because of time limitations and the greater tendency of Mexican families to consider decisions at length, the number of rounds in the family game in Mexico was reduced to four. Each round represented 3 years, and the scores for Mexican and United States families were standardized by multiplying United States scores by .67.

[7] Ages for starting the child's game varied in the three communities studied. In the United States the starting age was 18, the average age of graduation from high school. In Zacapu, the industrial town in Mexico, the game began at age 17, the average age of graduation from preparatory school (roughly equivalent to United States high school). In villages where no preparatory school existed, the starting age was 16, which corresponds to the average age for finishing secondary school (roughly equivalent to a United States junior high school).

ferred to economic conditions that affected the players' job opportunities, teachers' attitudes that affected success in school, unexpected illness, and so forth. The cards also gave players a choice of moving to a new community to improve their job opportunities.

At the end of each round of both the family's and the child's game, the players' investments in each of the 13 game choices were recorded in terms of the time and money spent. In addition, school grades (related to amount of time invested) and degrees earned were recorded. The type of school and/or the type of job chosen and the amount and type of goods purchased in the store were recorded on a separate form. These data provided a round-by-round record of the strategies families and children employed in seeking their goals. (See Appendix 8 for the appropriate forms.)

In the second round a tape recorder was introduced to remind players of the choices that were available to them. In this round and in each subsequent round, the recorded voice asked questions such as, "Do you want to go to school?" or "Do you wish to buy anything at the store?" The questions were presented in a different order in every round to avoid possible response biases. The experimenter would turn off the recorder if the family wished to ask additional questions or wished to discuss an issue in detail. The principle reason for using the recorder was to hold as constant as possible the effects that different experimenters might have on families' performances and to facilitate families' progress through the simulation at a reasonably rapid rate.

During the family game, a trained observer coded interaction patterns among family members. Observations were made on family power and support, areas of conflict, and communication channels. Intercoder reliability checks yielded greater than 90% agreement between coders in each country. These observations were coded so as to identify the family member who sent a message, the family member who received the message, and whether the message was accepted, rejected, or ignored. Codings were made on a moving paper tape which provided a rough measurement of the passage of time and sequencing of events. A line was drawn across the tape at the end of each round. These data provided us with the means for determining the amount of conflict expressed within families (the proportion of messages rejected) and the degree of ambiguity tolerated (the proportion of all messages that were not acted upon immediately). The data also allowed us to assess the distribution of power (i.e., directives that were accepted) among family members, enabling us to characterize family interactions as primarily patriarchal, equalitarian, and so forth. In all instances our unit of measurement was the family, not the individual. (See Appendix 7 for coding instructions provided to observers.) All verbal communications during the game were tape recorded.

The Success–Failure Condition

The unplanned event cards were used to create conditions of success, failure, or neutrality. In the success conditions, a general aura of positiveness was created by cards providing statements such as the child was elected class president, or that the family was provided a tax refund,[8] or job promotion. In the failure conditions, difficulties were introduced by cards indicating a serious illness to the breadwinner, loss of jobs, house damage, and job demotions, and so forth. Neutral cards were balanced with the positive, and negative events presented so that external conditions would not have any consistent effect on the way the family could play the game. (See Appendix 3 for statements on unplanned event cards.) In addition, the family's score at the end of each round was compared with a hypothetical "average" score of families. These scores were manipulated so that families in the success condition always scored higher than the average and families in the failure condition scored lower than the average.

Creation of Social Change

In the child's game social change was introduced by means of the unplanned event cards at the beginning of the third round. In the first two rounds an assessment was made on the basis of the child's investments as to the type of career route the child planned. The experimenter then used a set of unplanned event cards which made opportunities in the child's chosen career increasingly more difficult and provided better opportunities in other areas. For example, if a child chose college and a business career, the unplanned event card in round three stated that there were too many people seeking jobs in business and the top positions were no longer available. The fourth round card stated that top jobs were available in agriculture or the tool and machinist fields. In addition, a new school was introduced which provided the training necessary for top jobs in other than the original occupation chosen, if the child was willing to invest $30 and 30 hours for each of two rounds. The child who did not choose to change routes or go to the new school found in subsequent rounds that the unplanned event cards demoted him or her one occupational level, increased the pay in alternative job routes, further reduced the salary in the original job route, and so forth. Through this procedure we could determine whether or not the child would adopt an alternative route in the face of change and how quickly he or she would make the alternative choices. (See Appendix 4 for content of the unplanned event cards for the child's game.)

---

[8] In Mexico, equivalent funds were given on the basis of winning money in a raffle.

Game Rules

The rules under which the game was played were intended to be isomorphic with the social structure the game simulated. By keeping the rules constant for all of our participants, we were holding the simulated social structure constant.

Procedural Rules. Procedural rules delineated the various activities and their order of occurrence. The procedure we used was as follows: The experimenter asked the family to sit in front of the game board. He or she then introduced the tape recorded instructions and explained that the instructions to the game were given on the recorder. After the taped instructions had been played, the experimenter asked for questions and attempted to clarify possible misunderstandings. Permission was obtained for audiotaping the session. Next, the experimenter read the unplanned event card for the first round and showed it to the family so that they could read it.

The coder began coding family interaction after the unplanned event card was read for the first round. At this time the participants allocated their available resources (time and money) as they wished. They could ask questions at any time. However, the experimenter only answered questions concerning the rules of the game. He or she did not encourage or discourage any particular move or game strategy. There was no set order in which the family was to allocate their resources. When all of the resources were allocated according to the rules, the experimenter went to a large scoreboard where all the possible activities were listed. The experimenter asked if the subjects participated in each activity and to what extent, and then he or she allocated the appropriate number of points. The total points for the round were added and then compared to the average family score for that round. These average scores, created in the manner reported earlier in our discussion of success–failure, were already posted on the blackboard, ostensibly to help the parents and child gauge their progress.

The points at the end of each round provided feedback concerning the players' relative progress. With this information, players could adjust their strategies by considering alternative occupational and educational routes or by reallocating their investments of time and money. However, investments such as savings or time in school were carried over from round to round. Similarly some debts were also carried over. Purchasing could be made on the installment plan and having children cost $15 from the family income in subsequent rounds.

After completion of the first round, the time chips and money were picked up from the game board, and the unplanned event card for the next round was read aloud and shown to the family. The experimenter explained

that for the remaining rounds, a recorded voice would go through every activity asking the family to decide if they wished to invest time and money in
each of the activities. If the family wished, the tape would be turned off and
the experimenter would answer any questions and wait until they were
ready to turn the recorder on again. The remaining four rounds were played
identically to round two.

When the game had been completed, the parents were taken to another
room for a postsimulation interview. This interview is detailed later in this
chapter. The child was given a review of the game instructions and then
played the game again alone. This time, however, no tape was used and the
coder was not present. Game choices were recorded by the experimenter.
When the child finished, the family was reunited, pleasantries were exchanged, a check was presented to the family for their participation, and
the family left.

Behavior Constraint Rules. These rules define the role and status obligations for each activity in which the participants may wish to engage. In the
SIMCAR game, the role obligations were represented by the time, money,
or level of proficiency required for each activity. For example, if a child
wished to play the role of college student, he or she had to allocate 30 hours
and $30 per round to this activity for four rounds, and must have success-
fully graduated from high school. To attain the role of a supervisor or chief
designer in the tool and machine work and clothing construction job category, the child needed a trade school diploma with four years' experience in
a lower-level job in the same occupation. If the subject wanted to play the
role of a consumer, he or she allocated different amounts of money depending on the item desired (e.g., $25 for a boat and $5 for clothes).

Environmental Response Rules. This rule represents the patterned responses of the environment to the players' decisions. The responses include both rewards and constraints. The points given to the players for
their activities are considered a rule of this type. The point schedule reflected the relative payoffs for the different activities. For example, the
more one studied while in school, the more points one attained (to a specified limit); school graduation and job promotions were also rewarded with
points. In general, the point system rested on one point for expenditure of
each dollar and one point for each hour of time. Another form of points was
given indirectly to the players through money received for working. Such
funds could be used for savings or purchases in subsequent rounds, leading
to additional points. An attempt was made to make these payoffs as realistic
as possible. For example, money earned through salaries in the game was
proportionate to the achievement of higher status positions. Similarly,

costs were greater for some decisions than for others (e.g., getting married and having children cost more than purchasing a car).

The unplanned event cards were equivalent to external constraints. They were designed to represent happenings that could conceivably affect people in the normal course of their lives.

Police Rules. Police rules determine the action to be taken against those who break any of the other game rules. In this game, there were no punishments as such. If a rule was broken, the experimenter (akin to a referee) informed the subjects of the illegality, but only at the end of the round when all of the hours and money had been allocated. After subjects were informed of an illegal allocation, they simply reallocated their money and hours to coincide with the rules. Although some families objected to the rules, none declined to continue the game.

Postsimulation Interview and Debriefing

At the conclusion of the family's participation in SIMCAR, the parents were interviewed by a member of the staff. The questions in this interview were open ended and the answers tape recorded. Questions focused on the parent's interpretation and evaluation of their game performance, as well as the rationale for their choices.

After this interview, the purpose of the game was explained to the parents. Special care was taken with parents who had experienced the failure condition. The debriefing took the following general form:

> As we told you at the outset, our purpose was to study how families go about choosing a career for their child. One of the ways we tried to find this out was by using "unplanned event" cards and "average family scores." Sometimes we made things easy for families. For example, their unplanned event cards gave them extra points, scholarships, and so forth. In your case (if a failure condition), you were assigned a different set of cards that made things difficult for you. . . . The reason for this is that sometimes people in real life have a series of misfortunes which make it hard for them to get what they want for their children. We wanted to study how people react to such misfortunes. Actually, you did very well, considering the cards you received . . . and so forth.

Most people responded positively to the game and the explanations of the success or failure manipulation.

RESEARCH DESIGN

We have identified four sources of data collection: (a) an initial interview with mothers and fathers who had a 12–15-year-old son or daughter in their family; (b) the joint participation of a mother, father, and son or daughter in playing SIMCAR; (c) the son or daughter playing SIMCAR alone; and (d) a mother–father interview after participating in SIMCAR. These methods were used in three different communities that typified three levels of social development: (a) the Twin Cities metropolitan area of Minnesota in the United States represented a highly industrialized social structure; (b) the city of Zacapu in central Mexico represented a modernizing structure; and (c) four peasant villages in the state of Michoacán, although changing, could still be considered as representing a premodern or preindustrializing social structure.

Before this research began, IMES conducted a key informant survey and a broad multifaceted general survey of the cities and rural villages in the western part of Michoacan. These surveys included the city of Zacapu and the villages that were part of our research. The surveys provided vital information about the demographics and human ecology of the Mexican communities we were about to study. They also provided contacts that facilitated carrying out the initial interviews for this project.

The initial interviews were used to identify and select those families who met the required conditions for participating in SIMCAR. We set no absolute number of interviews since we were not certain how many interviews would be necessary to find appropriate families. We believed that we would need approximately twice as many family interviews as were required for the SIMCAR phase of the research. In total, we had usable interviews from 109 village fathers and 112 village mothers. The interviews with Zacapu white-collar families yielded 75 fathers' and 77 mothers' usable responses. Among blue-collar Zacapu families, 85 father and 91 mother interviews could be used. In the Twin Cities, we were able to use 78 interviews each from white-collar fathers and mothers, and 70 father and 71 mother interviews from blue-collar families. In all, we obtained 846 interviews from this phase of our research.

In the two urban areas, we wished to measure the independent and interactive effects of three variables on family and child problem-solving behavior. Only one of these variables, the success–failure condition in the family, involved an experimental manipulation. The other two, sex of child and social class, were determined by sampling procedures and validated by data in the initial interview. Social class was dichotomized by means of the father's occupation into blue-collar (manual workers) and white-collar (non-manual workers, professionals, and executives). Sex of child by social class, by success, failure, and neutral conditions provided us with a $2 \times 2 \times 3$ block design yielding 12 cells. The initial plan called for six families per cell or a total of 72 families in Zacapu and 72 families in the Twin Cities.

As noted earlier, SIMCAR was played in two parts, once by the family and then by the child. The family game provided the data relevant to making inferences about socialization processes. These data took three forms: (*a*) data relevant to the success goals families advocated for their children; (*b*) data pertaining to the strategies parents employed for attaining these goals; and (*c*) data relevant to family interaction patterns (power, support, channels of communication). The child's game provided the data for assessing the child's goals and problem-solving performance. It seemed reasonable, therefore, that the family game precede the child's game.

Since the format of SIMCAR was the same for both the family's and the child's games (the latter game was altered only in that the child played for 10 rounds, a social change condition was introduced, and there was no success–failure condition), it was possible that the child's score would be influenced by a prior learning affect. To determine the strength of this affect, we doubled the size of the families in the neutral cell and assigned one-half of these families to a condition in which the child played the game prior to the family game. The differences in scores of children who played the game prior to their families and those children (in the neutral condition) who played the game subsequent to participating in the family game, we believed, could be attributed to learning affects. This added six families each to the SIMCAR phase of the research in Zacapu and in the Twin Cities.

The small number of families in each cell was necessitated by limits in our resources and our decision to study both sons and daughters. We were not overly concerned about this, however, because we did not anticipate analysis that would require four-way interactions, though such interactions were at least conceivable when we included communities in our comparisons. The sample size was adequate for studying the main effects of the variables and two-way interaction between variables.

Inasmuch as the villages were composed almost entirely of peasant families, the social class variable was inappropriate for this group. The neutral game condition and the condition that required the child playing the game prior to the family were also eliminated from the village phase of the research. These decisions were made because setting up SIMCAR in the villages was more complex and time consuming. For the villages we used a 2×2 block design. We doubled the number of families per cell, however, to provide an anticipated peasant sample of 48 families.

Tables 4.1 and 4.2 provide a summary depiction of our overall research plan and the design for the SIMCAR phase of the research.

Data Gathering: Procedures and Problems

The presimulation interviews in the Twin Cities were conducted by trained undergraduate and graduate students. They were supervised by graduate research assistants who participated in administrating the pretests

Table 4.1
Research Design: Sequence of Data Gathering Procedures

Phase	Research sites involved	Data gathering method
I	Villages, Zacapu, and Twin Cities	Separate but simultaneous interviews with parents
II	a. Zacapu, Twin Cities	SIMCAR: Child plays game prior to family game SIMCAR: Family game played prior to child game under success, failure, and neutral conditions
	b. Villages	Family game played prior to child game under only success and failure conditions
III	Villages, Zacapu, and Twin Cities	Post-family-game interview with parents

and contributed to subsequent revisions of the instruments. This staff served as experimenters and coders in the family SIMCAR sessions.

A similar procedure was used in Mexico, where the interviews were conducted by first-year undergraduate sociology and public administration students at Ibero–American University in Mexico City. The students were given credit for fulfilling half of a required field experience and were paid living and traveling expenses.[9]

The research offices in the Twin Cities were adjacent to, but not a part of, the University of Minnesota campus. The game was played in a large room with a conference table. Family members sat on one side of the table and the experimenter and coder sat across from them. On the table, the SIMCAR playing board was displayed so that families could examine it before the game started. The various choices available to families and the categories for tabulating the game scores were listed on a blackboard at the end of the room. As each round was completed, the experimenter would place on the blackboard the scores the family members earned for each category as well as the total points the family earned in a given round.

In Zacapu, the research center was a large house in a respectable, but not

[9] Unfortunately, many of the students involved viewed the occasion less than seriously. The students were given a quota of interviews and were told they could return to Mexico City when these interviews were completed. Upon completion of the interviews, it was found that 17% were fabricated. In addition, a number of the interviewers had not gathered data pertaining to perception of opportunities, and approximately 20 interviewers had not followed instructions in terms of the presentation of the pictures to parents, generally failing to present the pictures of the appropriate sex child.

Fortunately, we were able to identify and revisit all families where a fabrication of the interviews had occurred and to complete those interviews in which data were missing. Pablo Pindas suspended for a year all students who had fabricated interviews, and the staffs at IMES and the research site worked extremely hard to rectify this error.

Table 4.2
Research Design for SIMCAR Phase of Research: Basis of Allocation of Families to Cells.[a]

Level of development	Premodern		Modernizing				Industrialized			
Community	Villages (48)		Zacapu (72)				Twin Cities (72)			
Social position	Peasant (48)		Blue collar (36)		White collar (36)		Blue collar (36)		White collar (36)	
Sex of child	Male (24)	Female (24)	Male (18)	Female (18)	Male (18)	Female (18)	Male (18)	Female (18)	Male (18)	Female (18)
Game condition	S F	S F	S F N	S F N	S F N	S F N	S F N	S F N	S F N	S F N
	(12)(12)	(12)(12)	(6)(6)(6)	(6)(6)(6)	(6)(6)(6)	(6)(6)(6)	(6)(6)(6)	(6)(6)(6)	(6)(6)(6)	(6)(6)(6)

[a] Anticipated cell size in parentheses.

exclusive, area a block off the main plaza. One room of the house was set up to replicate as closely as possible the Twin Cities setting. The two settings were, in fact, quite similar with the exceptions that our recording instruments in Zacapu were less powerful; electrical failure was an occasional problem; and street noises were not as easy to shut out. As a consequence, the quality of our audio tapes was much better in the United States.

For the villages we devised a portable canvas blackboard with the same scoreboard used in the other settings. We borrowed a room in either the school or the village's administrative building if no school existed. The primary difference between the Zacapu and village simulations was that the staff attracted considerably more attention in the villages. During the first simulations in a village, crowds would often assemble outside the research site. The attitude of the crowds was positive, even festive. This was partly due to the Mexican staff's success in conveying the importance of the research. Each village research team consisted of one male and one female. If the child was a girl, the experimenter was always a female. It was also important, in keeping with local custom, that our female graduate assistants were not by themselves, unaccompanied after dark.[10]

We were, of course, concerned about the potential "experimenter effects" resulting from the differing interpretations of the role of the research staff by families in the various communities studied. Clearly the Mexican families perceived the research staff different than did the North American families. Also, as noted earlier, peasant families tended to see the occasion different from the way white- or blue-collar families did. What effect did these differences have on the game performances? Of course we cannot be certain. Our intent was to make the game so absorbing and the rules so explicit that the experimenter would seem insignificant in the face of the demands and challenges of the game. We shall return to this issue again in Chapter 7 when we discuss the validity of SIMCAR.

---

[10]Despite a generally positive aura, however, there was evidence of lack of sensitivity to some cultural and class differences within Mexico. Respondents treated graduate and undergraduate assistants in Mexico quite differently from how they were treated in the United States. The Mexican students were viewed with considerable deference, especially by the peasant families. In retrospect, we believe it would have been wiser to train Michoacanos of Tarascan heritage as village experimenters and interviewers. There were sufficient differences in culture and class to result in our Mexican staff being considered outsiders, despite their efforts to wear clothing like that worn in the local communities. Makeup and jewelry were deemphasized by the women researchers and the men kept their hair length short according to the local fashion. Yet the obvious difference in speech and mannerisms undoubtedly caused some uneasiness. Nevertheless, the staff did get invited to a wedding in one village and the entire staff (including the North Americans) was the recipient of gifts of food from families in other villages.

Sample Characteristics

Table 4.3 provides a summary description of the demographic characteristics for the various samples drawn for the interview phase of the research.
The Hollingshead (1957) Index of Occupations was used to classify parents
according to fathers' occupations as white-collar (nonmanual) and as blue-
collar (manual). The initial interview with parents centered around one specific early adolescent member of the family—the potential participant in
the game simulation. In the Twin Cities, this child was a daughter in 55%
of the families. The larger percentage of daughters was primarily attributable to the difficulties in filling some of the cells for females in the simulation phase of the research. The percentage difference in the sex of child in
the Mexican interview samples was inconsequential.

It can be seen from Table 4.3 that the white-collar fathers and mothers in
both the Twin Cities and Zacapu were more likely to have come from other
states than parents in the blue-collar and village samples. The numbers of
children per family were considerably higher in Mexico than in the United
States. Surprisingly, the largest numbers of children were among Zacapu
white-collar families. Nevertheless, the average number of children in the
Twin Cities sample was above the national average of children per family.
Only 8.6% of United States families in 1972 had over four children (Bureau
of the Census, 1977, Table 56, p. 42). The discrepancy can be accounted
for, in part, by the fact that almost one-half of our sample was Catholic.
When we control for religion, the Catholic average raises to 5.8 children per
family and the non-Catholic average drops to 3.7.

The educational attainment of our respondents generally matched our
expectations. The Mexican village sample averaged less than 1 year of
schooling, and the Zacapu blue-collar sample was slightly higher, averaging
2 years. Both the white- and blue-collar United States families averaged
considerably more education than even white-collar Mexican families. The
Twin Cities white-collar sample generally attained some training beyond
high school, and the blue-collar sample achieved slightly less than a high
school education.

Similar patterns were apparent for income distribution across our
samples. The average income category for Twin Cities white-collar families
was between $15,000 and $20,000 a year; for blue-collar families, it was between $10,000 and $15,000 a year. In Zacapu, the average income category
for white-collar families was between $3800 and $4400 a year, much lower
than we had anticipated; and for blue-collar families, it dropped to between
$1900 and $2400 per year. Village families in Michoacan averaged between
$900 and $1400 a year. The most surprising fact in these data is the income

Table 4.3
Demographic Characteristics of Samples

Item	Villages Mother N = 104	Villages Father N = 105	Zacapu White collar Mother N = 78	Zacapu White collar Father N = 75	Zacapu Blue collar Mother N = 91	Zacapu Blue collar Father N = 85	Twin Cities White collar Mother N = 78	Twin Cities White collar Father N = 78	Twin Cities Blue collar Mother N = 71	Twin Cities Blue collar Father N = 71
Mean age	39	42	38	43	38	43	42	43	40	42
Mean number of children	6.5	6.1	7.2	7.2	6.4	6.4	4.5	4.5	4.9	5.0
Mean number of children Catholics (U.S. only)							5.8	5.8	5.9	5.9
Non-Catholics (U.S. only)							3.7	3.7	3.9	3.9
Education Median number of years schooling	0.7	0.9	8.0	6.0	2.0	2.0	13.0	16.0	11.9	11.9
Median annual family income category in U.S. dollars	960	1400	3800 / 4400	3800 / 4400	1900 / 2400	1900 / 2400	15,000 / 20,000	15,000 / 20,000	10,000 / 15,000	10,000 / 15,000
Percentage Catholic	94.7	89.9	93.6	92.0	96.7	95.3	42.0	41.0	51.7	50.7
Percentage born within state	92.0	98.2	71.8	62.7	79.1	82.1	62.8	64.1	81.7	81.7

gap between village and blue-collar families in Mexico. Our impression had been that the differences in income were minimal between unskilled blue-collar workers and peasants (see, for example, Pi Sunyer's, 1972, pp. 33–34, ethnographic study of the Michoacan city of Zamora). It is likely that we selected the more economically stable elements of Zacapu's blue-collar community. It is also likely that the Celenese plant in Zacapu provided a salary base for its union workers in excess of what was available in other communities.

It should be noted that these data were obtained from the parents' interviews and were not validated by other sources. Such indicators as age and income must be evaluated in this perspective. The only checks on accuracy were the comparisons between the independent responses of fathers and mothers to similar questions. On key issues such as family income, we found little disagreement between spouses.

Our theory assumed that with social development and/or increased socioeconomic status there was a corresponding increase in occupational choices. There are data in support of this assumption (Apter, 1971; Marsh, 1967, pp. 329–336). However, we sought to determine if our data reflected this choice differentiation by levels of development and social class. It can be seen from Table 4.4 that the number of occupations was positively associated with social class and level of development. It is of interest, however, that the anticipated class differences were not present in the Twin Cities sample.

The large differential between the number of occupations held by husbands as compared to wives in all communities except the Mexican villages suggests the extent to which structural opportunities differ for males and females. We shall consider this issue in greater detail in Chapter 6.

SUMMARY

This research was designed to provide a means for assessing the impact of the community social structure, as mediated by families, on 12–15-year-old children's problem-solving skills. Families were sampled from the Twin Cities, Minnesota in the United States, and from Zacapu, Michoacan, Mexico, and four rural villages in Michoacan. The United States sample represented people living at the highest levels of industrialization, whereas Mexico was considered as a "modernizing" country.

To measure social position, samples were drawn from families in which the father held a white- or blue-collar job in the Twin Cities and Zacapu. The impact of these structural variables on the family and family socialization was measured by comparing families from these different communi-

Table 4.4
Number of Different Primary Occupations Reported by Fathers and Mothers by Community and Social Class

Villages		Zacapu				Twin Cities			
		White collar		Blue collar		White collar		Blue collar	
Father N = 105	Mother N = 104	Father N = 75	Mother N = 78	Father N = 85	Mother N = 91	Father N = 78	Mother N = 78	Father N = 71	Mother N = 71
14	5	26	6	20	3	30	9	32	15

ties on their values, aspirations, expectations, and perceptions of opportunities for their sons and daughters. These data were gathered through interviews. Families' interactions while playing SIMCAR were observed and coded to provide data relevant to hierarchical structures, tolerance of ambiguity, tolerance of conflict, and social problem-solving skills. All of these measures were obtained under conditions of family success or failure in the simulation game.

The family interaction variables were hypothesized to influence the child's problem-solving ability and, therefore, the child's capacity to cope effectively with social change. To test this last critical variable the child played the simulation game alone under conditions of simulated social change.

5 | The Findings: Testing the Theory

The theoretical framework developed for this research was designed to explain how families prepared their children for a changing society by (a) identifying the conditions in the community social structure that influence how the family mediates the social structure for its members; and (b) identifying the elements in the mediation process as it takes place in the parent–child relationship. The key aspect of this relationship is a socialization process in which offspring learn to problem solve under conditions of social change.

In this chapter we will test propositions from the theory with the data gathered from the Michoacan Twin Cities families we studied. The analysis will follow the format proposed in the causal model presented in Chapter 3. We begin with the largest units of analysis, the community and the family, then consider the impact of these structures on parent–child socialization, and finally examine the findings pertaining to adolescent problem solving.

THE COMMUNITY AND THE FAMILY

Life Goals

The theory's first theorem held that families living under conditions of material deprivation will be more likely to emphasize attaining material success and those living under conditions of comparative abundance will be

111

more likely to emphasize interpersonal satisfactions. Thus, white-collar families, when compared to blue-collar and peasant families, and United States families, when compared to Mexican families, should be more inclined to emphasize goals stressing interpersonal satisfaction. Furthermore, peasant village families should show the greatest tendency to emphasize material attainment, and Twin Cities white-collar families should show a greater tendency to emphasize interpersonal satisfaction. This hypothesis was first tested comparing families on SIMCAR choices that emphasized the priority of family or interpersonal relationships. Five game choices were used as indicators of this value: (a) the decision to marry; (b) the decision to have children; (c) the time invested in work around the house; (d) time and money invested in visiting relatives; and (e) time and money invested in visiting friends.

The findings indicate that Twin Cities families were more likely to emphasize interpersonal and family goals than the Michoacan families. As shown in Table 5.1, virtually all (92%) of the village families decided not to have their children marry during the family game, and only slightly fewer urban Mexicans made the same choice (84% Zacapu blue-collar families and 83% Zacapu white-collar families). On the other hand, only 13% of the Twin Cities blue-collar sample and 12% of the Twin Cities white-collar sample decided that the child should not marry. Given these data, it is not surprising that only 4 families in all of the Mexican sample decided to have a child during the game. In comparison, 26 United States families decided to have one child and 14 families decided to have 2 children.

When the parents were interviewed about the reasons for these choices, virtually none of the Mexicans opposed marriage. Rather, they focused on the necessity for adequate financial readiness and maturity. This comment by an unskilled laborer from Zacapu typifies the attitude, "What is important is that a person be prepared—and later he can do what he wants. . . . I have seen many cases where people weren't concerned about preparation and sometimes didn't even have a job—and later in life it is extremely difficult. So I think it is better to have a good preparation first."

Consider, on the other hand, the following comments by a Twin Cities postman and his wife in response to the question, "Why did your son get married in the third round of the game?"

Wife: *Just a good age. I suppose he's gonna get married, he's working you know.*
Father: *And he's a family boy. He loves the family. He loves children. He's gonna be a good parent.*

The two quotes emphasize a major point. Mexican and United States families want to have both material attainment and a good family life. The ques-

Table 5.1
Family Game Choices on Indicators of Familistic and Interpersonal Preferences by Community and Class[a]

	Villages	Zacapu		Twin Cities		Significant effects[b] (p < .05)		
Indicators	N = 50	Blue collar N = 43	White collar N = 42	Blue collar N = 47	White collar N = 57	Community	Class	Village versus Zacapu
Chose to have child marry (%)	8	16	17	87	88	X		X
Chose to have children (%)	4	0	5	28	44	X	X	
Investments in housework (means)[c]	3.51	3.3	3.2	4.31	3.8	X		
Investments in visiting relatives (means)[c]	1.5	.99	.60	1.91	1.75	X		X
Investments in visiting friends (means)[c]	1.71	2.0	2.59	4.33	4.11	X		

[a] Comparison of percentages used the chi square test; comparisons of means based on two-way analysis of variance.
[b] No interaction effects were statistically significant; significant main effects are indicated by X.
[c] Game scores are proportional to number of rounds families played.

tion, however, is which is valued more highly, that is, which would be chosen if one must be chosen over the other. These data, both quantitatively and qualitatively, suggest that North American families place a higher value on family relations than Mexican families.

The findings comparing the amount of time and money spent during the game on visiting friends suggest that the stress on interpersonal relations is not limited only to family members for Twin Cities families. The data also indicate that within Mexico there is a positive relationship between family socioeconomic status and investments in visiting friends. Among Mexicans, the white-collar Zacapu families were the most likely to have their children spend time and money visiting friends.

The reluctance of the peasant families to invest in this type of activity also suggests the greater suspiciousness of strangers attributed to peasants by a number of investigators of peasant cultures (Foster, 1967; Nash, 1967; Rogers, 1969a). The following response to the question about the importance of visiting friends is an example of the ambivalence peasants feel toward strangers, "Yes, it's important on the one hand . . . in order to cultivate friendship. But one can do himself damage through his friends besides benefiting himself. . . . (F)riendships do help them (children) to develop socially, but there are also friendships that (wife interjects, "better none of these") . . . instead of teaching them something new or benefiting them, they go off in a different direction." Such responses were in sharp contrast to the typical replies of Zacapu blue- and white-collar parents which stressed the normalcy of friends and dates in the child's life. Twin Cities parents were virtually unanimous in saying that friends are extremely important; in fact, many parents tended to use the question as a springboard for analyzing their child's personality. A Twin Cities store manager, for example, replied to the question by describing his daughter as still very embarrassed "around boys," as "serious and picky," and finally, "bossy, bossy is the word I want. She wants people to do . . . things that are right. Not that she does them right, but she likes to be the one to tell them you're doing what's wrong—she's a critic."

In general, Twin Cities parents seemed concerned with what made their children tick, how they thought, and what they felt. They focused on the special or unique aspects of their child's individual personality. On the other hand, Michoacan parents seemed unconcerned with their children's personality characteristics or idiosyncrasies, paying more attention to their capacities to take advantage of opportunities available in the social structure.

In contrast to the emphasis Twin Cities families placed on personal and interpersonal satisfactions for their children, Michoacan families played SIMCAR in a way that stressed enhancing children's careers and incomes.

Table 5.2 shows the proportion of families from each community that selected a given career route; it also divides the career routes into those that
require or do not require post-high-school education. A surprising 49% of
the Twin Cities families from both social classes chose not to take the
higher paying career routes that required education beyond high school.
Among Michoacan families, the peasant and white-collar groups were the
most likely to choose education careers that were limited to a high school
education. But this represented only 14% of the families in each group.

For the North Americans, these data suggest less willingness to defer
gratifications in the early rounds of the game. The findings are also con-
founded by differences between boys and girls which are more pronounced
for North Americans than for Mexicans. These sex differences will be considered in detail in Chapter 6. For the Mexicans, these findings imply more
than the commonly acknowledged high value placed on education (Miller,
1973); they also reflect their readiness to advocate other sacrifices to reach
their career goals. This is evidenced in the data pertaining to families' acceptance of geographical mobility opportunities. In the third round of the
game families were given the following option: "You have a chance to get a
job which will provide $35 more than you can earn where you are. If you are
in school, you can go to school in the other town free. You must pay $20 to
travel to this town. You may choose whether you wish to move or not." The

Table 5.2
Career Routes Chosen during Family Game by Community (% of Families)

	Villages	Zacapu		Twin Cities	
		Blue collar	White collar	Blue collar	White collar
Career routes	N^a = 49	N = 40	N = 42	N = 47	N = 57
High school prerequi-sites only					
Office work	10		9.5	34	38
Factory work	4		4.5	9	2
Farming		2.5		6	9
Post-high-school train-ing required					
Office management	29	47.5	29	28	37
Manufacturing	24	17.5	29	19	9
Agriculture	33	32.5	29	4	5
Total	100	100	101	100	100

[a]N refers to number of families (father, mother, and child).
High school versus post-high-school training by community, χ^2 = 55.13, df = 4, p < .001.
United States versus Mexico, χ^2 = 4.13. df = 1, p < .05 (Yates correction for continuity).

family could take advantage of this option in subsequent rounds if it so wished. As shown in Table 5.3, Mexican families accepted the mobility option significantly more frequently than United States families. Although peasants were more likely than any other group to choose this option, differences between classes within Mexico and the United States were not statistically significant.

These data do not support the stereotypic view of the myopic Mexican peasant committed to tradition and closed to new opportunities; however, they are in accord with survey research findings indicating that the Mexican poor are willing to migrate if they think opportunities exist for improving their lot (Cone, 1976; Lomnitz, 1977, pp. 42–46). Rapid urban growth in Latin America, including Mexico, comes primarily from the rural poor who contribute to the enormous growth of shantytown populations in most of the major Latin American countries (Portes & Walton, 1976, pp. 38–43).

A common phrase used throughout the game by Mexican families of all social classes was *to better oneself*. Mobility was advocated because one had to better oneself. The United States families, on the other hand, tended to take longer to consider the mobility choice and were much more likely to take into account the impact of mobility on interpersonal relations. Thus, a father wanted his son to think carefully about accepting the option because, "at that time you would have too many friends you would be giving up." Another father rejected the mobility choice because the child could not live at home while she went to college. Based on the amount of time taken to discuss this choice and the content of the discussions, it seemed that United States families considered the migration issue more seriously than did the Mexican families. The content of the discussions supported the conclusion that more United States families than Mexican families were concerned with the impact of migration on family, interpersonal relations, and personal rather than material considerations.

To summarize the data pertaining to the families' valuation of life goals

Table 5.3
Percentage Choosing Mobility Option in Family Game by Community

	Villages	Zacapu		Twin Cities	
	$N = 50$	Blue collar $N = 43$	White collar $N = 42$	Blue collar $N = 47$	White collar $N = 57$
Percentage choosing mobility option	96	84	81	49	51

Communities, $x^2 = 39.91$, $df = 4$, $p < .001$. Mexicans versus United States, $x^2 = 40.03$, $df = 1$, $p < .0001$. Villages versus Zacapu, $x^2 = 5.32$, $df = 1$, $p < .05$.

for their children, Mexican families were more likely to make SIMCAR choices that optimized chances for material success, whereas North Americans made choices emphasizing interpersonal satisfaction and personal happiness. The Mexicans seemed aware that attaining material success, both in the game and in real life, required deferring such sources of gratification as marriage and children and committing oneself to education, saving money, and accepting opportunities even at the cost of leaving home. In interviews, they repeatedly stressed the importance of "bettering oneself." In contrast, the United States parents were not only more concerned with maximizing interpersonal satisfactions, but they also seemed oriented primarily toward facilitating their child's happiness without regard to status or economic concerns.

Despite tendencies of peasant families to invest in visiting relatives and their distrust of friends being greater than that of urban Michaocanos, and despite the tendency of blue-collar Twin Cities families to place less stress on having children than white-collar families, the overall differences between the two societies were more pronounced than the class differences within the societies. The consistency of the statistically significant differences between the Mexican and United States families combined with the relative lack of statistically significant differences between classes within the societies raises the question of whether a cultural explanation would be more appropriate than the structural explanation proposed in our theory. If we accept the commonly held definition of culture as shared belief systems, ideologies, and value orientations then it appears that a cultural explanation is less appropriate than the one proposed in our theory. From the cultural perspective we would predict greater familism in Mexico than in the United States (see for example Leñero, 1968, and Elu de Leñero, 1969) and greater emphasis on the work ethic in the United States. We do not imply that cultural influences are not operative, only that culture does not provide an adequate alternative explanation to the one proposed in our theory. In the next chapter we consider the cultural versus structural argument in more detail as it relates to the role of women in the two societies.

Family Power Structure

According to our theory, diversity in information and role choices within a community social structure should be associated with egalitarianism within the nuclear family (proposition 14 and theorem 5). Using as our indicator of structural diversity the number of role choices in a community and the diversity of tasks within given roles, Michoacan villages represent the least diverse structure, followed by Zacapu blue-collar workers, then by Zacapu white-collar workers, and, finally, by Twin Cities blue- and white-collar workers (see Table 4.4, Chapter 4). Since we anticipated that blue- and white-collar families would have different access to information by virtue of their social position, we also hypothesized that blue-collar families would be less equalitarian than white-collar families within their respective communities.

Power within families was measured by the proportion of directives each member of the family sent to the other members of the family that were accepted and acted upon. For example, if during a game trial a father said to his son, "I think it is time for you to buy a car," and the son said, "O.K." and bought the car, this would be coded by the observer as F → CP+ (father to child power—plus). The total number of each family member's power–plus messages were divided by the total number of messages sent within the family, providing us with a control for family differences in verbosity. The findings, reported in Table 5.4, are in accord with our hypothesis. Mexican families are more patriarchal than United States families and power was more equally distributed across the three family members among United States families.

The children's power in the Twin Cities sample was equal to, or, in the case of white-collar families, greater than any other family member. This allocation of power to children in the United States sample was acknowledged by parents in their postsimulation interviews. The initial and most common answer to questions asking parents why they invested resources in particular game choices was that it was their child's decision. The differences between Mexican and United States families in this regard were glaring. With two exceptions, Mexican parents never attributed responsibility for the family decisions to the child. Rather, their answers consistently reflected an emphasis on necessary conditions for achieving success within the social structure without regard to their children's desires or goals.

The distribution of power as a component of family structure is more clearly illustrated in Table 5.5. This table depicts the modal distribution of

Table 5.4

Mean Proportion of Power Messages Sent by Family Members, Acted upon by Other Family Members by Community

Family member	Villages $N = 50$	Zacapu		Twin Cities		F	p
		Blue collar $N = 40$	White collar $N = 41$	Blue collar $N = 47$	White collar $N = 57$		
Father	.50	.48	.45	.25	.20	26.93	$< .001$
Mother	.36	.25	.28	.21	.15	15.6	$< .001$
Child	.09	.18	.15	.25	.33	19.4	$< .001$

Table 5.5
Distribution of Power between Family Members While Playing SIMCAR (% by Communities)

Type of family power constellation	Villages $N^a = 50$	Zacapu		Twin Cities	
		Blue collar $N = 40$	White collar $N = 41$	Blue collar $N = 47$	White collar $N = 57$
One family member dominates	68	51	59	48	48
Which family member?					
Father	44	30	41	12	17
Mother	24	06	18	16	0
Child	0	15	0	20	31
Coalitions	22	39	30	32	21
Which family members?					
Father–mother	16	27	19	0	0
Father–child	02	06	11	16	21
Mother–child	04	06	0	16	0
Equalitarian (equal power with all family members)	10	09	11	20	31

^{a}N refers to number of families.

power in families in each of the five communities studied. Three types of power distribution were classified. If one family member sent 55% or more of the power messages, the family was classified as being dominated by a single person. If no family member sent 55% of the messages and two members combined to send 69% or more of the power messages, the family was considered to be dominated by a coalition. If neither of these two distributions occurred, the family was classified as egalitarian. Table 5.5 shows that 68% of peasant families were dominated by either the father or the mother, whereas at the other end of the continuum, only 17% of the Twin Cities white-collar families were dominated by a parent. The dominance of parents in the Mexican sample is also apparent in the data pertaining to coalitions. The primary coalitions in the Mexican sample were between parents; among United States families, the coalitions were most likely to include the child.

The class differences between urban blue- and white-collar families in either Zacapu or the Twin Cities were not statistically significant. However, the significantly greater equalitarianism of the white-collar Twin Cities families and the greater dominance by one parent in village families offers support for the hypothesis linking structural diversity with family equalitarianism.

COMMUNITY CONTEXT AND
PARENT–CHILD SOCIALIZATION

Many of the linkages between community structure, family structure, and parent–child socialization are not amenable to direct testing. It is only through parent's responses and observation of parent–child interactions that we are able to make inferences about family structures. In this section we examine the relationship between community structural conditions and parent–child socialization inferring the mediation of an intervening family structure. For example, our model proposes two aspects of the parent–child relationship that provide clues about the family structure within which these relationships function: The first is the parents' interpretation of the social structure to their child; the second is patterns of interaction between parents and children that replicate aspects of social structure.

Parent's Interpretation of the Social Structure

Propositions 5 and 6 of our theory proposed that parental optimism about opportunities in the social structure would be positively associated with children's problem-solving success. However, this principle was thought to hold only under social structural conditions that validate such optimism (theorems 3 and 4). We expected that lower-class parents would be less optimistic than upper-class parents, and parents living under conditions of rapid social change would be more optimistic than parents living under conditions in which positive change was less apparent. Thus, we hypothesized that peasant and blue-collar parents would be less optimistic than white-collar parents and United States parents would be less optimistic than Mexican parents. To test this hypothesis, we examined parent's estimates of their children's life chances, their perceptions of future opportunities for their children, and their aspirations and expectations for the 10 occupations they were asked to rank during the initial interview. It will be recalled that these occupations were presented to parents in the form of pictures, each on a separate card, with each card bearing the title of the pictured occupation. The pictures were selected and pretested to offer gradations in status and income as well as comparability across the cultures. Parents were asked to rank the pictures in terms of the jobs they most wanted for their children, then they were asked to rate whether they thought the chances of attaining that job were "good," "so-so," or "poor." Finally, they were asked to rank the 10 occupations in the order of their expectations for their particular child. That is, which of the 10 occupations did they think their child was most likely to attain, second most likely to attain, and so forth.

Table 5.6 presents the parent's average (modal) responses to the second of these questions. It appears from these data that the "reality" hypothesis holds. Blue-collar parents within both societies were more likely to consider their children's life chances as so-so or poor than white-collar parents. Only the differences between Twin Cities' blue- and white-collar mothers were not statistically significant. When parents in the two societies were compared, Mexican fathers were more likely to believe their children's chances were good and United States fathers were more inclined to use the so-so or poor category, $\chi^2 = 3.92$, $p < .05$ using Yates's correction. Differences between mothers in the two countries were not statistically significant.

Zacapu white-collar fathers were the most optimistic group in the study—an optimism probably based on the fact that the middle-class was the group that benefited most from the rapid industrialization taking place in Mexico. The optimism of the peasant and blue-collar Mexican parents, however, was not concordant with objective conditions. Underemployment in Mexico was estimated at 35–40% of the labor force in 1970, much greater than in the United States (Lomnitz, 1977). The situation was no better in Michoacan than in the rest of Mexico. If anything, the underemployment situation was greater in Michoacan than in the larger industrial areas. The rate of migration to the United States and Mexico City from Michoacan was higher than most other Mexican states (Lomnitz, 1977, p. 43). In our initial investigation of Zacapu as a research site, we were informed by the personnel director of the primary industrial plant in Zacapu that the employment situation was precarious for young people because the plant, which was the major employer in the city, was not expanding and there was very little turnover of workers. However, our hypothesis that Mexican parents would be more optimistic about their children's life chances than United States parents was not based on the premise that conditions in Mexico were good or perceived as such by the Mexicans. Rather, we thought that the rapid rate of change within Mexico fostered the sense that conditions would be improving. To test the degree to which the parents in our study were optimistic about the future of their children, we compared parents' responses to the following item taken from the Kluckhohn and Strodtbeck (1961) time orientation index.

> Three older people were talking about what they thought their children would have when they were grown. Here is what each one said:
> a. "I really expect my children to have more than I have had if they work hard and plan right. There are always good chances for people who try."
> b. "I don't know whether my children will be better off, worse off, or just the same. Things always go up and down even if one works hard, so we can't really tell."
> c. "I expect my children to have just about the same as I have had or bring things back as they once were. It is their job to work hard and find ways to keep things going as they have been in the past."

Table 5.6

Percentage of Fathers and Mothers Who Used Good, So-So, or Poor as Their Modal Category in Assessing Children's Life Chances (Based on 10 Occupational Pictures)

	Mexico						United States			
	Villages		Zacapu				Twin Cities			
			Blue collar		White collar		Blue collar		White collar	
Category	Father N = 105	Mother N = 104	Father N = 84	Mother N = 89	Father N = 73	Mother N = 77	Father N = 71	Mother N = 71	Father N = 78	Mother N = 78
Good	45	46	49	37	67	57	39	45	44	57
So-So	28	29	30	38	23	35	44	34	24	26
Poor	28	25	21	25	10	8	17	21	32	17
Total	101	100	100	100	100	100	100	100	100	100

Mothers, $\chi^2 = 16.41$, $df = 8$, $p < .05$.
Fathers, $\chi^2 = 19.95$, $df = 8$, $p < .02$.
Social class fathers (Mexico), $\chi^2 = 12.2$, $df = 4$, $p < .02$ (includes peasants).
Social class mothers (Mexico), $\chi^2 = 10.75$, $df = 4$, $p < .02$ (includes peasants).
Social class fathers (U.S.), $\chi^2 = 7.7$, $df = 2$, $p < .05$.
United States white-collar fathers versus Mexican white-collar fathers, $\chi^2 = 12.85$, $df = 2$, $p < .01$.

Parents were asked to choose which of the statements more closely approximated their own views. Responses "a" were coded as future oriented, "b" as present oriented, and "c" as past oriented.

The greater future orientation of Mexicans of all classes as compared with the pronounced tendency of Twin Cities parents (especially white-collar) to choose the statement indicating a present orientation is evident in the findings presented in Table 5.7. There were also class differences for Twin Cities fathers, primarily due to the greater present orientation of the white-collar fathers. Mexican peasant mothers were significantly less future oriented than other groups of Mexican mothers.

The greater optimism of Mexican parents is also apparent when we examine the data pertaining to parental aspirations and expectations. These data were obtained from parents' rankings of the 10 occupations pictured on cards. Tables 5.8 and 5.9 present the aspiration and expectation rankings for the five highest ranked occupations for daughters and the four highest ranked occupations for sons. Table 5.10 presents the relevant F ratios and levels of significance for mothers' and fathers' rankings for each of the ranked occupations.

Mexican parents of both boys and girls tended to have higher aspirations and expectations for their children becoming physicians than United States parents. However, the clearest indication of the greater optimism among Mexican parents comes from the mean discrepancy scores. These scores reflect the differences between the occupations parents want for their child and the occupations they expect their child will be able to obtain. Mexican mothers and fathers had significantly lower discrepancy scores than United States parents (see Table 5.10).

Class differences were more pronounced for sons than for daughters. Within societies, white-collar mothers of sons had significantly higher aspirations and expectations than lower-class mothers. Furthermore, the discrepancy between aspirations and expectations was lower for white-collar mothers than for mothers in the lower social strata. Significant class differences occurred for fathers only for expectations. White-collar fathers, in both Mexico and the United States, tended to have higher expectations than fathers in the other social classes. The significant interaction between class and community on discrepancy scores for fathers of sons reflects differences in the average discrepancy score for white-collar Mexican fathers of sons as compared to blue-collar Mexican fathers. Differences between white-collar and blue-collar United States fathers are minor.

The only social class differences for daughters were for mothers' aspirations. White-collar mothers had significantly higher aspirations than blue-collar and peasant mothers.

The data pertaining to teachers show that (with the exception of Twin

Table 5.7

Percentage of Parents Who Expected Their Children Would Be Better Off in the Past, Present, or Future by Community and Sex of Parent

| | Villages | | Zacapu | | | | Twin Cities | | | |
| | | | Blue collar | | White collar | | Blue collar | | White collar | |
Item	Father $N = 103$	Mother $N = 113$	Father $N = 84$	Mother $N = 90$	Father $N = 75$	Mother $N = 76$	Father $N = 70$	Mother $N = 71$	Father $N = 78$	Mother $N = 78$
Past	9	16	6	9	12	9	19	11	6	16
Present	9	14	8	7	5	4	27	38	46	51
Future	82	70	86	84	83	87	54	51	47	39

Mexican–United States differences for fathers, $\chi^2 = 59.5$, $df = 2$, $p < .001$.
Mexican–United States differences for mothers, $\chi^2 = 76.4$, $df = 2$, $p < .001$.
United States blue-collar–white-collar differences for fathers, $\chi^2 = 8.44$, $df = 2$, $p < .02$.
Peasant mothers differences from urban Mexican mothers, $\chi^2 = 11.4$, $df = 2$, $p < .01$.

Table 5.8

Mean Parental Aspirations, Expectations, and Discrepancy Scores for Daughters by Region, Social Class, and Sex of Parent[a]

| | Villages | | Zacapu | | | | Twin Cities | | | |
| | | | Blue collar | | White collar | | Blue collar | | White collar | |
	Father N = 52	Mother N = 52	Father N = 45	Mother N = 46	Father N = 37	Mother N = 37	Father N = 38	Mother N = 38	Father N = 44	Mother N = 44
Physician										
$\bar{X}$ aspiration	2.42	2.90	1.91	3.26	2.49	1.50	2.84	3.84	3.07	3.27
$\bar{X}$ expectation	2.86	5.07	3.68	4.15	2.89	2.94	6.16	6.29	5.95	5.77
$\bar{X}$ discrepancy	-2.48	-2.16	-1.75	-.87	-.47	-1.50	-3.32	-2.45	-2.89	-2.50
Teacher										
$\bar{X}$ aspiration	3.52	3.40	3.64	4.14	4.11	3.89	3.21	2.68	2.52	2.50
$\bar{X}$ expectation	3.51	3.19	4.00	4.12	3.94	3.88	2.84	2.08	2.43	2.20
$\bar{X}$ discrepancy	-.02	.28	-.32	.02	.21	-.09	.37	.61	.09	.30
Office employee										
$\bar{X}$ aspiration	3.92	3.60	3.23	3.24	4.06	4.29	3.55	3.71	4.23	3.25
$\bar{X}$ expectation	3.50	4.02	3.41	3.57	3.82	3.78	3.68	3.79	3.54	3.41
$\bar{X}$ discrepancy	.23	-.52	-.32	-.22	.39	.28	-.13	-.08	.68	-.16
Skilled worker										
$\bar{X}$ aspiration	3.54	3.07	4.49	2.88	4.00	3.49	5.16	4.45	6.34	5.18
$\bar{X}$ expectation	3.87	3.50	3.50	2.95	3.78	3.03	3.47	3.18	4.34	3.75
$\bar{X}$ discrepancy	-.24	-.31	.78	-.07	.39	.44	1.68	1.26	2.00	1.43
Wife–mother										
$\bar{X}$ aspiration	5.96	5.62	6.07	5.49	4.71	5.00	3.21	3.37	2.84	4.48
$\bar{X}$ expectation	4.87	4.44	3.98	4.51	4.37	4.55	2.24	3.68	2.30	3.98
$\bar{X}$ discrepancy	1.26	.96	2.03	1.00	.26	.65	.97	-.32	.55	.50

[a] Low mean scores indicate high aspirations or expectations. Minus signs indicate that aspirations are higher than expectations.

125

Table 5.9

Mean Parental Aspirations, Expectations, and Discrepancy Scores for Sons by Region, Social Class, and Sex of Parent[a]

| | Villages | | Zacapu | | | | Twin Cities | | | |
| | | | Blue collar | | White collar | | Blue collar | | White collar | |
	Father N = 53	Mother N = 52	Father N = 40	Mother N = 45	Father N = 38	Mother N = 41	Father N = 33	Mother N = 33	Father N = 34	Mother N = 34
Physician										
$\overline{X}$ aspiration	2.76	2.94	1.60	2.04	1.35	1.50	2.39	3.06	1.88	2.18
$\overline{X}$ expectation	4.02	4.60	4.60	3.93	2.09	1.93	6.12	6.60	6.00	4.56
$\overline{X}$ discrepancy	-1.17	-1.70	-3.00	-2.07	-.71	-.45	-3.73	-3.55	-4.12	-2.38
Teacher										
$\overline{X}$ aspiration	3.22	2.90	3.85	3.86	3.03	4.05	2.73	2.73	2.76	3.03
$\overline{X}$ expectation	3.43	3.02	3.95	4.17	3.22	4.15	3.27	3.88	2.38	2.74
$\overline{X}$ discrepancy	-.12	-.13	-.10	-.26	-.16	-.10	-.55	-1.15	.38	.29
Office employee										
$\overline{X}$ aspiration	3.82	3.68	4.13	3.86	4.63	4.24	5.88	5.24	6.21	5.91
$\overline{X}$ expectation	3.96	3.91	4.10	3.63	4.59	3.93	4.09	3.55	4.00	4.26
$\overline{X}$ discrepancy	-.29	.31	.03	.16	.06	.32	1.79	1.70	2.21	1.65
Skilled worker										
$\overline{X}$ aspiration	4.57	5.56	5.88	5.70	5.50	5.95	3.88	4.42	4.82	5.24
$\overline{X}$ expectation	3.71	4.70	4.18	3.97	5.09	5.78	2.39	2.85	3.97	3.26
$\overline{X}$ discrepancy	.96	.80	1.70	1.74	.41	.18	1.03	1.26	1.56	2.03

[a]Low mean scores indicate high aspirations or expectations. Minus signs indicate that aspirations are higher than expectations.

126

Cities blue-collar parents of sons) parents in both Mexico and the United States who wanted their children to be teachers believed it was possible for them to attain that goal. The discrepancy scores between parents' aspirations and expectations for children becoming teachers was considerably less than it was for the occupation of physician. (In general, United States parents ranked teaching higher than Mexican parents.)

The high discrepancy scores for United States parents' rankings of office work reflects their tendency to rank the occupation relatively low while indicating a moderately high expectation that their child will eventually hold an office position. United States parents were also more likely than Mexican parents to aspire for and expect their sons to be skilled workers. This latter finding may reflect the lower status and income of skilled manual workers in Mexico.

The data reflecting parents' aspirations and expectations support the conclusion that Mexican parents are more likely to want their offspring to hold higher status and higher income jobs. The United States parents not only were less likely to aspire to high status positions for their children, they were also less optimistic that their children could attain such positions. Within the two societies, white-collar parents were more optimistic than blue-collar parents.

In summary, our findings suggest that Mexican families interpreted the social structure to their offspring by stressing the importance of material attainment and by suggesting that the chances of such attainment would be improving in the future. White-collar families were more optimistic than blue-collar and peasant families. The United States families were generally less optimistic about the future, believing that opportunities for their children would not improve appreciably over current conditions. These families also were more concerned about children's self-fulfillment, happiness, and interpersonal satisfactions than about material advancement.

Parent–Child Interaction Patterns

According to our theory high levels of access to information and diversity of available roles within communities would be associated with egalitarianism in families and by communication patterns that were characterized by tolerance of conflicting ideas and tolerance of ambiguity (theorem 5).

The data presented earlier in Tables 5.4 and 5.5 are relevant to the hypothesis as it pertains to family egalitarianism. It will be remembered that the Twin Cities families in the study were significantly more likely to evidence an equal distribution of decision-making power than the Michoacan families. Moreover, the Michoacan peasant families were most likely to be dominated by one family member and the Twin Cities white-collar families were most likely to be egalitarian—all in accord with the hypothesis.

Table 5.10

F Ratios and Probabilities Indicating Significant Differences in Parents' Aspirations, Expectations, and Discrepancy Scores on Ranking of Various Professions for Sons and Daughters by Community and Social Class

	Parental aspirations			Parental expectations			Discrepancy score between aspirations and expectations		
	Community	Class	Interaction	Community	Class	Interaction	Community	Class	Interaction
PHYSICIANS									
Fathers with sons	$F = 8.26$; $p < .001$	NS	NS	$F = 12.72$; $p < .001$	$F = 5.53$; $p < .02$	$F = 4.32$; $p < .05$	$F = 11.50$; $p < .001$	NS	$F = 5.40$; $p < .05$
Fathers with daughters	$F = 3.13$; $p < .05$	NS	NS	$F = 20.25$; $p < .001$	NS	NS	$F = 7.17$; $p < .01$	NS	NS
Mothers with sons	$F = 7.11$; $p = .001$	$F = 6.43$; $p = .012$	NS	$F = 15.47$; $p = .001$	$F = 21.39$; $p = .001$	NS	$F = 6.00$; $p = .003$	$F = 9.41$; $p = .003$	NS
Mothers with daughters	$F = 5.02$; $p < .01$	$F = 11.13$; $p < .01$	NS	$F = 15.10$; $p < .001$	NS	NS	$F = 3.64$; $p < .05$	NS	NS
TEACHERS									
Fathers with sons	$F = 3.5$; $p < .03$	NS	NS	NS	$F = 6.0$; $p < .02$		NS	NS	NS
Fathers with daughters	$F = .464$; $p < .001$			$F = 9.67$; $p < .0001$				$F = 4.7$; $p < .03$	$F = 7.344$; $p = .007$
Mothers with sons	$F = 9.9$; $p = .0001$			$F = 5.35$; $p < .004$	NS	NS	NS	NS	NS
Mothers with daughters	$F = 14.65$; $p < .0001$	NS	NS	$F = 19.88$; $p < .0001$	NS	NS	NS	NS	NS

OFFICE WORKERS

Fathers with sons	F = 27.75; p < .0001	NS	NS	NS	NS	F = 19.95; p < .0001	NS	NS
Fathers with daughters	F = 26.2; p = .0001	NS	F = 7.34; p = .007	NS	NS	F = 15.6; p < .0001	NS	NS
Mothers with sons	F = 17.5; p < .0001	NS	NS	F = 4.36; p = .036	NS	F = 11.8; p < .0001	NS	NS
Mothers with daughters	F = 24.6; p < .0001	F = 4.96; p = .026	NS	NS	NS	F = 15.3; p < .0001	NS	NS

SKILLED WORKERS

Fathers with sons	F = 9.8; p = .001	F = 5.74	F = 7.3; p < .01	NS	NS	NS	NS	F = 6.12; p = .014
Fathers with daughters	NS	F = 6.4; p = .012	NS	NS	NS	NS	F = 8.9; p = .004	NS
Mothers with sons	F = 5.4; p = .005	NS	F = 11.5; p < .001	F = 9.4; p = .003	NS	NS	F = 10.9; p = .002	NS
Mothers with daughters	NS	NS	F = 5.3; p = .02	NS	NS	NS	NS	NS

We used as our measure of tolerance of conflict the proportion of power messages sent that were explicitly rejected within a family. For instance, if a father suggested that the child buy a car and the child said, "No, I'd better save the money for awhile," the exchange would be coded as $F \rightarrow CP-$. We then divided the $P-$ messages for a given family member by all the power messages sent in the family. In general, the findings are in the expected direction. As indicated in Table 5.11, United States families engaged in significantly more conflict during the game than Mexican families. Only the data for mothers did not reach an acceptable level of statistical significance. Class differences within the urban communities were not statistically significant. The peasant families, however, had significantly lower conflict scores than families in the other communities and the Twin Cities white-collar families tended to have the highest conflict scores.

Our measure of tolerance of ambiguity also derived from the coded observations of family communication patterns. We computed the average number of all messages sent that did not result in any questions, disagreements, challenges, failures to react, or qualifying statements. Put another way, they represent the degree of efficaciousness of the message. Since tolerance for ambiguity implies a willingness to hold decisions in abeyance, families that displayed a high level of efficacious messages should, we believed, display a low tolerance for ambiguity. For example, family members who responded to a directive from another family member such as, "We should spend $5 and 5 hours a week in church," with comments such as "Let's wait and see," or "Maybe we should save the money," or simply would not act on the suggestion, would score low on our efficacious measure and therefore high on tolerance for ambiguity.

Table 5.11

Mean Proportion of Power Messages Refused, Rejected, or Ignored (Conflict) by One or More Family Members[a] by Communities and Social Class[b]

		Zacapu		Twin Cities			
	Villages	Blue collar	White collar	Blue collar	White collar	F	p
Entire family	.018	.033	.037	.055	.059	10.27	< .001
Messages sent by father	.005	.013	.012	.019	.024	8.48	< .001
Messages sent by mother	.011	.014	.017	.016	.025	NS	NS
Messages sent by child	.001	.007	.008	.013	.019	11.44	< .001

[a] Computed by dividing total number of power messages rejected by all power messages sent in a given family.
[b] Social class differences were not statistically significant.

Table 5.12 presents the findings in terms of efficaciousness of messages. Peasant families sent the most efficacious messages, followed by urban Mexican families; Twin Cities families had the lowest efficacious scores. These findings generally support our hypotheses. Only when we examine children's efficacy scores does the pattern break down. In the Mexican sample, particularly among peasant and blue-collar families, children's efficacy scores are relatively low. As we have seen previously, children in the Mexican family sent very few messages and played a minor role in the decision process; these data thus reflect a tendency by the Mexican parents to ignore children, rather than to question, challenge, or evaluate statements made by the child.

These data are consonant with other research which suggests greater intellectual flexibility among people who live and work in complex social structures (Kohn & Schooler, 1978; Luria, 1976; Schooler, 1972). Moreover since the findings suggest a greater problem-solving orientation among families in industrial communities than among families living in preindustrial communities, they are in accord with much of the available theory on social development and modernization (Apter, 1971; Inkeles, 1969; Kahl, 1968).

The question, as yet unanswered, is how do these elements of family structure and parent–child relationships affect the adolescents' abilities to problem solve under conditions of social change? An adequate answer to this question requires observing the performance of children from different communities and different socialization experiences as they seek to solve the same problem in a changing social structure. SIMCAR provided a means for introducing the same changes for all the adolescents in the study regardless of background.

Table 5.12

Proportion of Efficacious[a] Messages Sent by Father, Mother, and Child by Community and Class[b]

Messages sent by	Villages N = 50	Zacapu		Twin Cities		F	p
		Blue collar N = 33	White collar N = 27	Blue collar N = 25	White collar N = 29		
Father	.92	.88	.85	.48	.50	91.58	< .001
Mother	.90	.79	.80	.48	.48	76.12	< .001
Child	.65	.66	.77	.49	.52	4.58	< .02
Entire family	.94	.91	.86	.48	.50	172.89	< .001

[a] Messages sent without disagreement from other family members.
[b] Social class differences were not statistically significant.

COMMUNITY CONTEXT AND
CHILDREN'S PERFORMANCE

Before examining the child's performance data, a brief reminder of the differences between the family game and the child's game seems appropriate. With the exception of 12 cases all families played SIMCAR prior to the child's playing the game alone.[1] The families played the game under conditions of success, neutrality, or failure for four rounds in Zacapu and six rounds in the Twin Cities. The neutral condition was eliminated in the villages, where SIMCAR was played only under success–failure conditions. When the family game was completed, the parents were interviewed by a staff member. During this time, the child played the game again for 10 rounds representing 10 years of the child's life beginning at age 16. In the third round, the social change simulation was introduced.

Whereas the family game provided data on family goals, family structure, and patterns of interaction, the child's game provided detailed information on the individual child's goals, strategies, and problem-solving behaviors. The family game data are relevant to socialization processes and the child game data are relevant to socialization outcomes. The analyses that follow test hypotheses linking the processes to the outcomes.

Children's Life-Styles: Goals and Strategies

The children's game performances were in close accord with the values parents expressed in the interviews and family game. The data on income earned and job rank achieved during the game provide support for the hypothesis that Mexican children, like their parents, place a greater value on material advancement than United States children (see Table 5.13). It is also worth noting that the village children earned more income than the Zacapu white-collar children whereas the white-collar children attained a somewhat higher job rank. Although these differences are minor, they are suggestive of a greater concern among village children for material advancement than for job status. A similar discrepancy occurred in the Twin Cities sample, where white-collar children obtained a slightly higher job status than blue-collar children. Zacapu blue-collar children outscored all other groups on both measures although differences in job rank were not significant.

To test the commitment of the children to familistic goals, we con-

---

[1] The 12 cases were used to determine the extent to which prior playing of the game had a learning effect on subsequent performances. Having assured ourselves that a learning effect was indeed present, we eliminated these cases from subsequent analyses.

Table 5.13
Mean Income Earned and Mean Job Rank in Child's Game by Community and Class

	Villages	Zacapu		Twin Cities	
		Blue collar	White collar	Blue collar	White collar
	N = 50	N = 33	N = 27	N = 25	N = 29
Mean income[a]	455.6	481.9	434.4	280.8	281.1
Mean job rank[b]	1.6	1.35	1.39	2.12	1.83

[a] Main effect for community, $F = 33.2, p < .0001$.
  Main effect for class, $F = 3.6, p < .06$.
[b] Highest job rank $= 1.00$.
  Main effect for community, $F = 18.00, p < .001$.
  No main effects for class.

structed an index that included the SIMCAR choices on marriage, number of children decided upon, hours spent in housework, and hours spent visiting relatives. These data are presented in Table 5.14.

In keeping with the findings reported earlier on the family game, Twin Cities children were more likely to invest their game time and money in family oriented activities than village or Zacapu children. Significant differences existed between the villages, Zacapu, and Twin Cities. However, differences between social classes in Zacapu and the Twin Cities were not significant. The hypothesis that United States children are more concerned with interpersonal satisfactions and Mexican children are more concerned with material payoffs is further supported by data presented in Table 5.15. These data summarize investments in 11 of the 13 game choices. The table also provides a basis for inferring the types of strategies the adolescents employed in seeking their goals. For example, the table indicates that Mexican children were less likely to get married, have children, visit friends, and spend time in housework. At the same time, certain differences emerged in the strategies employed by the Mexican children. Peasant children spent more time and money on visiting relatives than any other group in the

Table 5.14
Mean Familism Score for Child's Game by Community[a]

Villages	Zacapu		Twin Cities	
	Blue collar	White collar	Blue collar	White collar
N = 50	N = 40	N = 41	N = 47	N = 57
8.84	11.30	11.32	12.64	13.30

[a] Familism score is based on whether child married, number of children decided upon, hours spent in housework, and hours spent visiting relatives.
  Main effect community, $F = 20.88, p < .001$.

Table 5.15

Mean Scores of Child Game Activities Based on Investments of Time and Money and Percentage Choosing Social Mobility or Marriage by Community and Class

Activities	Villages N = 50	Zacapu Blue collar N = 43	Zacapu White collar N = 42	Twin Cities Blue collar N = 47	Twin Cities White collar N = 57	Significant effects[b] ($p < .05$) Community	Class
Means[a]							
Athletics	31.0	24.8	20.7	25.7	21.0		X
Television and radio	22.4	21.6	17.5	25.7	17.5		
Friends	17.6	15.8	19.4	33.8	30.8	X	X
Housework	35.3	35.0	36.7	47.7	45.2	X	X
Relatives	24.9	19.7	11.3	23.4	18.6	X	X
Money saved	124.9	134.2	108.0	110.5	90.3		
Money spent at store	160.7	188.5	181.2	82.1	79.9	X	
Church	22.0	16.1	14.5	18.6	19.6	X	
Number of children	.34	.75	.85	.94	1.33	X	X
Ratio of savings to earnings	1.81	.73	.62	1.54	1.73	X	
Percentages[a]							
Percentage accepting social mobility option	78	67	79	32	33	X	
Percentage married	44	79	86	83	93	X	

[a] Comparison of means based on two-way analysis of variance. Comparison of percentages based on chi square.

[b] No interactions between community and class were statistically significant.

study, an activity which seemingly runs contrary to the hypothesis that they have a major commitment to obtain material rewards. However, when we consider the evidence indicating that Mexican peasants depend upon kin to obtain jobs and other material advantages (Foster, 1967; Lomnitz, 1977; Miller, 1973), this behavior can be interpreted as another component in a strategy for attaining material payoffs.

The data pertaining to savings, money spent at the store, and the ratio of savings to money spent suggest that Zacapu blue- and white-collar children not only used their higher earnings to save more money than other children in the study, but also in the latter rounds spent a larger proportion of their savings than other groups of children. This type of behavior is suggestive of Apter's (1971) assertion that people living in countries in the final stages of modernization become "embourgeoised," placing great stress on the accumulation and consumption of consumer goods.

The greater tendency among white-collar adolescents in both Zacapu and the Twin Cities to have children lends additional support to the proposition that familism is more pronounced among more affluent groups. Also, the finding that peasant and blue-collar adolescents were significantly more likely than white-collar adolescents to save money lends credence to the inference that money is more highly valued among poorer people. Peasants and blue-collar children were also more likely than white-collar children to invest time in television and radio. This evidence of a higher value placed on mass media by the working-class and peasant children as compared to white-collar children is consistent with other data indicating that peasants and/or working-class persons depend more heavily than the middle class on the mass media for information as well as education (Rogers, 1969b; Wade & Schramm, 1969; Willensky, 1964).

A clearer picture of the types of strategies children employed is gained from examining the investments of time and money made over successive rounds of the game. The savings and spending patterns, for example, provide data relevant to the hypothesis that deferred gratification is more likely to occur among Mexicans and among poorer people. Figure 5.1 presents the saving patterns for children from each of the five communities sampled in this study. It can be seen that the Mexican adolescents began saving in large amounts during the sixth and seventh rounds of the game. This is about the time that their investments in education and training came to fruition in the better paying jobs. It is also of interest that the Mexican blue-collar and peasant children saved more than any of the other groups during this period. Figure 5.2 illustrates the children's spending patterns. In the last round of the game the Mexican children spent considerably more on consumer goods than United States children. Among the Mexicans, white-collar children were the highest spenders followed by blue-collar and peasant

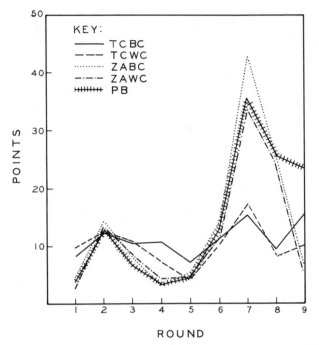

Figure 5.1. *Adolescent saving patterns over game rounds by community. The points are equivalent to money saved. TCBC is Twin Cities blue collar (means); TCWC is Twin Cities white collar; ZABC is Zacapu blue collar; ZAWC is Zacapu white collar; PB is Villages.*

children. Comparing Figures 5.1 and 5.2, it is clear that Mexican children were more likely to adopt a strategy of saving during the middle of the game and spending in the last round of the game. This strategy is not only suggestive of an awareness among the Mexican children of the advantages of deferred gratification in real life, it is also conducive to performing well in the game. It allows players to accumulate points for saving and then to accumulate points for purchasing without carrying over the costs of such purchases in subsequent rounds.

The tendency of the United States children to invest time and money in friends, marriage, and having children was manifested in a steady pattern that persisted from the first to the last rounds of the game. Figure 5.3 provides the per round data for investments in friends and Figure 5.4 provides similar information for number of children. From the first round to the last, the United States children seemed to place a higher priority on friends than the Mexican children. Only in the sixth, seventh, and eighth rounds did the Zacapu white-collar children match the United States sample in these investments. A similar pattern is apparent when we examine Figure 5.4. Mex-

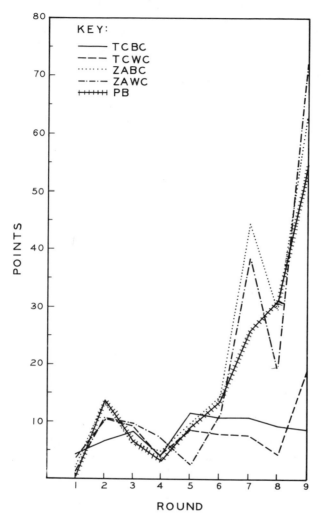

Figure 5.2. *Adolescent store purchases per game round by community. The points are cummulated amount of purchases (means). TCBC is Twin Cities blue collar; TCWC is Twin Cities white collar; ZABC is Zacapu blue collar; ZAWC is Zacapu white collar; PB is Villages.*

ican children showed no inclination to have children until the sixth round, and it was only during the eighth and ninth rounds of the game (after occupational careers had been established) that they made any substantial investment in children. On the other hand, some United States white-collar adolescents began to commit themselves to children as early as the second round of the game.

In summary, the data presented in these figures illustrate the Mexican

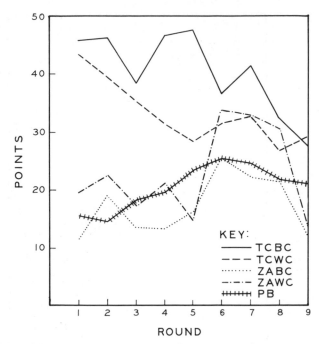

Figure 5.3. *Adolescent investment in visiting friends per round by community. Points are time and money spent (means). TCBC is Twin Cities blue collar; TCWC is Twin Cities white collar; ZABC is Zacapu blue collar; ZAWC is Zacapu white collar; PB is Villages.*

adolescent tendencies toward deferring gratification by saving, refraining from marriage and children, and spending only after sufficient funds had been accumulated. The Twin Cities children were more inclined to establish the life-style they desired early in the game. Their strategy seemed to be the early formation and continued maintenance of positive interpersonal relationships. The data also suggest that, within societies, blue-collar and peasant adolescents tend to be somewhat more financially conservative than white-collar adolescents.

The Effects of Family Success or Failure

Theorem 7 asserts that children with a history of family success in solving problems in designated situations will be more willing to take reasonable risks when engaging in problem-solving activities in similar situations than would children whose families had a history of failure in such endeavors. During the family game, urban families were randomly assigned to three conditions—failure, neutral, and success. The peasant families were assigned to two conditions—failure and success. In this section we compare

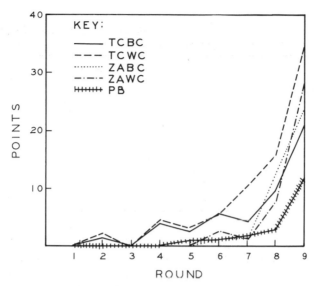

Figure 5.4. *Decision to have children per round by community. Points are 15 per child (means). TCBC is Twin Cities blue collar; TCWC is Twin cities white collar; ZABC is Zacapu blue collar; ZAWC is Zacapu white collar; PB is Villages.*

the child game performances of children who experience success or failure in the family game. The analyses, which included peasant families, required elimination of the neutral cases.

One test of children's willingness to take reasonable risks was their acceptance or refusal of the mobility option. We predicted that those children who were part of the failure condition in the family game would be inhibited from expending the initial costs involved in accepting a geographical move for a potential long-term gain when they played the game alone. As shown in Table 5.16, a significantly larger proportion of children from all communities who experienced the success condition during the family game accepted the mobility option.

Partly because of the mobility option, the success–failure condition was also associated with other outcomes of children's game performance. Table 5.17 presents data indicating that prior experiences of family success or fail-

Table 5.16
Relationship between Success–Failure Game Condition and Adolescents' Choice of Social Mobility Option in all Communities

	Success N = 73	Failure N = 72	Chi square	p
Percentage accepted mobility option	.74	.53	7.04	< .01

Table 5.17

Mean Income in Child's Game for Adolescents Who Experience Success or Failure in the Family Game by Community and Sex of Adolescent

Game condition	Villages		Zacapu		Twin Cities	
	Male	Female	Male	Female	Male	Female
Success	493.1	471.5	481.3	426.6	297.7	273.8
Failure	398.6	451.2	441.3	466.8	264.7	269.2
Main effect	F	p				
Community	33.48	$<.001$				
Success–failure condition	4.81	$<.04$				
Interaction						
Sex by success–failure	6.02	$<.02$				

ure were linked to the amount of income children earned in the game. The significant interaction between sex of the child and game condition, however, points to the fact that the failure condition had a more depressing effect on the performance of boys than on girls. In all three communities, the discrepancies between scores of those who experienced success and those who experienced failure was greater for boys than for girls. In fact, in Zacapu, girls who experienced the failure condition earned more than those who had a success experience. We will return to this issue in the next chapter when we consider sex differences in detail. Class differences were not statistically significant.

We anticipated that children in the success condition would adopt new career routes when their original routes were blocked sooner than those with a failure experience; we expected a similar response in terms of the readiness of the children to accept the "new school" alternative. Neither of these hypotheses were supported by the findings. The Mexican adolescents showed a greater readiness to exercise these options regardless of the conditions under which they played the family game.

In brief, our findings provide only partial support for the hypothesis that children's risk taking and performance is effected by prior success or failure. We will reconsider family success or failure again when we test the theory's predictions for adolescent problem solving.

ADOLESCENT PROBLEM SOLVING

Initially, we established two indicators of adolescent problem-solving ability; the round in the game in which the adolescent changed career routes, and the round in which the adolescent graduated from the new school. The new school proved to be the more appropriate of the two measures. It offered the child an opportunity to recover from a deteriorating situation in which obstructions were continually blocking the way to the child's original career choice.

The child could change career routes without entering the new school, thereby avoiding a $60 cost. This alternative, however, made it impossible for the players to reach the highest occupational levels and to earn the highest incomes. In fact, this was a relatively poor stratagem. If we assume that the initial career choice represents the adolescents' most desired type of work activity, it would follow that those adolescents who gave up this activity and did not avail themselves of the advancement opportunities provided by the new school forfeited both the symbolic rewards of working in the most desired field and the practical chance to attain the highest income and status position provided by the game. Table 5.18 presents the percentages of children from each community who chose to change career routes and chose to enter the new school. Mexican children were significantly more likely than United States children to make these choices, probably because of their materialistic orientation. Of special interest was the finding, indirectly reflected in Table 5.18, that those white-collar children who chose to change their career routes were significantly more likely than blue-collar or peasant children to also choose to enter the new school, $x^2 = 5.29$, $p < .025$. Of the white-collar children, 92% in the United States and 91% in Mexico choosing to change routes also chose the new school; the percentages drop to about 80 for peasant and Mexican blue-collar children and the lowest percentage (58) was among the United States blue-collar children. From this perspective, the Twin Cities blue-collar children seem to be the poorest problem solvers in the study.

The round in which the adolescent graduated from the new school provides a more discriminate measure of problem solving than does the dichot-

Table 5.18
Percentage Adolescents Who Chose to Change Routes and Chose to Enter the New School during Child Game by Community and Social Class

	Villages	Zacapu		Twin Cities	
	N = 50	Blue collar N = 40	White collar N = 41	Blue collar N = 47	White collar N = 57
Change of routes[a]	92	85	78	51	46
Entered new school[b]	74	72	71	30	42

[a] Chi square for all communities = 49.29, df = 4, p<.001.
  Chi square for Mexican–United States comparison = 47.17, df = 1, p < .001.
[b] Chi square for all communities = 32.24, df = 4, p < .001.
  Chi square for Mexican–United States comparisons = 30.55, df = 1, p < .001.

omous choice of whether or not to go to the new school. SIMCAR was constructed so that the earlier the player chose the new school—providing he or she graduated—the better his or her chances of obtaining a high status or high income position. In fact, if the player waited to enter the school until either of the last two rounds, income would be lower than if he or she had never chosen to enter the school in the first place. Some adolescents chose to enter the new school, drop out for a round to earn money, and then return to graduate. This strategy was not as effective as completing the 2 years sequentially. It was also possible to enter the new school and not complete the 2 years (rounds) required for graduation. Such a course of action would place the adolescent at a particular disadvantage because a year (round) of income was lost without gaining the advantages of graduation. The sooner the adolescent graduated from the new school, the sooner he or she could begin working up the economic and status ladder in the new occupation. Thus, the round in which the child graduated from the new school provided the best indicator of problem-solving ability.

Problem solving involves overcoming barriers to achieving desired goals; measuring problem solving therefore requires comparing persons with similar goals. This measurement could not be made on the decision of whether or not the new school was chosen. Players who decided on career routes because they seemed intrinsically satisfying or because they merely provided a means of support might have been less willing to change career routes than those who sought the highest status jobs and the most money. On the other hand, if we compare only players who chose the new school, we can assume that they wanted to achieve their goals of success sufficiently strongly to give up their original career choices. For this group, the round in which the child graduated from the new school appears to be the best indicator of problem-solving ability, because, as we noted earlier, the earlier the child graduated, the higher would be his or her potential income and status. Since the phrase, *round graduated from the new school,* is lengthy and awkward, we shall simply refer to this behavior as "problem-solving ability." However, the reader should keep in mind its specific meaning and its game context.

The model presented in Chapter 3 proposed that parents' interpretation of children's opportunities in the social structure combined with family success or failure experiences and parent–child interaction patterns to influence the development of adolescent problem-solving skills in social situations. The theory holds that the parent–adolescent socialization relationship provides the experiential nexus within which the adolescent learns problem-solving skills. We have seen that white-collar families tend to be more optimistic than blue-collar families and that Mexican families are more optimistic than United States families. Also, Mexican families were more future oriented and had higher aspirations than United States families. Moreover, the data show that United States families especially the white-collar families are more egalitarian than Mexican families (peasant families being the least egalitarian) and that United States families also show greater tolerance of ambiguity and conflict than Mexican families.

We turn now to the hypotheses that predict that egalitarianism, tolerance of ambiguity, and tolerance of conflict within families are positively related to adolescent problem-solving ability. Although the theory predicts that these experiential variables are affected by social structures, the influence of these variables on adolescent problem-solving ability should hold for all children in the study regardless of social structure. Thus, in the section that follows we shall test our hypotheses linking these variables (as well as success–failure) with adolescent problem-solving ability, ignoring, for the moment, the role of community. Once these tests are completed we will conclude our analyses by testing hypotheses predicting which communities produce the best problem solvers.

The basic test of the theory does not depend upon the impact of single independent variables, but on the combined affects of the variables discussed earlier. These variables, in combination, were expected to have an additive affect on adolescents' problem-solving ability (proposition 11 and theorem 7).

Parent–Child Relationship, Family Success–Failure Experiences, and Adolescent Problem Solving

To test the additive affect of the independent variables designated by the theory, we included the relevant variables in a multiple regression analysis. This analysis also allowed us to assess the specific contribution of each individual variable to the adolescents' problem-solving score, controlling for some of the confounding affects of the other variables. The data are presented in Table 5.19. In combination they produce a multiple correlation of .58, explaining 34% of the variance associated with adolescent problem solving.

Six of the 11 independent variables—equalitarianism, mothers' aspirations, mothers' expectations, family success–failure, fathers' time orientation, and tolerance of ambiguity—had a statistically significant, $p < .05$, association with problem solving. The independent influence of each of these variables is indicated by the standardized betas reported in Table 5.19. Of the 6 significant independent variables, 3 were measures of the parents' interpretation of the social structure, two were parent–child interaction patterns, and one (the success–failure condition) was a family structural component. In sum, the essential components designated in our

Table 5.19

Multiple Regression of Variables Depicting Parents Interpretation of the Social Structure, Parents–Child Interaction, and Family Success–Failure Experience on Adolescent Problem Solving

Variable	Simple r	Beta	Standardized beta	F
Family equalitarianism	−.33	−.29	−.23	4.668*
Family conflict	−.12	−1.46	−.06	.294
Father aspirations	−.03	−.03	−.06	.324
Father expectations	−.20	−.23	−.11	1.68
Mother aspirations	.10	.08	.23	4.754*
Mother expectations	.34	.63	.28	6.352*
Father time orientation	.16	.21	.19	3.796*
Mother time orientation	.03	.007	.005	.663
Parents perception of opportunity	.01	.01	.005	.663
Family success–failure	.22	.51	.25	6.685*
Family tolerance of ambiguity	.20	1.17	.17	2.454*

*Standardized betas, $p < .05$.
Multiple $R = .58$.
Multiple $R^2 = .34$.

model as influencing the socialization process all indicated significant effects on the socialization outcome we sought to explain.

Nonetheless, the theory requires modification. Not only did variables such as parents' perception of children's opportunity and tolerance of conflict have little affect on the outcome, but, egalitarianism—a variable that had a significant affect—was related to the outcome variable in a direction opposite to that predicted by the theory. In speculating on the possible reasons for this finding, it gradually became clear to us that the concept of equalitarianism has two separate meanings, as we interpreted it. It referred to both the power to make decisions and to openness of communication. Indeed, our measure reflected the power to make decisions more accurately than it reflected openness of communication. The distinction between these two behaviors is critical, since it is possible for decisions to be made by a single family member, even though all of the family members contributed information toward the problem solution. In fact, as we suggested in Chapters 2 and 3, such a combination of behaviors would be positively associated with problem solving in career-planning problems. The best approximation we have that both centralized authority and the free flow of information may positively affect the child's socialization as a problem solver is the association between our measure of egalitarianism and adolescent problem solving, combined with the positive association between tolerance of ambiguity and problem solving. Reconceptualizing the measure of egalitarianism into centralization of decision making allows us to merely change the signs of the correlation with adolescent problem solving, that is, from −.33 to +.33.

We offer such a rearrangement as a reasonable revision of the original theory.

The fact that only mothers' expectations and aspirations were positively associated with adolescent problem solving, whereas only fathers' future orientation significantly influenced problem solving, once again raises the important issue of sex differences. Again, we remind the reader that we shall defer the discussion of these findings and this issue to the next chapter.[2]

Community Context

We must still address the question of how adolescent problem solving differs in the five communities studied. The communities, it will be remembered, were selected so that they differentiated on such dimensions as available resources, number and diversity of role choices, and access to information. The theory, applied to these communities, predicted that Twin Cities and white-collar adolescents would be the best problem solvers. The prediction is also in line with most of the available explanations of differences between modernizing and industrialized countries. We expected (and found) that Twin Cities parents were not overly optimistic, they seemed to be realistic about their children's life chances; they were egalitarian; and they had high tolerances for conflict and ambiguity—all variables considered to be associated with problem solving. Also, as expected, peasant families were the least likely to be egalitarian and tolerate ambiguity and conflict. They did, however, have a high degree of optimism about their children's future, a trait shared with other Mexican families. In general, the data pertaining to family interpretations of social structure and family patterns of interaction were in accord with our hypothesis. Overall, the combined variables were able to explain 34% of the variance on adolescent problem-solving behavior (Table 5.19).

Despite these findings, the data did not support the hypothesis predicting the direction of community differences in problem solving. As shown in Table 5.20, the peasant adolescents were the group most likely to graduate early from the new school, even when Twin Cities adolescents chose the new school, they were more likely to graduate later than other groups in the

[2] We considered the question of colinearity with the items of mother and father aspirations, expectations, and time perception. Not only were the interitem correlations between these items relatively low, but when we eliminated single items and ran the multiple regressions with all other items, it was clear that the variables that were included had an independent effect on the dependent variable—an effect which was not appreciably influenced by the exclusion or inclusion of other variables.

Table 5.20
Mean Round Adolescent Graduated from the New School

	Villages	Zacapu		Twin Cities	
		Blue collar	White collar	Blue collar	White collar
	N = 32	N = 27	N = 29	N = 13	N = 20
Mean round	5.84	6.0	6.03	6.54	6.80

$F = 14.44, p < .001.$

study. This trend was most apparent for the Twin Cities white-collar children.

One possible explanation for this result is that the independent variables in the model were associated differently with problem solving within the different communities we studied. Efforts to test this possibility by doing separate multiple regression analyses within each community provided unstable and unreliable results (basically because of the reduced sample size). In essence, we are left with a model that predicts a reasonable amount of variance on our measure of problem solving but does not explain the differences between communities.

Two *post-datum* explanations for these findings are worth considering. The first is simply that Mexican children in our sample are better problem solvers than the United States children. This explanation, however, ignores the evidence that Mexican (particularly peasant) families indicated significantly less psychological flexibility than the United States families. Our own data show that such flexibility is associated with problem solving.

We believe the more plausible explanation is to drop the assumption that all children who chose to go to the new school shared the same success goal—that is, the differences reported in Table 5.20 reflect differences in degree of commitment to the goal of material success. The important condition provided by SIMCAR in the child's game was that everyone has an equal chance to obtain material and status payoff, if they make the right choices. Given this condition, data from the Mexican adolescents indicated that they had the ability to adopt strategies appropriate for achieving the goals of high income and high status jobs. But what if one's life goals were less materialistic and status-oriented? The greater delay evidenced by the Twin Cities white-collar children in choosing the new school may be due to the higher perceived costs associated with making such a choice. If the primary reason for choosing the original career route was a means for earning a good living or attaining a high status position, an alternative route offering better opportunities poses no serious difficulty. However, if the original route was chosen for reasons of personal satisfaction (e.g., the job represents the kind of work one wants to do; the people one works with are likely to be pleasant; or the job is consonant with one's sense of one's own identity), the cost of choosing an alternative career is greatly increased. Given the perceived costs in changing career routes, there may be a tendency to delay the decision in favor of seeking more information in subsequent rounds. Such information would be seen as either altering the direction of events or confirming the necessity of choosing the new school (Leik & Tallman, 1977).

Unfortunately, the available data do not enable us to test this interpretation. We have seen repeatedly, however, that United States families and children sought to invest in choices that involved family, children, and friends, whereas the Mexicans tended to emphasize material gains. What we did not realize was how powerful these goals would be in determining SIMCAR performance. In constructing SIMCAR, we expected that participants would be able to respond to it both as a game and as a simulation of real-life situations. What occurred was that the family members' readiness to play out the life of the adolescent child as they would like it to be was so powerful that the game aspect was completely submerged. We successfully predicted the differences in life-style goals that emerged from our research—we had not anticipated that these differences would so completely affect game strategies that they would create essentially problems different from the one we thought was being posed for the children (i.e., how to get ahead in a changing society). In Chapter 7 this issue is discussed in greater detail.

TESTING ALTERNATIVE EXPLANATIONS

In this section, the possibility that our findings may be spurious is considered. Only those potentially spurious relationships that can be checked against available data will be examined. Other alternative explanations resulting from weaknesses in design, varying perspectives as to the meaning of data derived from game simulations, and different possible interpretations of our findings will be discussed in Chapter 7.

One possible contribution to spuriousness may have resulted from the variations in our methods of sampling families in Michoacan and the Twin Cities. The greater emphasis on family and interpersonal satisfaction among Twin Cities families and children could be attributed to our use of church membership roles as a sample source. It can be argued that such people would tend to reinforce family values more than those whose religious convictions were weaker. Fortunately, about a third of our Twin Cities sample was drawn from YMCA, Boy Scout, and suburban city

(Edina, St. Louis Park, and Columbia Heights) directories. We compared the families in this group to those drawn from church rosters. Thirty non-church-affiliated families were eligible for comparison; they included 15 families with girls and 15 families with boys, as well as 13 blue-collar and 17 white-collar families. Thus, it does not appear that either sex or social class represents a systematic bias in this particular subsample. The church and nonchurch subsamples drawn from the Twin Cities sample were compared on adolescent SIMCAR performance scores such as familism, income earned, total game score, highest occupation rank attained, and adolescent problem solving. We found no statistically significant differences between the subsamples on any of these variables. We also compared Catholic, Lutheran, and other Protestant families (there were only three Jewish families in the study) on the same criterion variables; again, we found no significant differences between groups.

Families in both Mexico and the United States were compared on parent's education, family size, child's ordinal position, and family income. Since education and income distributions differed between Michoacan and the Twin Cities (see Table 4.3 in Chapter 4), we did our analysis separately for Mexico and the United States. Our findings were generally negative. A few comparisons yielded significant results, but their impact on the findings were limited at best. For example, Michoacan family income was positively associated with adolescent's familism, a finding that further supports the hypothesis that familism is a consequence of affluence. However, family income was not associated with any other criterion variables in either Michoacan or the Twin Cities. Within the Twin Cities sample, father's education was significantly related to occupational rank in the adolescent game. The relationship was curvilinear, with the middle ranks being positively associated with father's education.

We had fully expected that family size and ordinal position would be associated with adolescent's problem solving, but neither of these variables yielded significant associations with any of the criterion variables (despite the fact that virtually every possible combination of ordinal position was analyzed).

CONCLUSIONS

In this chapter we tested hypotheses derived from a theory developed to explain the processes through which parents socialize their children to solve problems in a changing social system. The theory was intended to (a) identify components of the family relationships that contributed to children learning problem-solving skills; and (b) identify the social structural conditions that influenced variations in these relationships. We hoped the theory would contribute not only toward explaining socialization for problem solving, but also toward the effects of social structural conditions on the socialization process, and through this process, on the course of social change. How successful were we? On the one hand, the ability to explain a reasonable amount of variance on adolescent problem solving in career problems seemed promising; on the other hand, the effort to use the theory as a contribution to a theory of social change was not successful.

The attempt to link our theory of socialization to social change was based on the premise that the more highly developed social structures would provide the conditions through which children would learn to be the most effective problem solvers under conditions of social change. It followed that peasant adolescents, coming from the least developed social structures, should be the group least able to take advantage of the opportunities when structural conditions changed. This is not the way it turned out. The peasant adolescent children in our sample seemed unencumbered by tradition, family loyalties, lack of cognitive flexibility, or any other constraint that we could detect, from taking advantage of the opportunities for success provided in SIMCAR. It is possible, of course, that in the "real" world peasant children would not be able to compete for the top jobs because they could not do as well as white collar children in school, or they do not have the cognitive skills necessary to grasp and integrate the necessary abstract ideas. The data reported here are not relevant to that supposition. They are relevant, however, to the question of whether peasant children have the intellectual acumen and flexibility to know the kinds of acts and choices that would facilitate achieving their social goals while playing SIMCAR. Since SIMCAR is a reasonable replication of opportunity aspects of the social structure in Mexico and the United States, we can infer that they are able to take advantage of the opportunities extant in such social structures—more able, or at least more ready, than any other group in our study.

Problem solving was considered to be a consequence of developing certain cognitive skills through parent–child interaction. Interestingly, the interaction patterns we observed and the cognitive styles they represented were in accord with the hypotheses. Peasant families were most likely to be dominated by one parent, most often the father; they were also most likely to display an absence of tolerance for ambiguity and conflict of ideas. The Twin Cities white-collar families, at the other end of the developmental continuum, were the most egalitarian and the most likely to tolerate ambiguity and conflict of ideas.

Our hypotheses were also reasonably accurate with regard to the impact of family success–failure experiences and parents' perceptions of the social structure. There was a slight significant positive relationship between family success as manipulated in the family portion of the game and the adolescents' problem-solving performance. In addition, Michoacan parents were more optimistic about their children's future than were Twin Cities parents. At the same time, within the Mexican and United States samples, white-collar parents tended to be more optimistic than blue-collar families. Mexican families tended to believe that their children's life chances would be better than their own in the future, whereas United States parents believed that their children's chances would be no better than their own. When we tested our overall model by combining these variables we found that we could explain a significant amount of the variance with the variables identified by the model. Why then were we not able to predict the relationship between community and adolescent problem-solving performance?

The answer probably lies in the failure to give sufficient weight to the value participants placed on their life goals. We expected that Mexicans would be committed to materialistic payoffs and North Americans would be committed to interpersonal satisfactions, but we did not fully appreciate how prevailing these commitments were. In retrospect most of the data point to considèrable flexibility on the part of the adolescent peasant and his or her family when confronted with issues of material advancement; they were more ready than any other group to accept the option to be geographically mobile in both the family and the child's game. They were also more willing to change career routes and they indicated less commitment to any particular type of career (see Table 5.2). More generally, the data suggest that all Mexicans displayed a hard-nosed, rational commitment to achievement, a relatively clear set of standards as to how to reach goals, and a readiness (at least at the ideological level) to make the necessary personal and interpersonal sacrifices required to "better oneself." The Mexican families and their children were much more ready to commit themselves to a "work ethic" than North Americans.

We had expected that the North American families would place a high value on familism, and we were also not surprised at the degree to which such families tended to be child centered. However, we did not understand the full implications of this orientation. The Twin Cities parents in our study were concerned with the specialness of their child; their efforts were directed toward meeting their children's unique individual needs. Status or material attainment seemed a secondary concern at best. Consequently, the children seemed to interpret the problems posed by SIMCAR in terms of attaining personal satisfaction through interpersonal relations.

It is conceivable, then, that the Mexican and United States adolescent children who played SIMCAR differed in their perceptions of the problem that confronted them. Different problems require different strategies. For

Mexican children seeking material gain, the appropriate strategy would be to aggressively take advantage of all opportunities leading to advancement and to defer gratification as long as possible. For the United States children, on the other hand, an appropriate strategy might be to maintain one's personally desired style of life at the least possible cost. The Mexicans would, therefore, seek to take advantage of change; the North Americans would seek to establish a life-style, maintain it, and seek to avoid change. Figures 5.1 through 5.4 suggest that these, in fact, were the strategies employed by both groups.

The tendency of United States parents to consider their children's life chances to be no better than their own, in contrast with the Mexican parents' belief that their children had a chance to be much better off than themselves in the future, suggests that the United States children would have less incentive to either delay gratification or positively orient themselves toward a changing world.

The findings indicate that our theoretical model needs revision, not only in terms of the weighting we give to life goals, but also to the relationship between family decision making and open channels of communication. However, these revisions must wait until we consider one additional factor affecting the socialization of adolescents. Whether the adolescent is male or female makes a difference; we consider these differences in the next chapter.

6 Sex Differences

No field of social science investigation has grown more rapidly in recent years than the study of sex roles and sex differences. It is with some embarrassment, therefore, that we must admit that the original design of this research included only families with sons. The addition of daughters occurred after some months of planning, and only on the insistence of a graduate assistant, Rosalyn Lindner Cohen. Cohen repeatedly sought an explanation for the exclusion of females and refused to accept as justification the fact that adding daughters would greatly complicate the research design. We are now grateful to Dr. Cohen for her persistence. The inclusion of females in the study resulted in a set of findings that has added considerably to our understanding of parental roles in socialization for problem solving. For the most part, these findings were unanticipated. Many do not fit the prevailing stereotypes about sex roles in either Mexico or the United States, and some appear contradictory. Thus, one of the tasks of this chapter is to provide theoretical frameworks for explaining these data. Unlike the previous analyses, these frameworks were developed after the data were collected.

Three types of data comparisons will be made. First, we consider how sex roles differ in the five communities included in this study. Second, we consider the sex differences that hold across all five communities. Finally, we consider how the sex of a child interacting with the sex of a parent influences socialization for problem solving.

SEX DIFFERENCES BY SOCIETY AND CLASS

Male–female relationships have been a subject of investigation in both Mexico and the United States for the past decade. Both the popular and scientific literature in this field have tended to emphasize the greater dominance of Mexican males and the greater egalitarianism between males and females in the United States. National and regional surveys of Mexicans (Elu de Leñero, 1969; Fagen & Toughy, 1972; Kahl, 1968; Leñero, 1968), as well as ethnographic studies of specific communities (Erasmus, 1961; Lewis, 1959, 1961; McGinn, 1966), seem to corroborate the following description of male–female relations presented by the poet Octavio Paz (1961):

> Like almost all other people, the Mexican considers woman to be an instrument, sometimes of masculine desires, sometimes of the ends assigned to her by morality, society and law. It must be admitted that she has never been asked to consent to these ends and that she participates in their realization only passively, as a "repository" for certain values. Whether as a prostitute, goddess, *grande dame,* or mistress, woman transmits or preserves . . . the values or energies entrusted to her by nature or society. In a world made in man's image, woman is only a reflection of masculine will and desire. When passive, she becomes a goddess, a beloved one, a being who embodies the ancient stable elements, of the universe: the earth, motherhood, virginity. When active she is always function and means, a receptacle and a channel. Womanhood, unlike manhood, is never an end in itself (pp. 35–36).

Paz goes on to describe the idealization of Mexican women as "long suffering" with the strength to endure, albeit passively, a constant array of misfortunes. This view of male dominance and the submissiveness of women received almost universal support from the data available in 1972. Men were considered relatively free to be unfaithful to their wives and their lovers, but were still duty bound to guard the fidelity of their wives, even to the point of violence.

We expected to find evidence of the "machismo" tradition in all social classes in Mexico. We anticipated, however, that this evidence would be more characteristic of the less educated and poorer groups in Mexican society, primarily because they tend to be more traditional and less aware of alternative life-styles.

As for the United States, we expected greater equality between the sexes. We accepted the popular social-scientific view that industrialization and urbanization produces nuclear families, which in combination with increased opportunity for geographical mobility, produces an emphasis on achievement and individualism—all of which foster democratization of family relationships (Goode, 1963). We recognized, of course, that a double standard continued to exist in the United States. Men in the United States, as in Mexico, had greater freedom of choice in sexual partners, in available recreation alternatives, in education and job opportunities, and in income earning potentials (Hole & Levine, 1971; I. Reiss, 1960). Nevertheless, the prevalent viewpoint was that differences between the sexes would be greater in a developing country such as Mexico than in an industrialized country like the United States (Goode, 1963; Young & Wilmott, 1973). Aware of the increasing number of women in the United States work force, cognizant of the visibility of the women's movement in North America and the consequent raising of "consciousness" for both males and females concerning sexual inequalities, and sensitive to the equalitarian norm which dominated North American cultural values, we believed that there would be greater sexual equality in the United States than in Mexico.

Male and Female Power: Ideology versus Behavior

Initial impressions of Zacapu and the villages reinforced the expectations of greater equality between the sexes in the United States than in Mexico. The villages still practiced the custom of "robo," the kidnapping of a girl by her suitor, thereby forcing the parents to negotiate a marriage (see Diaz, 1967, and Foster, 1967, pp. 67–74, for detailed discussions of this ritual). True, the kidnapping was usually more an elopement than a forced abduction, and the young girl was more a willing accomplice than a victim; nevertheless, the symbolism was clear—the woman was passive and helpless when confronted with the will and the power of the man.

Our interviews with parents yielded data further supporting the conclusion that sexual inequality was greater in Mexico than in the United States. For example, we posed the following situation to parents: "A husband and wife have an argument as to how to spend some extra money for fixing the house. As the argument goes on, the husband realizes his wife is right but if he gives in to her he feels he will lose respect. What should he do?" Respondents were given the choice of two possible answers: "Give in to his wife," or "Maintain his own opinion." To endorse the latter statement was to support the traditional claim to male superiority as birthright, since in the situation posed, the male clearly did not *earn* the right to hold his position. The data, presented in Table 6.1, indicate that the Mexicans were more likely than the North Americans to state that husbands should not give in to wives, and blue-collar and peasant parents were more likely than white-collar parents to advocate this view. The largest proportion (almost half) of the respondents who advocated male dominance were Zacapu blue-collar wives. Generally, the male superiority position was adhered to more by wives than by husbands.

Table 6.1

Parents' Responses to the Question, "Should a Husband Give in to His Wife When He is Proved Wrong?" by Sex of Parent, Community, and Class (%)

| | Villages | | Zacapu | | | | Twin Cities | | | |
| | | | Blue collar | | White collar | | Blue collar | | White collar | |
	Father N = 108	Mother N = 112	Father N = 85	Mother N = 89	Father N = 75	Mother N = 77	Father N = 70	Mother N = 71	Father N = 78	Mother N = 78
Keep own opinion	24.1	28.6	22.4	46.1	12.0	19.5	8.6	12.7	1.3	1.3

$\chi^2 = 92.94$, $df = 9$, $p < .001$.

When respondents were asked to explain their choices, the responses of Mexicans who were in favor of the man holding to his position were generally unambiguous. "He rules," "He is the man," "At home one does what the man of the house does," and so forth. One male went so far as to indicate that such action nipped future problems in the bud, "Because he is man of the house, and if he gives in it will continue." Although many of the Mexicans who answered that the husband should give in to the wife based their judgment on the principle that "right is right," others (especially males) applied a *noblesse oblige* orientation: "One does not have to go against what is reasonable just because he is the boss." Many males and females in both societies refused to accept the question's premise that the husband would lose respect if he admitted he was wrong. Some Mexicans argued that, to the contrary, a husband who admitted he was wrong would gain respect.

The few United States respondents who maintained that the husband should not give in used the head of the house principle or assumed (despite the question's clear implication to the contrary) that the husband would end up being right. It should also be noted from Table 6.1 that virtually no United States white-collar males or females responded in favor of the male's holding his position.

Parents were asked another question pertaining to male–female differences. The question posed was "Imagine you have a daughter, aged 20, and a son, aged 17, and both of them need money to stay in college. You have only enough money for one of them. Whom would you give the money to?"

Again, as indicated in Table 6.2, the Twin Cities white-collar parents seemed the least likely to indicate a traditional male preference. Also, Twin Cities white-collar mothers were the only group of women in the study who were more likely than their husbands to choose daughters. The data in Table 6.2 lend general support for the frequently reported liaison between Mexican mothers and their sons (see Romanucci–Ross, 1973, pp. 56–74, for a discussion of this relationship among peasant families). They also suggest a similar orientation for United States blue-collar mothers. In fact, the Twin Cities blue-collar mothers were the least likely of any of the subsamples to support preferences for daughters over sons.

The most common justification for choosing the son given by parents in both Mexico and the United States was that the male would eventually be the chief family provider, and, therefore, he needed the education more. A sizable proportion of Mexican men and women also claimed that the male was more likely to work harder or was more capable of making use of educational opportunities. Those who chose daughters tended to emphasize the age differential and suggested the possibility that the son might have his

Table 6.2
Parents' Choice of Older Daughter over Younger Son to Stay in College by Sex of Parent, Community, and Class (%)

| | Villages | | Zacapu | | | | Twin Cities | | | |
| | | | Blue collar | | White collar | | Blue collar | | White collar | |
	Father $N = 105$	Mother $N = 110$	Father $N = 82$	Mother $N = 91$	Father $N = 69$	Mother $N = 76$	Father $N = 68$	Mother $N = 68$	Father $N = 74$	Mother $N = 69$
Choice of daughter	21.9	16.4	31.7	18.7	24.6	19.7	29.4	10.7	43.2	53.6

$\chi^2 = 51.64, df = 9, p < .001.$

chance later. Many Mexicans emphasized the importance of the husband's maintaining authority and stressed the inevitability that the "wife suffers." Such phrases did not occur in the United States white-collar responses and rarely occurred among United States blue-collar parents.

In summary, the data presented in Tables 6.1 and 6.2 suggest that Mexicans are more likely than North Americans to adhere to the value of male dominance, and women (except for United States white-collar women) are somewhat more likely to hold this view than their husbands. The findings seem in accord with the previous surveys measuring sexual attitudes in Mexico and in the United States. However, they are not in agreement with the data previously reported in Chapter 5, indicating that Twin Cities white-collar wives exercised the least power of any group observed in our study (see Tables 6.3 and 6.4). Twin Cities white-collar families were the only families in which there were no dominant mothers, and in which the mother was not involved in a single dominant coalition (Table 6.4). Only in the 31% of the families that were egalitarian did the United States white-collar women make a sizable contribution to family decision making. Thus although the Twin Cities white-collar families were the most egalitarian in the sample, when all forms of power relations are considered, the Twin Cities white-collar mothers were found to be the least likely to exercise power. Conversely, although Mexican peasant fathers were the most dominant group of fathers, their wives also exercised more power than any other group of women in the study. They were the most likely women to be the dominant person and, along with Zacapu blue-collar women, they were more likely to be part of dominant coalitions. The fact that 40% of the peasant women were either dominant or shared dominance with their husbands, compared with none of the United States white-collar women, provides a dramatic contrast to the amount of power exercised. It also runs contrary to our expectations.

The data reported in Tables 6.1 and 6.2 were gathered by means of interviews in which parents were asked to respond to hypothetical situations. As such, they tend to reflect what parents wanted others to think about their attitudes toward male–female relations. The data reported in Tables 6.3 and 6.4 were the result of observers coding family interaction while families were absorbed in activities having nothing to do with the behaviors that were being coded; as such, these data provide us with patterns of behavior that family members are not consciously revealing. In brief, the interview data are more likely to reflect the parent's ideologies pertaining to relations between the sexes, and the observational data are more likely to reflect habitual behavioral patterns.

The sharpest differences in Tables 6.1–6.4 are between peasant and Twin Cities white-collar wives. These two groups not only represent the

Table 6.3
Mean Proportion of Power Messages Sent by Father, Mother, and Child by Community, Class, and Sex of Child

| Messages sent by | Villages | | Zacapu | | | | Twin Cities | | | | F | p |
	Male N = 26	Female N = 24	Blue collar Male N = 20	Female N = 20	White collar Male N = 22	Female N = 19	Blue collar Male N = 24	Female N = 23	White collar Male N = 27	Female N = 30		
Father	62.4	48	55	48	56	47	29	33	30	40	26.93	<.001
Mother	37.5	41	30	26	27	37	37	25	25	15	15.60	<.001
Child	0.1	11	15	26	17	16	34	42	45	45	19.40	<.001

Table 6.4
Distribution of Power between Family Members While Playing SIMCAR by Community

Type of family power constellation	Villages N = 50	Zacapu		Twin Cities	
		Blue collar N = 33	White collar N = 27	Blue collar N = 25	White collar N = 29
One family member dominates	.68	.51	.59	.48	.48
Which family member?					
Father	.44	.30	.41	.12	.27
Mother	.24	.06	.18	.16	0
Child	0	.15	0	.20	.31
Coalitions	.22	.39	.30	.32	.24
Which family members?					
Father–Mother	.16	.27	.19	0	0
Father–Child	.02	.06	.11	.16	.24
Mother–Child	.04	.06	0	.16	0
Equalitarian (equal power with all family members)	.10	.09	.11	.20	.31

greatest differences in life-style, but also serve as prototypes for women in preindustrial and in highly industrialized or postindustrialized societies. It appears that the peasant woman is faced with the contradiction of a normative standard that belies her actual power. Romanucci–Ross (1973) described elements of this contradiction in the following passage:

> The Mexican woman expects to be abandoned by a weak, irresponsible, child-like man, who is likely as well to be arbitrarily violent toward her and her children, alcoholic (or nearly), and a philanderer, whose adulteries will be an endless threat to her. Better men have been known to exist and one can always hope, but no woman can discount the near certainty that this is the kind of man she is going to have. She has been conditioned to this image from birth by her mother, from whom she also learns the female defenses of *independence* and *self-reliance* on the one hand, and *token submission* and minimal expectations on the other (emphasis added by the authors, p. 56).

For such women, Romanucci–Ross claims children provide solace, companionship, and, eventually, protection. It is not likely that these women will leave the planning of their children's future entirely to their husbands. Unlike the North American white-collar mother, the Mexican peasant mother may wish to relinquish responsibility to her husband, but, given the realities of her situation, is often unable to trust him.

The Twin Cities white-collar wife appears to be faced with the converse problem. She is sensitive to her rights to equal status with her husband, but, perhaps because she is more often less experienced in the work world, she is less willing to exert her influence in directing her child's career plans. It is also possible that the Twin Cities father and child share this perception of the mother as being less competent in career planning, and, therefore, they give less credence to her opinions.

Toward an Explanation

Until recently, the prevailing viewpoint among sociologists was that industrialization and urbanization contributed to the formation of families into nuclear family forms. Industrialization and urbanization also were considered to increase the value placed on individualism, competition, and geographical mobility. All these factors were thought to contribute to an ideology of equal opportunity and greater equality between husband and wife. It was argued that two factors—the nuclear family and the ideology of equality—combined to improve the woman's bargaining position within the family, increasing her authority and, consequently, improving her relative power (see Goode, 1963, pp. 368–378, for a discussion of this perspective). Our data support this argument insofar as it is limited to ideology, but it clearly does not support the premise that this ideology affects the woman's power position within the home. The prevailing viewpoint, therefore, does not fit our data and we must look elsewhere for an explanation.

Recently family historians and ethnographers have challenged some previously accepted assumptions concerning family power relations in preindustrial and industrial societies. For example, Tamara Hareven (1976) claims, "The work of French, English, and American historical demographers studying preindustrial Western Europe and the United States has shown that the families during that period were rarely 'the great extended families' that have been part of the folklore. . . . Households and families . . . were not drastically different in their organization from contemporary families (p. 89)." What was different, according to Hareven, was the congruence between household and productive work, "In pre-industrial society most of the work took place at home (p. 97)." "As long as the family was a productive unit," she notes, "housework was inseparable from domestic industries or agricultural work and was valued, therefore, for its economic contribution (p. 98)." Thus, in preindustrial social structures, males may be quite dependent on the work of their wives for sustenance, maintenance, and survival. This dependence on women's contributions to family maintenance is further attested to by Lee (1977, pp. 233–242). In his review of ethnographic studies he states:

> There are numerous recent reports of the extent of female authority in horticultural societies based upon ethnographic observations. Riegelhaupt (1967) shows that Portuguese women have a great deal of power because of a rigid division of labor between spouses in which the wife is charged with the responsibility for allocating family resources. Friedl (1967) shows that a similar process occurs among Greek peasantry. Women receive land from their families as dowries when they marry, thus they contribute important resources to the marriage; they also manage domestic affairs, which include many important areas of family decision-making. And Rogers' (1975) research on a French peasant village showed that women's contributions to subsistence were such that it was quite possible for a woman to survive, and even support children, without a husband, but if a man lost his wife she would have to be replaced. Although women's tasks might be categorized as "domestic," they were of such importance that men were heavily dependent upon them for subsistence; consequently the balance of power in peasant families resided with women (p. 236).

How does industrialization alter this balance of power? Lee suggests "the man's dependency upon his wife's contribution to subsistence is reduced. Industry brings a money economy. Money is earned by wage labor. Men are more likely to be recruited into the labor force than women, particularly for the more prestigious supervisory positions (p. 236)." If, as Lee indicates, men in an industrial society obtain the more prestigious (and better paying) positions, then it follows that male dependency on wives should decrease in the middle class more than in the working class. This is because middle-class husbands earn more money and have higher status positions than working-class husbands. Conversely, middle-class wives should become more dependent on their husbands than working-class wives. Hareven (1976) states that industrialization, "had a dramatic effect on the experience of the middle-class, it produced a sharp distinction between home and work place, greater role segregation between husband and wife, and restricted women's activities to the home along with a glorification of their domestic roles as housekeepers and mothers... (p. 103)." The net effect is the lessening of the wife's perceived contribution to family maintenance, and, therefore, of the husband's perceived dependence on the wife.

Our data provide some support for Hareven's conclusion that there is a more clearly defined division of family labor in industrial societies. Table 6.5 presents the mean time investments the adolescents made in housework while playing SIMCAR. There is virtually no difference in investments between males and females from the villages and Zacapu blue-collar families. Zacapu white-collar and the Twin Cities adolescents, on the other hand, were more likely to evidence a "traditional" division of labor through their investments. Females in these groups assumed household activities more frequently, whereas males tended to shun this option. It is important to remember that the data in Table 6.5 reflect options voluntarily chosen by the adolescent. The experimenter was explicitly restrained from guiding the child in choosing any of the 13 game alternatives; and the child, playing alone, was free of the influence of parents, peers, siblings, or other norm setters. These data, therefore, suggest that the "traditional" sex-role division of labor of women doing housework has been internalized by the children in industrial structures to a greater extent than by children in preindustrial structures. An even more vivid example of the greater tendency of the Twin Cities families to emphasize a clear-cut gender-linked division of labor can be seen from the findings of career routes chosen during the family game. These data are presented in Table 6.6. As indicated in this table, 53% of the Twin Cities white-collar girls, as compared with 44% of the white-collar boys, made occupational choices that did not include post-high-school education. Even more dramatically, 69% of the Twin Cities blue-collar girls, as compared to 29% of the boys, did not choose post-high-school educational routes. In the Mexican samples, virtually all families chose higher educational routes, and gender differences were minor.

However, as the earlier quotation from Lee indicates, the family division of labor, in itself, does not necessarily imply greater power for males. A key variable appears to be the particular activities associated with that division of labor and the resulting dependence each spouse has on the other for services. One factor that seems to contribute to the greater dependence of

Table 6.5

Mean Scores Indicating Amount of Time Adolescents Invested in Housework during SIMCAR by Community, Class, and Sex of Child

Villages		Zacapu				Twin Cities			
		Blue collar		White collar		Blue collar		White collar	
Male $N = 26$	Female $N = 24$	Male $N = 20$	Female $N = 39$	Male $N = 22$	Female $N = 20$	Male $N = 24$	Female $N = 23$	Male $N = 27$	Female $N = 30$
32.0	39.0	31.0	39.2	23.0	52.6	33.4	62.5	34.1	55.2

Analysis of variance (Main effects): Community: $F = 4.04$, $p < .02$;
Sex: $F = 33.06$, $p < .001$;
Interaction: $F = 4.77$, $p < .01$.

Table 6.6
Career Routes Chosen during Family Game by Community and Sex of Child (% of families)

| | Villages | | Zacapu | | | | Twin Cities | | | |
| | | | Blue Collar | | White Collar | | Blue Collar | | White Collar | |
Career Routes	Male $N^a = 23$	Female $N = 26$	Male $N = 21$	Female $N = 22$	Male $N = 22$	Female $N = 20$	Male $N = 24$	Female $N = 23$	Male $N = 27$	Female $N = 30$
High school prerequisites only										
Office work	4	15	—	—	4	15	8	61	33	43
Factory work	—	8	—	—	9	—	12	4	4	—
Farming	—	—	—	5	—	—	8	4	7	10
Post-high-school training required										
Office management	39	19	48	47	23	35	38	17	44	30
Management	22	27	33	—	32	25	33	4	7	10
Agriculture	35	31	19	47	32	25	—	9	4	7
Total	100	100	100	99	100	100	99	99	99	100

[a] N refers to number of families (father, mother, and child).
High school versus post–high school by sex, $\chi^2 = 7.68$, $df = 1$, $p < .01$.
High school versus post–high school by sex within the United States, $\chi^2 = 5.08$, $df = 1$, $p < .05$.
High school versus post–high school by sex within Mexico, N.S.

wives on husbands in the middle class is money. The more the husband earns, the more likely the wife is to play a dependent role and consequently to exert less power (Blood & Wolfe, 1960; McKinley, 1964). Hareven (1976, p. 111) suggests two additional factors that are associated with sex-role differentiation and that tend to increase the wife's dependency on her husband. She claims the modern woman is isolated because of the combined emphasis of the wife's role as childrearer and the focus on family autonomy and privacy. Hareven argues that women trained for homemaking and motherhood tasks find that the training becomes obsolete relatively early in their marital lives. More than half of the women's married life is spent without children in the household. Thus, even if the active mother is highly valued, it is relatively short-lived. Consequently, without job training and isolated by the norms of family privacy and autonomy, these women are likely to be more dependent on their husbands for companionship as well as for economic support.[1]

Some recent studies of family relations challenge the above conclusions, maintaining that symmetrical power relations between spouses are more likely to occur in Western industrial societies and among the middle classes. In fact, Young and Wilmott (1973) claim that the future trend in industrial societies is toward increased equalitarian relations between husbands and wives. They hold that the increased ability to control births and the larger number of working wives and mothers results in a less segregated division of labor within the household and, consequently, more symmetrical power relations. We have already indicated that the data in this study and historical and cross-cultural data suggest that role segregation is increasing rather than decreasing in white-collar industrial families. It is evident from our data that the division of labor is more pronounced in the Twin Cities sample than in the Michoacan sample. Moreover, we would argue that this division of labor is internalized as a desirable set of options for coming generations of husbands and wives (Marotz-Baden, 1976).

The claim that women in industrialized societies are employed outside of the home in increasingly greater numbers is incontrovertible (Strober, 1976). Our findings indicate that a greater proportion of Twin Cities wives held part- and full-time jobs outside the home than did Mexican wives. The data presented in Table 6.7 show that 42% of the wives in Twin Cities blue-collar families and 37% in white-collar families had jobs outside the home.

---

[1] Although working-class wives tend to complain more than middle-class wives about lack of communication with husbands, they are more likely to maintain open communication lines with their mothers and with old girl friends (Komarovsky, 1967, pp. 148–151; Rainwater, Coleman, & Handel, 1962, pp. 244–245; Tallman, 1969). It is only when working-class wives are forced into middle-class patterns, such as moving to the suburbs, that they tend to experience this sense of isolation and, consequently, an increase in marital tension (Tallman, 1969).

Table 6.7
Percentage of Full- and Part-Time Working Wives by Community and Class[a]

	Villages	Zacapu		Twin Cities	
	N = 93	Blue collar N = 85	White collar N = 75	Blue collar N = 78	White collar N = 78
Full-time housewife	95	90	85	58	63
Full-time employed	0	0	5	13	10
Part-time employed	5	10	10	29	27

Differences between Mexico and United States, χ^2 = 51.6, df = 2, p < .001.

The highest percentage of employed wives among Mexican families was 15% for the white-collar sample.

The assumption made by Young and Wilmott, among others (see also Blood & Wolfe, 1960), is that the wife's ability to earn income outside the home increases her independence and, therefore, her power inside the home. Our data do not support this assumption. We found no such relationship between working wives and decision-making power in the Twin Cities samples. When taken in conjunction with data indicating that village wives had more power than any other group of wives in our study, and Twin Cities white-collar wives had the least amount of power, this finding raises reasonable doubt concerning Young and Wilmott's assertion that married partners in Western industrialized countries are more symmetrical in their power relationships.

It is important to note that Young and Wilmott do not deny that power relationships are unequal in modern Western families or that they may have been more equal in preindustrial families; rather, they hold that the trends indicate a return to a more symmetrical power relationship than previously was true in industrial societies. Our data offered a unique opportunity to test this hypothesis. We were able to compare conjugal relations among families living under preindustrial, industrializing, and highly industrialized conditions. As we have seen, despite more egalitarianism in Twin Cities families, the wives of these families tended to exercise less power than wives living under preindustrialized and industrializing conditions.

A Power-Dependency Explanation

Clearly these findings are not definitive. We did not set out to test the hypothesis that industrialization leads to power symmetry between spouses, nor were our samples sufficiently representative of various levels of industrialization to warrant reaching any firm conclusion. However, taken as a whole, the findings are strong enough to suggest an alternative explanation of power relationships to that provided by Young and Wilmott,

Blood and Wolfe, and others. Implicit in the work of these scholars is a set of principles that have loosely been referred to as "resource theory." Briefly stated, this orientation seeks to explain the distribution of power between spouses on the basis of control of key resources, primarily income. The relationship between resources and power is thought to be linear: the more key resource a family member holds, the more power the family member holds. From this perspective, it follows that the more wives earn in income outside the home, the more power they will have.

The explanation we propose differs slightly but, we think, significantly, from the one presented by the resource theorists. In our explanation we draw on Richard Emerson's (1962) theory of power and dependency. Rather than considering only resources, we also consider the degree of dependence each partner has on the other. Of equal importance to the degree of dependence is the symmetry or balance between the partners. A couple may be very dependent on each other for income, affection, advice, and so forth, but if that dependence is mutual (i.e., symmetrical), the power relations should be equal. Similarly, couples may be relatively independent of each other and have an equal power relationship. Only if partner A is more dependent on partner B than partner B is on partner A, would we infer that B has greater power than A. The data presented thus far suggest that such an imbalance appears to be more characteristic of middle-class couples living in the Twin Cities than of couples living in peasant preindustrialized social structures in Mexico. This was true for wives employed outside the home as well as full-time housewives. The wife working outside the home could increase her power only if she decreased her dependency on her husband or increased his dependency on her. In our sample, white-collar Twin Cities working wives generally held clerical jobs and contributed about one-third of their families incomes. Clearly, in most families, this is an important contribution, but it would not sufficiently change the income pattern to make the wife–mother less dependent upon her husband. It is not likely that wives earning one-half to one-third of their husbands' salary could live adequately without their husbands' assistance. Conversely, the middle-class husband who earned what he probably considered to be a decent living in 1972 could more easily conceive of living on his income with or without his wife's contribution.

This proportion of husband–wife income is not peculiar to this sample. Using United States census data, Myra Strober (1976, p. 122) demonstrated that, although there was a sizable increase in the employment of wives between 1940 and 1970, this increase was not reflected in the type of work women did when employed (see also Gross, 1968). Socialization into traditional female and male occupations has relegated females to clerical or service occupations—55% compared to 14% of the male work force (Strober,

1976, p. 126). Even those women who were classified as being in the professional and technical occupations tended to be represented primarily in four of the lowest paying occupations: school teacher, registered nurse, social and recreational worker, and librarian. These occupations accounted for ⅔ of professional women and only 15% of professional men. Thus, women earned considerably less than men did at all occupational and educational levels (Hole & Levine, 1971). The net result is that women tend to be employed in the more crowded, lower paying, and generally less desirable jobs (see Strober, 1976, p. 133). This appears to be the case for the United States working women in our study. It seems reasonable to infer that these conditions would increase rather than decrease women's dependence on men.

Additional evidence of the asymmetry in Twin Cities white-collar spousal power–dependency relationships as compared to peasant families, comes from interview data on decision making. The two items in the interview schedule, taken from Blood and Wolfe's (1960) scales, pertain to whether the husband, wife, or both partners make the final decisions concerning (a) the husband's job; and (b) the wife's working outside the home. As shown in Table 6.8, the majority of peasant husbands and wives stated they jointly participated in decisions pertaining to husband's job, whereas virtually 90% of the Twin Cities white-collar husbands and wives state that this was the husband's decision alone. The finding takes on special relevance when we compare it with the data pertaining to wives' working. Of the Twin Cities white-collar wives 94% stated that their husbands should make the final decision concerning their (the husband's) jobs, but only 36% of these wives thought they should make such a decision alone when their own jobs were at issue. This percentage changes slightly when we compare those wives who worked outside the home with those who did not have outside employment. Of the "employed" wives 48% would make such a decision alone, as compared to 29% of the nonemployed wives. However, the differences between the two groups were not statistically significant.

Although very few peasant wives compared to Twin Cities white-collar wives believed they should make such a decision alone, 41% said it should be made jointly with their husbands. Since 64% of these women compared to 6% of their United States white-collar counterparts thought decisions pertaining to husband's jobs should be made jointly, the symmetry between the two decisions was much greater for peasant wives than it was for Twin Cities white-collar wives.

This difference in the degree of perceived mutuality of decision making may be due, in large part, to the reliance spouses have on each other for carrying out vital daily activities. In the peasant family, the wife's activities are perceived as being essential for survival (Bossen, 1975; Rogers, 1975); the middle-class wife's work in and out of the household tends either to be trivialized or viewed as peripheral to individual family survival. Oakley (1974) argues that being a housewife in an industrial society not only has a relatively low status regardless of the husband's occupation (see also Haavio–Mannila, 1971), but housework as such is rarely acknowledged as work. In fact, we have the anomaly of women working more than the ordinary 40 hours per week at housework (see Oakley, 1974), but not having such work recognized by their families or by the community. Strober (1976) claims that "working wives, on the average, do not appear to receive more assistance from husbands or children than other wives (p. 136)." The net effect is that wives who are employed outside the home have considerably less leisure time than wives not so employed (Robinson, Converse, & Szalai, 1972).

Despite the data, there is reason to believe that members of the middle class continue to cling to the notion that housewives make up a leisure class, living in their own homes, surrounded by labor saving devices, free to decorate, furnish, and cast their individual stamps on these homes. Theirs is thought to be a creative life, free of the oppressive dominance of a boss (Oakley, 1974, pp. 41–60). This orientation may derive from the combination of material abundance and the norm of conjugal equalitarianism.

The modal middle-class husband apparently does not see himself as being dependent on his wife. The money he earns makes him economically independent. He often finds his work interesting; he works hard and he views himself as successful. He may feel admired and is self-satisfied. More-

Table 6.8

Village and Twin Cities White-Collar Husbands' and Wives' Responses regarding Which Spouse Makes Final Decision Pertaining to Jobs (%)

	Villages		Twin Cities white collar	
Who makes final decision?	Husband $N = 109$	Wife $N = 109$	Husband $N = 78$	Wife $N = 78$
Husband's work[a]				
Husband	46.8	33.9	89.7	93.6
Wife	1.8	1.8	1.3	0
Together	51.4	64.3	9.0	6.4
Wife's work[b]				
Husband	59.6	53.6	23.1	20.5
Wife	5.5	5.5	46.2	35.9
Together	34.9	40.9	30.8	43.6

[a]Husband's work—differences between villages and Twin Cities. Husbands, $\chi^2 = 37.3$, $df = 2$, $p < .001$. Wives, $\chi^2 = 68.6$, $df = 2$, $p < .001$.

[b]Wife's work—differences between villages and Twin Cities. Husbands, $\chi^2 = 47.4$, $df = 2$, $p < .001$. Wives, $\chi^2 = 35.4$, $df = 2$, $p < .001$.

over, he tends to view his wife as being in a fortunate position. Her respon-
sibilities are limited; her freedom is great; she does not have to participate
in the "rat race." The husband seems hardly conscious of the fact that he
makes most major decisions and has the dominant family influence. If he is
aware of this fact, he attributes it, perhaps accurately, to his greater knowledge of the specific areas around which decisions are made: His wife certainly would be deferred to if she had the appropriate knowledge. They are
equals, after all.

Our data provide some support for the above description of middle-class
male attitudes. The findings pertaining to parents' aspirations and expectations for daughters indicate that white-collar fathers were more likely than
any other group in our study to rank the wife–mother occupation high.
These data were reported in Table 5.3 of the previous chapter. Twin Cities
white-collar fathers' rankings of aspirations for their daughters placed the
wife–mother occupation a close second to teacher. This is particularly important, because the aspiration data represented parents' occupational
rankings based on the occupations they would want for their daughters *if it
were a perfect world* and the daughter could attain any occupation she
wanted. Thus, it seems that the Twin Cities white-collar fathers view the
wife–mother occupation as highly desirable. No other group in our study
reflected such conceptions of the benefits of this particular occupation. It is
also important to note that the Twin Cities white-collar wives differed significantly from their husbands in the ranking of the wife–mother role, placing it fourth. The discrepancy between the Twin Cities white-collar husbands and wives on these rankings was greater than any discrepancy
between spouses reported in Table 5.3.

The power-dependency theory seems to provide a reasonable set of principles for explaining our data and the data of others pertaining to the relationship between societal development, socioeconomic conditions, and
conjugal power, but it does not provide principles that adequately, or at
least easily, account for the normative data.[2] However, if we define norms

---

[2]Colleen Johnson (1975) has used a theoretical model which approximates power dependency in attempting to explain the discrepancy between the "authority" vested in Hawaiian
Japanese–American husbands and the greater daily decision-making power of the
Japanese–American wife. Johnson suggests that by bestowing status on the husband, the wife
is increasing the husband's "ego investment" in the family and fostering his dependency on
the wife and family for such deference. Conversely, she argues that the husband "by relegat-
ing his power through the exercise of authority, he is constraining his wife into compliance.
Her rewards come from the power given her to make decisions and in the assurances of the
husband's higher investment in the family (p. 191)." This exchange of deference for actual
power may account in part for our findings indicating the greater power among Mexican peasant women and their greater readiness to adopt male dominant norms. We find ourselves

as valued outcomes, a structural explanation for the development of norms of male dominance or egalitarianism is possible.[3] Applying the principle of diminishing marginal utility, and given the two choices of male dominance or egalitarianism, we suggest that the different norms advocated in Mexico and the United States represent scarce values. There is evidence to suggest that peasant wives of Mexico would like to have husbands who are strong, responsible, mature, and faithful (Romanucci–Ross, 1973). Allowing such a strong man the privilege of being boss may seem an almost pleasant alternative to their current life-style of poverty and uncertainty. For peasants, exercising power implies burden, suffering, and undue responsibility. Conversely, the peasant men would probably like to be sufficiently successful to adequately care for their families. In short, both men and women may want the men to provide protective leadership—that is, to have the resources and the attributes of white-collar men, rare commodities in the peasant's world. Romanucci–Ross (1973) implies that the Mexican peasant woman wishes that her husband would have these attributes, while all the time she expects the worst of him. Komarovsky (1967) and Rainwater, Coleman, and Handel (1962) indicate somewhat similar orientations in North American blue-collar women. Elliot Liebow (1967) and Ulf Hannerz (1969) have argued that the poor man's resorting to alcohol and extramarital sexual exploits are a means of compensating for the failure to meet the masculine standards of caring for and protecting the family. Drinking and womanizing are used to rationalize, justify, and alleviate the pain associated with the man's sense of failure. Hyman Rodman's (1963) concept of "the lower-class value stretch" reflects, in some ways, the same idea; the poor person, although he may adhere to the prevailing middle-class standards, has difficulty in meeting those standards and, therefore, develops a more flexible value system. The patriarchal ideology of male dominance, at least for the poor, represents a hoped for circumstance; as such, it is an ideal the Mexican husband and wife present to the public and perhaps in a somewhat self-delusionary way, to themselves. To view themselves in this way enhances the self-esteem of both the wife and the husband—she because (by implication) she has attracted a rare phenomenon, a strong man; he because he has social approval.

Ideologies, therefore, may have behavioral consequences, especially in

---

unable, however, to make a similar argument with regard to the Twin Cities white-collar families—that is, husbands are exchanging an egalitarian norm for the privilege of actual decision-making power.

[3] Our explanation does not consider female dominance as an alternative, primarily because it did not occur in this or other studies. An explanation for the fact that no modern society advocates female dominance requires a more thorough and lengthy sociohistorical analysis than is warranted here.

public arenas. Such behavior is often designed to camouflage self-perceived inadequacies. For example, Foster (1967) says in his study of the Mexican village Tzintzuntzan, "Wife beating is common and some women even believe that a good husband should occasionally beat his spouse simply to remind her who is boss. Men, too, are much afraid of being accused of being dominated by their wives, and some beating is certainly due to the desire to impress one's associates with his *machismo,* or the desire to avoid the charge that a wife has the upper hand (pp. 60–61)." What Foster suggests, then, is that these behaviors may be show or "public" actions, designed to enhance flagging self-esteem. Our findings suggest that, despite this public presentation of male dominance, in the daily process of decision making, peasant wives exercise more power than their ideology concerning power would imply. There is, then, a distinction between the public presentation of family relations and the private reality. The public presentation is in keeping with a set of values that are desired but difficult to attain, a set of values which surface as ideology. The private reality may be less desirous but necessary to accomplish the goals of everyday life.

Similarly, we suggest that for Twin Cities white-collar families, the norm of male dominance is contrary to the prevailing values of a liberal capitalistic society built on the image of equal opportunity and individual initiative. Few white-collar husbands would admit to taking a power advantage over their wives, let alone accept approbation for such action. Blood and Wolfe (1960) conclude that in American society "the weight of evidence suggests that the patriarchal family is dead (p. 29)." Yet their own data indicate, as do ours, that middle-class families who adhere to the equalitarian norm have wives who exercise the least power. The public image seems to reflect how family members would like to treat each other, whereas private behaviors seem to reflect more directly the consequences of structural conditions, particularly those affecting the relative dependency of each family member on the other.

SIMILARITIES IN THE TWO SOCIETIES

Our comparison of sex differences in the Mexican and United States sample should not obscure the commonalities that we found in the two societies. Although Mexican and United States mothers differed in the amount of power they exerted, in neither society did we find mothers exercising *more* power than fathers. Similarly, although we found that sex-role differentiation was more pronounced in the United States than in Mexico, and more pronounced among white-collar families than blue-collar or peasant families, nevertheless, in both societies and in all three classes, females were more likely to indicate a preference for housework and visiting relatives than males (with the exception of Twin Cities blue-collar adolescents). Males, on the other hand, were more likely to show a preference for athletics and to accept the opportunities offered by geographical mobility (with the exception of village males).[4] The urban males both in Mexico and in the United States also tended to earn more money and reach higher job statuses while playing SIMCAR than was true of the females.

When we examined the types of purchases made in both the family and child game, we found that males in all groups were more likely than females to buy items such as cars, sporting goods, home improvements, and boats or bicycles. Females, on the other hand, were more likely to purchase domestic appliances and clothing.

Over 80% of all mothers in our study, regardless of class or culture, stated it was important that their husbands be at least equal to them in intelligence, and at least 83% of all mothers stated it was desirable for mothers to remain at home. These data, as well as impressions from the postgame interviews and our initial interviews with parents, suggest that both societies continue to socialize their children into sex-linked roles in which males are expected to exercise greater independence and enjoy greater freedom to venture from the household, whereas females are expected to emphasize appearance and domesticity.

Such findings, of course, were not unexpected. They are consistent with considerable cross-national and cross-cultural research that indicates that, despite variations, females in most societies tend to be taught nurturant and domestic roles, whereas males are taught independence, self-reliance, and productive activities carried on outside the home (see as some examples, Barry *et al.*, 1957; Draper, 1975; Lee, 1977; Whiting & Whiting, 1971). They are reported here to avoid any possible misconception concerning the thrust of our findings. We did not find strong evidences of sexual equality or symmetry either in Mexico or in the United States.

One finding that held across virtually all the groups in our study was of special interest. Participation in the success–failure condition was associated with total game scores for boys, but not for girls[5] (see Table 6.9). Boys who played SIMCAR under failure conditions scored considerably lower than boys who participated in the success condition. The girls' performance was not affected in a consistent way by the game condition.

One possible explanation for this finding is that the conditions created

[4] The relevant data are presented in Table 5.14.
[5] Overall performance or "game score" is the accumulation of all points players made during the game. This includes points for purchases, savings, investments, and achievements such as graduating from school. See Appendix for a description of point system.

Table 6.9
Child Total Game Score by Community, Class, Sex, and Game Condition

| | Villages | | Zacapu | | | | Twin Cities | | | |
| | | | Blue collar | | White collar | | Blue collar | | White collar | |
Game condition	Male	Female	Male	Female	Male	Female	Male	Female	Male	Female
Success	667.0	659.0	714.6	697.1	725.7	591.5	610.0	603.5	640.6	631.0
Failure	625.8	629.0	699.2	714.0	666.3	700.5	519.6	580.0	609.4	650.0

Analysis of variance: Mean effect for communities: $F = 7.54, p < .001$; Interaction between class and communities: $F = 3.35, p < .05$; Interaction between sex and game condition: $F = 3.65, p < .05$.

by SIMCAR were more salient for sons than for daughters. It is possible that there is greater pressure placed on sons to perform successfully in competitive situations and that they respond with greater anxiety when confronted with possible failure situations (Bronfenbrenner, 1961). It is also possible that such competitive situations are not perceived as either potentially rewarding or punishing to daughters (see Harter, 1978, for a discussion of how children internalize and discriminate between relevant and irrelevant goals). There is evidence that males have higher achievement motivations than females (McClelland, Atkinson, Clark, & Lowell, 1953; Hoyenga & Hoyenga, 1979, pp. 263-274) and some data indicate that males are more competitive in achievement situations than females (Horner, 1972; Walker & Heyns, 1962). There is also evidence suggesting that parents put greater achievement pressure on boys than on girls. Parents in industrial countries such as England, Germany, and the United States are more communicative toward their sons when they are nonachievers than they are toward their daughters when they fail to achieve (Devereux et al., 1962). Pearlin (1971) concluded from his studies of families in the industrial city of Turin, Italy, that parents with high aspirations for their sons were more likely than parents with low aspirations to use physical punishment as a method of socialization.

Our data indicate that parental pressure to succeed was associated with poor game performance for those boys who experienced the failure condition. These data are presented in Table 6.10. Sons whose parents had high perceptions of opportunity for them and who underwent the failure condition should have been the most likely group to perform poorly while playing SIMCAR. The table presents the findings comparing boys' and girls' game scores by community, the success–failure condition, and fathers' perceptions of opportunities. Sons in the failure condition whose fathers held high perception of opportunities scores had the lowest game scores. The perception of opportunity measure is an indication of the fathers' anticipation that the child will reach the goal set for him or her. If we interpret this measure as an expectation that the child will perform well, then it appears that the greater the pressure on the son to succeed, the more likely he is to perform poorly after undergoing a failure experience. It is important to note these findings hold only for fathers' perceptions of opportunities. Mothers' perceptions did not produce any systematic results. Perceptions of opportunities by either fathers or mothers did not seem to explain the behavior of daughters in our study.

The difference between urban sons and daughters as well as the ambiguity surrounding the behavior of the females seems even more pronounced when we include the children who experienced the neutral family game condition. These data are presented in Table 6.11. Village children were ex-

Table 6.10
Mean Child Score by Community, Sex, Perception of Opportunity, and Game Condition

Perception of opportunity	Villages		Zacapu		Twin Cities	
	Male	Female	Male	Female	Male	Female
High perception						
Success condition	662.3	577.6	728.3	631.8	658.6	622.0
Failure condition	552.4	622.0	649.8	731.9	621.4	670.0
Low perception						
Success condition	598.8	670.3	687.8	658.8	678.2	690.7
Failure condition	576.6	614.8	686.1	679.7	629.0	580.8

Analysis of variance: Main effect for communities: $F = 6.078, p < .01$; Interaction between sex, perception of opportunity, and game condition: $F = 6.381, p < .01$.

cluded from this table because the neutral condition was not used with village families. The most striking aspect of Table 6.11 is that the neutral boys scored almost as high as the success boys, and the neutral girls scored lower than the girls in the other game conditions. These data suggest that the impact on the male child performance came primarily from the failure conditions. Apparently success conditions did little to accelerate the child's performance because there is little difference between sons who underwent the success condition and those who underwent the neutral condition. The major difference was that sons who underwent the failure condition had scores significantly lower than those of sons in the other two conditions.

The only possible explanation we have to offer for the fact that urban girls did more poorly under neutral conditions than those who experienced either success or failure is that the latter conditions increased the salience of the game for the girls which, as we have already surmised, was lower than it was for boys.

SEX DIFFERENCES AND SOCIALIZATION FOR PROBLEM SOLVING

We turn now to the question of whether socialization for problem solving differs for boys and girls. The primary indicators of problem solving under conditions of social change are the readiness of the game participants to change routes and adopt the new school option when confronted with blocked opportunities for attaining high status or high income positions in their original career routes. The overall differences between Mexican and United States adolescents on these two behaviors were reported in the previous chapter. When we introduce sex comparisons, we find that only the Twin Cities white-collar boys and girls differed significantly on these two

Table 6.11
*Mean Child Game Scores for Urban Males
and Females by Game Conditions*

Game condition	Male N = 61	Female N = 58
Success	681.8	636.3
Failure	630.6	671.4
Neutral	679.1	592.0

behaviors; furthermore, the Twin Cities white-collar girls were the least likely group in the study to change career routes (see Table 6.12).

The final question we sought to answer was whether the same set of family and parent–child experiences had similar effects on boys' and girls' problem-solving performances. To answer this question, we computed a multiple regression analysis, regressing the measures of parents' interpretation of the social structure, parent–child communication and interaction, and family success–failure on adolescent problem-solving scores, separately for boys and girls (see Table 6.13).

Table 6.13 shows not only that different parent–child behaviors influence boys' and girls' problem-solving abilities differently, but the data also explain more of the variance for boys than they do for girls. Also, the beta coefficients for four variables—family equalitarianism, father's aspirations, mother's aspirations, and family success–failure—were statistically significant in the boys' analysis, whereas only two beta coefficients—mother's expectations and father's time orientation—were significant for girls.

Of particular interest are the indications in Table 6.13 that fathers and mothers have different effects on sons' performances. Fathers' aspirations and expectations were negatively associated with the sons' problem solving whereas mothers' aspirations showed a strong positive association with sons' problem solving. On the other hand, both fathers' future orientation and mothers' expectations were positively associated with girls' problem solving. These findings are suggestive of Bronfenbrenner's (1961) conclusion that fathers are more likely than mothers to treat their sons and daughters differently and that boys are subjected to greater pressure and discipline. The finding further supports our supposition that fathers' expectations and aspirations are interpreted by sons as pressures that increase their anxiety about performances and inhibit their tendency to take reasonable risks while solving problems.

The negative relationship between family equalitarianism and adolescent problem solving noted in Chapter 5 holds for both boys and girls as does the positive relationship between tolerance of ambiguity and problem

Table 6.12

Percentage of Adolescents Who Changed Career Routes and Graduated from New School by Sex of Child and Community

| | Villages | | Zacapu | | | | Twin Cities | | | |
| | | | Blue collar | | White collar | | Blue collar | | White collar | |
	Boys N = 26	Girls N = 24	Boys N = 20	Girls N = 20	Boys N = 22	Girls N = 19	Boys N = 24	Girls N = 23	Boys N = 27	Girls N = 30
Changed career routes[a]	92	92	90	80	82	79	50	52	63	30
Graduated from new school[b]	62	67	60	75	64	79	25	30	48	23

[a] Mexico versus United States boys, $\chi^2 = 15.21$, $df = 1$, $p < .001$.
Mexico versus United States girls, $\chi^2 = 22.72$, $df = 1$, $p < .001$.
Twin Cities white-collar boys versus girls, $\chi^2 = 6.22$, $df = 1$, $p < .02$.
[b] Mexico versus United States boys, $\chi^2 = 7.0$, $df = 1$, $p < .01$.
Mexico versus United States girls, $\chi^2 = 24.37$, $df = 1$, $p < .001$.
Twin Cities white-collar boys versus girls, $\chi^2 = 3.84$, $df = 1$, $p < .05$.

Table 6.13
Multiple Regression of Independent Variables on Adolescent Problem Solving for Boys and Girls Separately

Variable	Simple r	Standardized beta	Unstandardized beta	F
Boys[a]				
Family equalitarianism	−.34	−.24	−.28	2.131[c]
Tolerance of conflict	.07	.01	.31	.003
Father's aspirations	−.14	−.23	−.13	2.284[c]
Father's expectations	−.30	−.10	−.20	.506
Mother's aspirations	.42	.42	.14	8.832[c]
Mother's expectations	.13	.12	.30	.496
Father's future orientation	.04	.03	.05	.06
Mother's future orientation	−.05	.02	.04	.03
Father's perception of opportunity	.19	.11	.21	.574
Family success–failure	.32	.33	.63	4.50[c]
Tolerance of ambiguity	.17	.18	.92	1.09
Girls[b]				
Family equalitarianism	−.31	−.14	−.18	.751
Tolerance of conflict	−.13	−.03	−.64	.03
Father's aspirations	.05	.02	.008	.015
Father's expectations	−.11	−.08	−.18	.273
Mother's aspirations	−.10	.09	.04	.365
Mother's expectations	.47	.38	.83	5.32[c]
Father's future orientation	.21	.25	.24	2.81[c]
Mother's future orientation	.09	.04	.02	.04
Father's perception of opportunity	.19	.15	.34	.81
Family success–failure	.14	.09	.19	.28
Tolerance of ambiguity	.29	.21	2.57	1.87

[a]Multiple $R = .70$, $R^2 = .50$
[b]Multiple $R = .62$, $R^2 = .39$
[c]$p < .05$

solving. The latter, however, is more strongly associated with problem solving for girls than it is for boys.

It appears that separate explanatory models are necessary to account for different patterns of socialization for boys and girls. Such models, however, cannot be fixed for all time and should vary in different communities. Unfortunately, our sample size did not allow us to compute reliable multiple regression analyses for the separate communities in the study. We cannot be certain, therefore, whether fathers' aspirations and expectations have a negative effect on sons' problem solving in all of the communities studied. Despite these limitations, certain conclusions seem warranted. The data suggest that sons are more susceptible to achievement pressures than daughters and that these pressures have a negative affect on sons' readiness to take risks in problem-solving situations. Girls' problem-solving abilities, on the other hand, are less likely to be affected by negative family experiences, perhaps because their identities are not as closely linked as boys' identities are to achievement and the need to demonstrate competence (Harter, 1978). Girls' problem-solving performances are more closely associated with parents' optimism and confidence that their daughter will attain their success goals. Finally, family interaction patterns in which one family member dominates (low equalitarianism) while the family avoids premature closure on issues, contributes to effective adolescent problem solving for both boys and girls.

CONCLUSIONS

Two behavioral dimensions seem important in understanding the relationship between males and females in any social system. One is the public presentation reflecting the gender characteristics individuals want to convey to others in their environment. Such behaviors are largely guided by public norms and ideologies. The second dimension is less self-conscious, more mundane, and more likely to represent how people go about solving their daily problems. This "private" dimension is primarily determined by opportunities and resources differentially available to males and females.

Our findings suggest that Mexicans and North Americans differ in important ways on both dimensions. The findings are linked to social structural conditions along a rough continuum ranging from Michoacan peasants representing a preindustrialized state, to Twin Cities white-collar families representing a highly industrialized state. At the public level, the peasant and poor urban families of Michoacan displayed what has come to be viewed as "traditional" norms advocating male dominance. At the other extreme, the Twin Cities white-collar husbands and wives were more committed to equalitarian relationships. At the private level, the data suggested that peasant wives exercised more power in decision making than the wives in any of the other communities, and the Twin Cities white-collar wives exercised the least amount of power.

The ideological or public behavior level is akin to Goffman's (1959, pp. 104–140) conception of "front-stage" behavior. People who are on front stage behave normatively and, consciously or unconsciously, conceal what goes on back stage. One illustration of such behavior, as well as the normative differences between the communities we studied, is the form wife beating may take in a peasant village and in a white-collar community. Foster (1967) indicates that in the Michoacan village of Tzintzuntzan, wives may be beaten for "show," that is, to demonstrate to the community the dominance of the husband. Conversely, when wife beating occurs in a United States white-collar home, every attempt is made to keep it secret (certainly by the man). In one case, it is a badge of honor; in the other, it is a disgrace. In the United States, a show of concern for one's wife is viewed as admirable; in Mexico, at least among the poor, it may be viewed as a sign of male weakness and may be the subject of scorn.

This public behavioral dimension is reported as representing essential aspects of family or sex-role behavior. Such a portrayal is inadequate, not because it is wrong, but because it is incomplete. SIMCAR provided a means for catching a glimpse of the less obvious and less self-conscious private, or "back stage," aspect of male–female relationships, thus placing the two behaviors—public and private—in some perspective.

The line between the two types of behavior cannot always be sharply drawn. Public behavior seeks to convey an ideal, and as such people try to implement it in their everyday life; but they frequently must do so against serious structural obstacles. The ideal of male dominance which characterizes peasant and Mexican blue-collar families is confronted with social conditions that make it difficult for husband–fathers to be adequate providers, whereas the services of wife–mothers are necessary for family survival. On the other hand, the middle-class ideal of equality between husband and wife is confronted with conditions in which the services of wife–mother are considered less than vital. Thus, although the peasant families were more often dominated by husbands than any other group in our study, they also were more often dominated by wives. Conversely, although the Twin Cities white-collar families were more often equalitarian than other groups, they were also likely to have wives who exercised less power than any other wives in the study.

We attributed the greater power of peasant wives to the greater mutuality of dependence between wives and husbands. White-collar wives in the United States, because of their isolation and limited income potential, were more dependent upon their husbands than their husbands were on them.

Although Michoacan boys and girls were both significantly more likely than their Twin Cities counterparts to make game choices geared toward occupational success and material attainment, in general, females in both societies were more likely to make choices appropriate for domestic roles and males were more likely to make choices emphasizing occupational achievement. The greater emphasis among males on occupational success becomes even clearer when we consider the impact of the success–failure condition on boys' and girls' performances. Failure in the family game was associated with lower SIMCAR and problem-solving scores for boys but not for girls in both Mexico and the United States. The data suggest that the pressure on boys to be successful is so strong that experiencing failure as part of a family inhibits their risk taking and problem-solving behavior. These data provide support for the claims of observers of slum and ghetto behavior that the frustrations resulting from repeated failures for males increases the probabilities of subsequent failures in school and other efforts to achieve life goals (Hannerz, 1969; Liebow, 1967).

The findings relevant to parent–child socialization and adolescent problem solving indicated that fathers' behaviors, unlike the behavior of mothers, had a differential effect upon the behaviors of sons and daughters. Fathers' optimism tended to be positively associated with their daughters' problem-solving skills, but fathers' aspirations and expectations were negatively associated with their sons' problem-solving performance. This latter finding tends to support other research suggesting that fathers put greater pressure on boys to be high achievers than they do on girls. Both the boys and girls who decided to go to the new school functioned more effectively if their family structure had one family member who was responsible for major decisions; at the same time they considered an array of information and avoided premature decisions.

In summary, three findings stand out most clearly:

1. Mexican peasant women were the most likely to be the dominant decision makers in the family and the United States white-collar women were the least likely.
2. Despite differences in both societies, females exercised less influence and power.
3. Mexican boys and girls alike were more ready than the United States adolescents to use the opportunities provided in SIMCAR.

This last finding has, as we shall see, some implications for a theory of social change.

7 From Iron Cage to the Age of Narcissism

The Puritan wanted to work in a calling; we are forced to do so. . . . In Baxter's view the care for external goods should only lie on the shoulders of the "saint like a light cloak, which can be thrown aside at any moment." But fate decreed that the cloak should be an iron cage. . . . No one knows who will live in this cage in the future, or whether at the end of this tremendous development entirely new prophets will arise, or there will be a great rebirth of old ideas and ideals, or, if neither, mechanized petrification, embellished with a sort of convulsive self-importance. For of the last stage of this cultural development, it might well be truly said: "Specialists without spirit, sensualists without heart; this nullity imagines that it has attained a level of civilization never before achieved" [Max Weber, 1930, The Protestant Ethic and the Spirit of Capitalism, pp. 181–182.].

Americans have retreated to purely personal preoccupations. Having no hope of improving their lives in any of the ways that matter, people have convinced themselves that what matters is chic self-improvement: getting in touch with one's feelings . . . learning how to "relate," overcoming "the fear of pleasure". . . . To live for the moment is the prevailing passion—to live for yourself, not for your predecessors or posterity. We are fast losing the sense of historical continuity, the sense of belonging to a succession of generations originating in the past and stretching into the future [Christopher Lasch, 1979, The Culture of Narcissism, pp. 29–30].

Were the Mexican families we studied pushing their children to enter the "iron cage" indifferent or unaware of the potential costs to the human spirit that troubled Weber? Were their adolescent children ready to commit themselves to a work ethic and a course of action in which the primary payoff would be material goods? The data reported in the previous two chap-

185

ters suggest that the answer to both of these questions is yes. Moreover, these data indicate that the poorer the families were, the more likely they were to adopt this orientation.

Were the North Americans in our study, living with relative abundance, able to escape the "iron cage" at long last, only to find themselves wallowing in the quicksand of purposeless self-indulgence without past and without future? The data suggest at least the possibility that this question, too, should be answered affirmatively.

We did not begin our research anticipating that we would be struggling with these issues in this final chapter. We began with a different question: How can parents prepare their children to cope with a changing society when they do not know how that society will change? We also began with an idea about what the answer to the question would be. We believed that the way to prepare children to cope with a changing society is to help them become effective problem solvers. We have learned in this research that although parents do not know how the world will change, they do know what they want their children to become. This fact has much to do with how children learn to deal with their social structures. The data suggest that through their interpretation of the social structure parents transmit to their offspring the life-style goals they would like their children to pursue. These goals determine the problems the child will identify and seek to solve.

Put simply, the data indicate that Mexican parents want their children to be rich, and North American parents want their children to be happy. These goals pose different problems and call for different strategies. The Mexicans played SIMCAR as if they were students of Adam Smith. They deferred gratifications, they studied, they saved money, they took advantage of mobility opportunities, and they changed career patterns when it was to their material advantage. They delayed marriage and childbearing and limited their time with friends. Their stated motives were self-interest: They valued money and status so that they could, in their own words, "better themselves." The North Americans, on the other hand, sought to establish a way of life they considered satisfying as quickly as possible. Income and status were less of a motivator for their game choices than personal satisfactions in their work and interpersonal relationships. This was evident in the comments made by parents and children when considering game choices and in the parents' postgame interviews. It was also evident in the game choices themselves. United States adolescents, more frequently than their Mexican counterparts, did not invest in higher education, rejected the mobility option, and were less willing to change career routes in the face of blocked opportunities for advancement. They were more likely to form families and have children early in the game and were more willing to spend their resources on friends. They were also more likely to make game choices that emphasized a traditional sex-linked division of labor. Only the findings indicating the greater tendency of North Americans to ignore education and to maintain traditional sex roles were unexpected. In general, the theory developed for this research predicted reasonably well the structural conditions and family experiences that were associated with adolescent behaviors while playing SIMCAR. The theory also correctly predicted that Mexicans would be more oriented toward materialistic goals and North Americans would be more oriented toward goals seeking familistic and interpersonal satisfactions.

Yet at this point we find ourselves with questions different from the ones with which we began our research. Life-style goals and the ideology that support them seem more important for explaining socialization outcomes relevant to social change, and simply learning the technical skills of problem solving seems less significant than anticipated. Thus, we have the paradox of a theory that is generally supported by the data but that nonetheless requires modification if it is to serve the purposes for which it was designed. The first step in unraveling this paradox is to reassess the theory in the face of the data collected.

EVALUATING THE THEORY

The theory, presented in Chapters 2 and 3, was intended to account for differences in adolescents' problem-solving abilities by stipulating a socialization process that was largely determined by conditions in the community social structure that affected the family structure, which, in turn, influenced parent–adolescent interaction patterns. The socialization process was thought to occur as an unintended corollary of parent–adolescent interaction as they engaged in planning the adolescent's career. We found, in accordance with our hypotheses, that Mexican families were more patriarchal and showed less tolerance for ambiguity and conflict than North American families in the study. Peasant and blue-collar families were more likely to display these traits than were white-collar families.

An underlying assumption that determined our selection of communities was that the level of industrial development of a community was positively associated with the complexity of its social structures. Thus, we conceived of a continuum of complexity with the simplest structures being in peasant villages and the most complex being in Twin Cities white-collar communities. All of the hypotheses pertaining to the effects of structural complexity on family structure and cognitive style were supported for comparisons between peasant and Twin Cities white-collar families.

The theory did not fare quite as well in predicting the differences between parents' interpretations of the social structure. The findings indicating that Mexicans were more optimistic about their children's chances than North Americans and white-collar parents were more optimistic than blue-collar or peasant parents were as anticipated. What was not expected, and what, in retrospect, seems critical was the finding that Mexican parents were significantly more likely to believe that their children's lives would be better than their own. United States parents were more likely to believe that their children's future would not be better than present conditions. The time-honored notion that North Americans looked to the future with hope and optimism did not hold for this sample.

When the full theoretical model was tested, it was evident that some relationships required specification by sex of parent and sex of child. Fathers' expectations, for example, were negatively associated with their sons' problem-solving performance whereas mothers' aspirations and expectations were positively associated with problem-solving performance for both sons and daughters. We also found that, contrary to expectation, adolescent problem solving while playing SIMCAR was positively associated with patterns of family decision making, characterized by the dominance of one family member. As predicted, tolerance of ambiguity was positively associated with adolescent problem-solving ability. These two findings suggest that both cognitive flexibility and centrality of decision making combine to influence the degree to which the child learns to solve problems effectively.

None of these changes, however, account for the finding that Mexican peasant adolescents have the highest problem-solving scores of any group in the study and Twin Cities white-collar adolescents have the worst problem-solving scores. It is this finding and the failure to predict it that led us to reassess the theory in terms of its essential theorems and their implications for a theory of socialization for change.

REVISING THE THEORY

Relevance of Problem Definition

The findings provide strong support for theorems 1, 2, and 4, and they suggest that theorem 3 be eliminated. Theorems 1 and 2 state that persons who enjoy economic abundance are more likely to define the attainment of interpersonal satisfactions as a problem and persons living under conditions of economic deprivation are more likely to define the attainment of material benefits as a problem. Theorem 3 holds that persons in lower strata are less likely to be motivated to solve problems than are persons in higher social strata. The data suggest, however, that when actors are faced with an opportunity structure that is equal for all participants, those from economically deprived backgrounds are more motivated to seek solutions than those from affluent backgrounds. Elder (1974) reports a similar finding. In his study of depression children, boys whose families were economically deprived tended to place greater emphasis on work than boys whose families were not deprived (p. 187). Elder adds an important note. During the depression, the United States had not given up its belief in a society of abundance nor in equal opportunity. President Roosevelt "set forth a New Deal for the American people which expressed his optimistic faith in the potential of the economy to benefit all ... [p. 284]." In short, there was little feeling in those bleak days that conditions would not be or could not be improved. We found similar optimism among Mexican families.

Thus, we conclude that persons living under conditions of relative economic deprivation are more likely to define the attainment of material goods as a problem if (a) they believe their chances of solving the problem are equal to those of other members of the social structure; and (b) they perceive the social structure as having sufficient resources to provide for the desired payoffs. These two conditions are specifications of the principle that "outcome expectations" are important motivating factors in problem-solving behavior (see Chapter 2, but more specifically, see Bandura, 1977a, pp. 79–80, and 1977b).[1] The assumption we make is that people will not define a situation as a problem (in the sense that *problem* is defined in Chapter 2) unless they think that opportunities exist for them to solve the problem. It follows that the two conditions, in different form, should also affect whether actors define the attainment of interpersonal satisfaction as a problem. That is, such perceptions are more likely to occur if (a) actors believe their chances of forming a satisfying relationship with someone else are equal to those of others in their environment; and (b) actors perceive that there are persons in their immediate environment who are attractive or likeable and have the potential for being attracted to and desirous of a relationship with the actor.

---

[1] Bandura considers both self-efficacy and outcome expectations as factors determining anticipated success. Our focus is on outcome expectations, because the primary emphasis remains on the impact of social structure. Self-efficacy is a learned evaluation of personal competency in a given situation. We have no measure of that evaluation. Bandura (1977a) notes that "outcome and efficacy expectations are differentiated because individuals can come to believe that a particular course of action will produce certain outcomes, but question whether they can perform those actions [p. 79]." The converse of this statement should also be true. People may believe they can behave in an efficacious way and believe also that, despite such behavior, positive outcomes may not be assured. This could happen because of discrimination, lack of access to persons of influence, or because of other perceived structural inequities beyond the control of the actor.

Theorem 4 also pertains to outcome expectations. It states that if the social structure changes in a direction that increases the chances of attaining desired family life goals, people's problem-solving motivation will increase. The evidence that Mexican adolescents were more willing to take appropriate risks in problem-solving situations than United States children lends some support to this theorem. In Chapter 1 we discussed the prevailing aura in Mexico that the economic future was bright. In the United States, on the other hand, despite economic well-being, the country was badly divided over the Vietnam War. Perhaps even more important, the United States was experiencing increasing rates of homicide, suicide, and divorce—conditions symptomatic of personal and interpersonal problems.

In light of the findings theorems 1, 2, and 4 take on added significance. In combination they emphasize the relevance of social conditions and opportunity structures in determining problem definition. The data illustrate a second point: Not all problems require the same problem-solving strategies. Consequently, the identification of different problems within a social structure implies different strategies for coping with the social structure. It also follows that if the way people act within social structures affects the structural changes that take place, different strategies should have different effects on the structure. Below we consider the different strategies that result from seeking to solve two different types of problems. Later in the chapter, we shall consider the implications of these strategies for changing the social structure.

Two Types of Problems

Both the objective and the qualitative data indicate that the problem for Mexicans was to obtain as much in the way of money and associated occupational prestige as SIMCAR was able to provide. The problem for North Americans was to play SIMCAR so that they could maintain family and interpersonal relationships as part of a satisfying life-style without going under financially.

For Mexicans, solutions to their problem had to be found outside of the family unit, that is, in the game and/or in situations the game symbolized. Solutions to external problems require seeking and processing information that is objective and verifiable (Kelley & Thibaut, 1969). Appropriate sources for such information would be persons who understand the workings of the social structure. In this research, such persons would most likely be the parents for the child, and the experimenter for the family. Our impression is that the Mexicans, especially peasant and blue-collar Mexicans, were much more likely to look to the experimenter for guidance than were North American families. The data show rather clearly that Mexican children in the study tended to rely more heavily on their parents for instructions and directions as to a course of action than United States children did.

The Mexicans played SIMCAR as a rule-bound game. To understand the payoff structure the players had to understand the kinds of investments and activities that the game (structure) would most likely reward. The rules were analogous to those in structures in which payoffs are linked to achieved status. If the goal was to gain the highest status position, knowledge of these rules would be essential.

Solutions to the problem faced by the United States families required knowledge from sources internal to the family. The information necessary had to do with the feelings, motivations, and desires of the persons involved with the actor. Such information is impressionistic, tentative, and variable (see Orne, 1962; Rosenthal, 1966). Furthermore, the resolution of interpersonal problems is not easily linked to any established set of rules. Accordingly, we found that United States families played SIMCAR with a greater focus on the child and his or her desires than was true of Mexican families, and we also noted greater variation in the way United States parents and children played the game. United States parents tended to mold their decisions to conform with the special characteristics of their children; Mexican parents rarely considered their children's unique or special aspects, emphasizing instead the societal requisites for advancement their children would have to meet.

In sum, the problem Mexicans faced was external, objective, and rule bound. The North Americans, on the other hand, were solving internal, subjective, non-rule-bound problems. How successful were the two groups? Since SIMCAR was designed as an external, objective, rule-bound problem, it is difficult to evaluate the performance of most of the United States adolescents. In fact, there is some question as to whether the North Americans were seeking solutions at all. They seemed "problem" rather than "solution" oriented (Maier, 1970). They concentrated on analyzing the elements of the interpersonal and personal problems faced by their children rather than indicating appropriate solutions. Solution orientations may be more effective for rule-bound problems since the group can move more quickly to discover the appropriate analytical or procedural rules necessary to solve the problem (see Tallman *et al.*, 1974).

Social Structure, Family Structure, and Cognitive Style

The findings support theorem 5, which holds that the complexity of the social structure is associated with family egalitarianism and flexible cognitive styles. The data indicate that families' tolerance of ambiguity, tolerance of conflict, and egalitarianism are all positively associated with the complexity of community social structures. Such findings are in accord with a growing body of research that links psychological flexibility with structural complexity and level of social development (Kohn & Schooler, 1973, 1978; Luria, 1976). What surprised us, however, was that these indicators of psychological flexibility were only mildly associated with problem solving and could not account for the fact that the Mexican peasant adolescents, the children whose families scored lowest on the meaures of cognitive flexibility, were the group most likely to accept the mobility option, change career routes, and graduate from the new school in early game rounds.

In brief, the data in this study showed no relationship between cognitive flexibility (measured in terms of verbal interactions) and behavioral flexibility (measured in terms of changing courses of action to adapt to changing situations). We cannot here adequately deal with the long-standing debate concerning the possible bias in measuring the cognitive processes and performance of lower-class persons (e.g., see R. Cohen, 1974; Klein & Hill, 1979; Miller & Riessman, 1964; Tallman & Miller, 1974). It is worth noting, however, that there is evidence indicating the propensity of peasants to move wherever work is available, even if such moves mean living in strange cities and foreign countries (e.g., see Lomnitz, 1977; Miller, 1973). Such moves have rarely been interpreted as indications of flexible behavior. Many arguments can be made concerning the motives of peasants to take such action: They have less to lose than those who are better off; they tend to follow in the path of kin, and so forth. Nevertheless, it cannot be argued that for people whose lives have been primarily agricultural and whose families have been identified for centuries with a given village, relocation is evidence of rigid, conservative, or traditional behavior. Whatever the push or pull motives of those who exhibit such behaviors, the actions clearly imply flexibility and a willingness to take risks.

What of the United States adolescents whose families evidence more cognitive flexibility than any other families in the study but whose SIMCAR behavior appears least flexible? Can this be explained solely on the basis that these families defined the problem posed by SIMCAR differently than Mexican families? If the United States adolescents perceived SIMCAR similarly, would they have performed as well or better than the Mexicans? The finding indicating a negative relationship between family egalitarianism and adolescent problem solving suggests that United States adolescents, whose families were the most egalitarian in the study, may not have been the most effective problem solvers, even if they played SIMCAR on the same terms as the Mexicans. Of course, it is conceivable that if United States families had tended to define the problem in objective rather than interpersonal and subjective terms, they would have placed more authority in the hands of the adult with knowledge of the external world. Unfortunately, this conjecture must remain purely speculative, since we have no further means of testing it in this study.

Somewhat less speculative is the inference that a family environment that provides centralized decision making and tolerance for ambiguity will be more likely to facilitate learning to solve problems that are external, objective, and rule bound; in other words, the types of problems involved in getting ahead in a social structure. This inference receives some support from other data in the group problem-solving literature indicating that central decision-making authority, when combined with a group climate that encourages contributions from all members and weighs those contributions critically, is positively associated with effective problem solving (Blau & Scott, 1962, pp. 116–128; see Tallman, 1970, for a review of this literature).

It was not possible to develop data to test theorem 6, which holds that complexity of the social structure is associated with children's level of information processing. Our original intention was to analyze verbatum transcripts of audio tapes to test levels of information processing, but the quality of the tapes and the costs of making transcriptions in Spanish made the plan impractical. We were able to transcribe the United States tapes and our findings generally supported the theorem. Reporting these data within the context of this comparative study, however, would take us far afield.

Family Success–Failure and Adolescent Problem Solving

The findings on sex differences suggest that theorem 7 requires additional specification. In essence, this theorem proposes that family success in problem solving activities is positively associated with an adolescent's willingness to define situations as problems and, therefore, to engage in a course of action designed to solve the problem. Conversely, those adolescents who experience failure in problem solving as members of a family will be more tentative and less willing to take appropriate risks when faced with barriers to attaining their goals. The data indicate that this relationship holds for boys but not for girls. Specifically, boys who experienced failure in the family game were more likely to have low SIMCAR game scores than were boys who experienced either the success or neutral family game condition. On the other hand, family success–failure had no systematic effect on girls' game performance.

The most plausible explanation for these sex differences is that SIMCAR was not as salient for girls as it was for boys. The findings linking fathers' perceptions of opportunity, aspirations, and expectations with sons' poor game performance suggested that boys were highly sensitive to achievement pressures. Girls, on the other hand, were more likely than boys to make game choices that were not relevant to career advancement. They were more likely to invest in housework and visiting friends, less likely to obtain high paying, high status jobs, and more likely to make store purchases in the areas of home appliances and clothing. In brief, the girls in this study tended to make traditional female choices. The ideological climate relevant to those choices is exemplified by the fact that 83% of all mothers in this study stated that it was desirable for mothers to stay home with their children rather than go to work. In sum, it appears that the girls were less likely to view a competitive–achievement focus, such as that implicit in SIMCAR, as salient to their lives and goals.

Why should the salience of the game have an intervening effect on the relationship between family success or failure and the child's game performance? After all, salient or not, SIMCAR was the only game being played at the time. Why should not successful family experiences have some carry-over effect when girls played the game alone? We think the answer lies in the reason SIMCAR was not salient to the girls; that is, their passivity made it difficult for them to link SIMCAR outcomes to the actions of their parents or themselves. Although Mexican mothers and United States mothers differed in the amount of power they displayed, in neither society did mothers exercise more power than fathers. Moreover, in Mexico, where they exercised the most power, women held most strongly to the belief that males *should* be powerful. This abrogation of power could result in daughters having a lower sense of efficacy particularly in areas outside their fields of expertise. If they felt that they could not influence external events, they would be more likely to perceive the success or failure of the family's problem-solving efforts as being beyond the control of the actors involved. In short, theorem 7 should hold true only if children perceive outcomes pertaining to family goals as directly attributable to the family's problem-solving activities.

The eighth and final theorem is eliminated from the theory because it holds, in part, that adolescents from communities with a complex social structure should be more effective problem solvers. The results do not support this prediction. Since the second part of theorem 8 is essentially the same as theorem 7, and since the first part is not supported, the theorem becomes redundant.

The Influence of Affluence

Despite the revisions reported earlier, many elements in the theory remain unchanged. The main units that make up the explanatory model, for example, seem to remain intact. Nothing in the data has warranted changing the proposed linkages between community social structure, family structure, parent–child relationships, and adolescent problem solving. The key structural elements—level of material abundance, access to information, and diversity of role choices—have provided useful indexes for linking position in social structure and/or level of development with individual performance. Furthermore, categorizing parent–child relationships in terms of parents' interpretation of the social structure and family patterns of communication and interaction provided a means of differentiating variables that were, as predicted, associated with adolescent problem solving.

The basic assumptions, derived from the exchange perspective that underlies the theory, have also proved useful. Whatever the limitations of this perspective, it provides directions for explaining decisions relevant to problem solving within the social structure. The assumptions that people attain their benefits through negotiations and exchanges with others, and that they are motivated in these exchanges to seek a favorable benefit–cost ratio, provide a heuristic framework for predicting and analyzing courses of action while playing SIMCAR. Since SIMCAR was developed to be an analog of social structure, we draw the same inference for social structures. The exchange perspective requires us to specify a priori the benefits and costs that are involved in given transactions in order to avoid tautological arguments. Having done so, it provides a means of putting into a rational decision-making framework behaviors that might otherwise be written off as irrational or attributed to vague wastebasket concepts, such as unconscious motivation or cultural differences.[2] The exchange perspective allows us to account for quite different performances on SIMCAR within a framework that can explain the relative value of nonmaterial as well as material goals and payoffs. In fact, applying the law of diminishing marginal utility within the exchange perspective leads to one of the main implications of this study, that is, that actors can have too much of a good thing. Material rewards can lose their attraction once they have been attained in sufficient quantity, and conversely, the importance of nonmaterial rewards pales in the face of material scarcity. The data suggest that the law of diminishing marginal utility can be viewed in social–psychological as well as economic terms. They also suggest that the relevant affluence of a community plays a critical role in socialization for social change. The perspective also provides a basis for explaining differences between ideology concerning male-fe-

---

[2] We believe that people can be motivated by unconscious drives or culturally learned preferences—we do not believe, however, that the terms themselves provide an explanation for behaviors without considerable specification. Furthermore, we think that if they were specified, they could fit into an exchange framework.

male power differentials and observed power relations. The power-dependency explanation, which derives from the exchange perspective, provides a reasonable explanation for the finding that peasant wives have more power than United States white-collar wives.

In summary, we suggest that:

1. The degree of affluence in the social structure and the distribution of resources within the social structure influence perception of the problems people will identify within the structure.
2. The more affluent the family and/or the greater the material resources available within the social structure, the more likely the family and its members will be to identify and seek to solve personal and interpersonal problems. Conversely, the fewer the family's material resources, the more likely it will be to define problems in terms of acquiring material goods.
3. The two types of problems require different types of information search. Personal and interpersonal problems require subjective information about motivations, desires, and feelings, whereas the attainment of material goods requires objective, verifiable information from authoritative sources concerning the opportunities and requisite activities necessary to attain the goods. The two types of problems also require different methods of information processing. Personal and interpersonal problems tend not to be rule bound, whereas obtaining material benefits generally involves discovering and using appropriate established rules. The resolution of rule-bound as compared to non-rule-bound problems implies different strategies. Non-rule-bound problems require that time be taken to form rules appropriate for solving each problem. Thus, of necessity, there is greater focus on diagnosing the nature of the problem. Accordingly, we have seen a greater tendency among United States parents to put time and effort into *analyzing* the individual characteristics and motivations of their children. Rule-bound problems, on the other hand, allow for solution oriented strategies; if the rules are understood, the task becomes one of behaving in ways that meet the requisites for finding a problem solution.
4. Although the data support the proposition that complexity of the social structure is associated with cognitive flexibility, it is not clear that cognitive flexibility is linked to behavioral flexibility, at least when it is measured in terms of a readiness to choose alternative routes for attaining material payoffs.
5. Prior success–failure experiences will affect the readiness of actors to engage in problem solving in similar situations only if actors attribute possible outcomes directly or indirectly to the actions they take.

COPING STRATEGIES IN MEXICO AND
IN THE UNITED STATES

How do these conclusions pertain to the socialization of children for dealing with a changing world? We have seen in these data the greater commitment among Mexicans to rules that have been promulgated as the route to material success since the days of Adam Smith. They displayed a commitment to the work ethic, to education, to deferred gratification, and to an impersonal, unsentimental search for practical solutions. The data suggest that Mexican adolescents were socialized to anticipate a changing world that would give them occupational opportunities greater than those of their parents. They learned the rules for success and, assuming necessary abilities and equal opportunities, were ready to apply the rules for the purposes of making more money. They would eagerly don an iron cloak, not for the purpose of everlasting grace, but for the satisfactions associated with material success.

The Twin Cities data present a more complex picture. The traditional view of the North American as optimistic, future oriented, status conscious, and obsessed by a hard driving commitment to financial success was not supported in this research. The parents of United States adolescents seemed simultaneously more realistic and more pessimistic than Mexican parents. United States parents were aware of the obstacles to their children acquiring more in the way of material goods than they were currently enjoying. Having attained material comforts, they seemed to recognize that the things money can buy do not meet all human needs. As individualistic as their forebearers had been, they focused on the problems of satisfying their children's unique potentialities. The interviews suggested that, more often than not, United States parents assumed the role of practicing psychologist, interpreting motives, attributing causes for actions, and analyzing their children's special personality characteristics. The overriding concern was that their children have a happy life. We can infer from the way both the parents and their adolescent children played SIMCAR that they believed such a life required friendships and stable family relationships. These orientations held for both blue- and white-collar families. In fact, throughout this study hypotheses predicting class differences in the United States sample were generally not supported.

How does this emphasis on interpersonal satisfaction prepare children to deal with changes in the social structure? The data indicate that they may simply ignore the changes. If, like SIMCAR, the social structure is primarily concerned with status and income opportunities and if the actors have little interest in such career goals, then structural changes affecting such attainment are irrelevant. This, of course, could change if the economy affected the desired life-styles of the actors. The data suggest that the United States families and their children were not psychologically inflexible—only uninterested in the type of changes created in SIMCAR. But these types of changes are the ones most likely to occur in social structures. The institutionalized channels for engaging in communication and interaction within social structures exist primarily for the purpose of exchanging goods and services, and the essential differentiations that take place within social structures are based on the control and distribution of goods and services. Thus, the question must be raised as to whether the United States parents' socialization of their children adequately prepares them for the realities of a changing world?

A number of critics claim that United States children raised during the past decade are ill-prepared to perform effectively or contribute meaningfully to a changing world. For example, Christopher Lasch (1979) states that

> the modern parent's attempt to make children feel loved and wanted does not conceal an underlying coolness . . . the remoteness of those who have little to pass on to the next generation and who, in any case, give priority to their own right to self-fulfillment. The combination of emotional detachment with attempts to convince a child of his favored position in the family is a good prescription for a narcissistic personality structure (pp. 101–102).

Urie Bronfenbrenner (1973), relying more heavily on the accumulation of research findings than does Lasch, is no less strident in his evaluation.

> As we read the evidence, both from our own research and that of others, we cannot escape the conclusion that, if the current trend persists, if the institutions of our society continue to remove parents, other adults, and older youth from active participation in the lives of children, and if the resulting vacuum is filled by the age-segregated peer group, *we can anticipate increased alienation, indifference, antagonism, and violence on the part of the younger generation in all segments of our society—middle-class children as well as the disadvantaged* (p. 121).

Lasch and Bronfenbrenner provide different causal explanations for growing normlessness among young people. Lasch attributes the problem to a changing ethos, the abandonment of the "culture of competitive individualism" for the sake of the self-indulgent pursuit of pleasure. Bronfenbrenner sees the problem as the consequence of "age segregation," which can be attributed to the growing residential isolation of families from other relatives, the separation of work from the home, the increased use of television, and a wide range of entertainments that are exclusively for either adults or children. Parents find themselves spending increasingly less time with their children. They also find themselves in the position of delegating responsibility for raising their children to others, primarily institutions like schools, or (and this is more problematic) to the street and the children's peers.

In some ways our data provide support for Lasch's thesis. The Twin Cities parents' tendency to focus attention on their children's psychological well-being and happiness, the children's SIMCAR choices that tended to eschew high status positions, and the adaptations of what appeared to be ideosyncratic life strategies, all suggest aspects of the culture of narcissism.

We have little direct evidence to support Bronfenbrenner's generalizations. We have no data measuring the amount of contact parents have with their children. Our informal observations, however, support Bronfenbrenner's claims. Comparing life-styles in the Twin Cities with life-styles of families in Zacapu and in the villages leaves little doubt that the simpler the community structure, the more frequent the daily contacts between parents and children.

Yet on one important point the data run contrary to the descriptions presented by Lasch and Bronfenbrenner. Far from putting their own needs before those of their children, the United States parents seemed to focus so completely on their children's wishes that they tended to abrogate their own desires and goals. Our observations and interviews confirmed that game decisions were based on the children's wishes rather than on those of their parents. These data cannot be attributed to the United States parents' relinquishing responsibility or disinterestedly acquiescing to whatever their children might want. The parents' detailed analyses of their children's feelings and motivations provides evidence of their deep involvement. A more reasonable interpretation of these data is that the parents deliberately sought not to foist their views onto their children. Such an orientation is consonant with strategies for solving interpersonal problems, because the subjective feelings of others are important criteria in reaching solutions.

This type of socialization could be a manifestation of the overpsychologizing that Lasch argues is a key element in the formation of the culture of narcissism. It is also possible that the parents' sensitivity and concern for the welfare of others is transmitted to their children. If the primary goal is the resolution of interpersonal problems, such sensitivity would be an essential skill. Concern for others in an era of nuclear weaponry and hardening ideological conflicts may prove to be functional in the years to come.

THE UTILITY OF SIMCAR

We have drawn extensive generalizations from data produced while families and their adolescent children played a game. We must now address the question of whether such data provide a justifiable basis for drawing inferences about life-style goals, socialization patterns, and ways of behaving in the real world. The question does not lend itself to an absolute answer. SIMCAR, like other instruments designed to measure behavior, records only a momentary slice of people's lives, and it is difficult to know just how representative or significant that slice is. This is especially true since SIM-CAR is a new instrument whose properties are just being tested. Moreover, the complex and multiple purposes to which SIMCAR was put make ordinary validity checks difficult to assess. Nevertheless, we cannot ignore the critical issue of how well the simulation game serves the purposes for which it was constructed. This is especially important if we wish to assess the claims made in Chapter 4 as to the applicability of this method for cross-national research. Three modes of analyses—face validity, predictive validity, and utility—are particularly relevant in appraising SIMCAR's applicability.

Face Validity[3]

Face validity describes the extent to which the game reproduces what it seeks to simulate. SIMCAR had greater face validity than we had anticipated. In fact, face validity may be a major reason for the failure to support the hypotheses concerning problem-solving behavior. The most unexpected finding in this study was that the peasant adolescents proved to be better problem solvers than United States adolescents. The measure of problem solving used was the adolescents' decision to change career routes and to take advantage of the new school, both important actions in making progress toward high income, high status positions. The finding was surprising even though we had predicted that the Mexicans' life-style goals would be materialistic and the North Americans' would be familistic and oriented toward interpersonal satisfactions. What had we expected? First, we had thought that the United States adolescents would seek to make money for the purpose of supporting families in a comfortable life-style. Second, we expected that the participants would treat SIMCAR as a *game* about real life, that is, all participants would be faced with the single problem of performing well in the game. We did not take into account how thoroughly the families would be absorbed in the simulation as a representation of the real world.

Participants in game simulations generally tend to view such games as consonant with their life experiences (Boocock, 1972; Hermann, 1967). To assess the game's realism or its similarity to the subjects' life experiences, we asked parents to discuss their game experiences in a postsimulation interview. Six questions were asked in an attempt to assess face validity.

---

[3] Parts of this discussion are drawn from Tallman and Wilson, 1974.

Parents were asked to explain why they invested time and money in education, marriage, religious activities, time spent with friends or on dates, time with relatives, and store purchases. Native coders then coded the responses into one of four categories: (a) game—subject's answer clearly indicates that choices during the game were a function of the game or game-related constraints and options; (b) real life—subject's answer clearly indicates that the choices reflect actual or potential real-life values or behaviors; (c) both—a combination of a and b; and (d) no answer. We also asked whether or not parents were playing for points or were behaving as they would in real life. Responses were coded in the same four categories. The data, which are presented in Table 7.1, clearly indicate that the vast majority of parents in each community were judged to have made their game choices on the basis of real-life considerations. The largest proportion of parents to indicate they made choices on the basis of game contingencies was only 10%. The conclusion that real-life considerations dominated game choices was further supported by the analysis of audiotape recordings and transcriptions of family discussions over specific issues such as accepting the mobility options and evaluating game performance at the end of each round. Almost universally, family members in both countries alluded to personal real-life situations in their environments while discussing their options.

We do not believe that these findings can be attributed to experimenter effects, because, if there was an experimenter bias, it was in the opposite direction. As noted earlier, we had expected that the participants would play SIMCAR more like a game.

The perceived parallel between the simulation game and life situations can be a confounding factor when testing hypotheses. In fact, the greater the parallelism, the greater the probability that personal values, memories, preconceptions, and orientations will be factors in the decisions that are made, thus adding considerable unmeasured variation to the hypothesis-testing situation. This is more problematic, however, if the simulation is used as an experiment or if the possible confounding factors cannot be identified. We do not believe that either of these conditions represent a major problem in this research because it was designed to use SIMCAR more as an observation technique than as an experimental situation. We wanted not only to test hypotheses but to remain open for further specifications or modifications of our theory.

The face validity of the game increased the chances of producing relevant, serendipitous findings while it decreased the chances for an exact test of any single hypothesis. For example, the failure of the daughters to respond as predicted to the success–failure condition provided additional insights about the conditions under which prior experience influences per-

Table 7.1
Percentage of Decisions Based on Game or Life Situations by Community and Type of Choice

Type of choice	Twin Cities (N = 96)				Zacapu (N = 77)				Villages (N = 50)			
	Game	Real life	Both	No answer	Game	Real life	Both	No answer	Game	Real life	Both	No answer
Education	6.2	84.4	2.1	7.3	1.3	82.3	7.6	8.8	10.0	80.0	0	10.0
Marriage	3.1	75.0	2.1	19.8	1.3	92.4	0	6.3	0	94.0	0	6.0
Religious activity	3.1	84.4	1.0	11.5	5.1	84.8	0	10.1	4.0	84.0	2.0	10.0
Friends and dates	3.1	84.4	3.1	9.4	0	97.5	0	2.5	0	96.0	0	4.0
Relatives	4.2	81.2	2.1	12.5	5.1	84.8	1.3	8.8	4.0	78.0	0	18.0
Store purchases	2.1	93.8	1.0	2.1	1.3	93.7	0	5.0	0	92.0	2.0	6.0
Total game	0	79.2	12.5	8.3	2.5	91.2	3.8	2.5	6.0	80.0	10.0	4.0

formance. The relative richness of SIMCAR allowed for testing other explanations when a given hypothesis was not supported. Thus, the game provided a number of indicators of the way the female role was played in the various communities, allowing us to examine the alternative hypothesis that the passive role of females made it difficult for the success–failure condition to be salient for daughters in the study. Our approach recalls Robert Merton's (1957) dictum that research, "does more than confirm or refute hypotheses. Research plays an active role: it performs at least four major functions which help shape the development of theory. It *initiates*, it *reformulates*, it *deflects* and it *clarifies* theory (p. 103)."

Predictive Validity

The ability to predict subsequent behavior or similar variables in other contexts is referred to as predictive validity (Nunnally, 1967, pp. 76–79). With simulation games such as SIMCAR predictions to nongame behavior pose theoretical and logical problems. For example, despite the apparent face validity of the game, we can not logically draw the inference that people will behave in real-life situations as they do in the game. Unlike the game simulation, opportunities in the real world are not held constant. The most reasonable interpretation of subjects' game choices is that they represent the way people would like to behave with regard to the simulated aspects of their social structure. The game simulation was intended to elicit evidence concerning peoples' values, success goals, strategies, behavioral flexibility, and information processing capacity. Adequate tests of such behavior in a nongame setting would require consistent observation over an extended period. We had hoped to conduct a longitudinal follow-up study of the children in both the Mexican and United States samples to assess the course of their work and family careers over a period of 10 years. Not only would this research have provided a reasonable test of the predictive validity of SIMCAR, but it would have allowed for an assessment of how career goals and anticipated strategies are affected by the constraints of real social structures. Unfortunately we were not able to obtain sufficient funding to carry out this research.

Although we cannot test how SIMCAR behaviors predict subsequent actions of the game participants, we can examine how these behaviors are reflected in relevant data describing current Mexican and United States populations. Even though our samples were not representative of Mexicans or North Americans, such comparisons have indirect implications for the predictive validity of SIMCAR. Equally important, such comparisons provide evidence relevant to the theory of socialization for change. We can compare family and adolescent problem-solving behavior measured in 1972 to current reports of behaviors in similar samples or populations. The children studied in 1972 are, at this writing, between 21 and 24 years old, an age when they are confronted with some of the behaviors they played out in SIMCAR. Although we do not know how the specific children in our study are behaving as young adults, we can estimate how closely the data approximate the reported data for similar people, 10 years later. Any theory of socialization that seeks to contribute to a theory of social change should link socialization practices at one period of time to later macro social behavioral patterns.

Let us begin with some specific game choices. One of the findings that surprised both North American and Mexican researchers with whom we shared these data was the greater restraint among Mexican families and adolescents in choosing to have children while playing SIMCAR. This restraint was not reflected in the population picture in Mexico at that time. The Mexican population had grown from 20 million in 1940 to 54 million in 1972. Until 1973 there was no official policy designed to discourage rapid population growth (Nagel, 1978). The finding thus seemed to be an anomaly. However, we were not measuring the number of children the participants in the game were having, but the value being inculcated in these children with regard to their having children. In brief, the data were relevant to how they were being socialized on this issue. The question then is whether such socialization has had an impact on the birth rates. By 1978 the population in Mexico had increased to 65 million; the annual growth rate, however, had slowed to 2.9%, a decline from a rate of 3.5% prior to 1973 (Nagel, 1978). In the decade from 1970 to 1980, fertility rates dropped from 44.2 births per thousand to 34.0 per thousand, a decrease of 25% (Zamarono, 1981). There was also a dramatic increase in contraceptive use.

Between 1973 and 1976, the use of contraceptives had doubled, and there was every indication that the rate of use would continue to increase at the same pace (Gallegos, Peña, Solis, & Keller, 1977). Thus it appears that the data gathered with SIMCAR in 1972 anticipated changes in the general Mexican population.

The greater willingness of Mexicans, particularly peasants, to accept the geographical mobility option also seemed to parallel the migration rates of Mexicans from rural areas to cities. This rate continues to increase (Cone, 1976; Lomnitz, 1977; Miller, 1973). The primary motive for such migration, as our data suggest, is financial betterment (see Lomnitz, 1977, p. 47). The following description of villagers by anthropologist Frank Miller (1973) provides validation for the findings generated by SIMCAR.

> The villager . . . no longer lives in a narrow world fatalistically resigned to a hard life. His horizons have been extended by schools, the mass media, and travel to urban centers or contact with relatives who have traveled. He has seen the benefits and comforts of modern technology, and he does not worry about its ill effects. In order to share

those benefits, he realizes that he needs a well paying job in the modern sector of the economy (pp. 125–126).

The emphasis on a well-paying job has become so important in the lives of Mexican villagers that they are leaving the villages and farms in ever increasing numbers (Cornelius, 1981).

We have noted the correspondence between the tendency of urban Mexicans to earn, save, and spend money on consumer goods and Apter's (1971, pp. 42–72) idea that "embourgeoisement" becomes a major orientation for people living in countries in the latter stages of modernization. According to Apter, "embourgeoisement" increases the pressure for consumer goods within the country. This makes it difficult for such countries to accumulate sufficient excess resources to reinvest in capital goods and continue industrialization. Mexico is currently facing this problem. The demand for consumer goods, particularly appliances made in the United States, is so great that Mexico has been forced to institute high tariffs and stringent restrictions against the importation of such goods in order to maintain a reasonable balance of payments. This is apparently true despite increasing production and exportation of petroleum and petrochemicals.

The Mexican gross national product growth rate has been above 7% per year since 1977, a reflection of the country's strong industrial expansion. At the same time, unemployment is somewhat over 25% of the work force and the inflation rate in 1980 was almost 30%. This combination of deprivation and changing opportunity may be a factor effecting the optimism and behavioral flexibility we found in our research.[4] People continue to be optimistic because they see new opportunities in a growing variety of industrial and service areas. These opportunities, however, require appropriate training. The data in this study indicate that in 1972 children of Mexican peasants and of blue- and white-collar workers were being socialized to look for and to take advantage of training wherever it was available. If these data are an accurate reflection of Mexican values and attitudes, Mexico is developing a committed work force, ready to seize education and economic opportunities wherever they lie. It is a work force with high expectations, willing to give much but also expecting much.

The finding that United States families and children place a higher value on family life than on jobs or career has been corroborated by a number of studies for at least 2 decades. However, these data have received little attention or emphasis. For example, Rokeach (1973) found in his nationwide random sample that "family security" ranks second only to "a world at peace" among 18 terminal values. The ranking holds for both males and females.

---

[4] See also Elder, 1974, who notes similar responses as a consequence of deprivation and the commitment to abundance during the depression.

Significantly, "a comfortable life" ranks below "family security" for both sexes (fourth for men and thirteenth for women). As early as 1960, a survey of American college students indicated that they ranked a happy family life as their primary life goal (Goldsen, Roseberg, Suchman, & Williams, 1960). "Quality of life" studies have also reported the importance of family life for Americans' feelings of well-being (Campbell, Converse, & Rogers, 1976).

Despite these data, there remains the myth that Americans are achievement oriented, hard driving, materialistic, status seekers who put family and interpersonal relations second to career. The move to the suburbs, for example, which characterized migration patterns of white-collar families for 2 decades after World War II, was popularly considered to be an example of upward striving and status seeking (see Whyte's *Organization Man,* 1957). This view was held in the face of consistent empirical evidence that the motives for moving had more to do with a better family life and relaxed life-style (see W. Bell, 1958; Martin, 1956; Mower, 1958; Wood, 1958; for a recent update, see Marshall, 1979).

The data that suggest the willingness of the United States adolescents to forego material gain if it is at the cost of psychological well-being seems to have support from the periodic "quality of life" studies carried out by the University of Michigan's Institute for Social Research. Angus Campbell, who directed this research, summed up the most recent findings as follows:

> What appears to have happened is that an increasing number of people have achieved a degree of economic security that has liberated them from an obsessive concern with income, with a consequent increase in the importance of nonmaterial needs—the need for a sensitive and responsive marital relationship, for challenging and significant work, for the respect and approval of friends, for identification with community, and for a stimulating and fulfilling life (reported in ISR Newsletter, Institute of Social Research, The University of Michigan, Spring, 1981b).

Campbell claimed that we are entering an era of the "psychological man." He goes on to state, "For the most part these people were talking about values that cannot be counted in dollars."

Some of the SIMCAR findings, however, do not square as easily with current data. For example, the findings that United States children and their families were more likely than the Mexicans to decide to have children during the game are not reflected in the United States fertility data. Moreover, a growing number of United States women indicate a desire to remain childless. Yet, a year after we collected our data, a Gallup Poll reported that only 1% of the Americans interviewed regarded the childless family as ideal (Reiss, 1980, p. 353). One possible explanation for this discrepancy derives from evidence that children are desired primarily because they are seen as providing their parents with personal happiness (Hoffman & Hoffman,

1973). Thus, when couples are faced with the actual decision of whether or not to have children, they may weigh more carefully the happiness-producing potential of the child. This interpretation is supported by those few studies of married people who do not wish to have children. The primary justification provided for not wanting children is that the child could weaken the basis upon which the couple has established a happy relationship (see Reiss, 1980, p. 356, for a review of the available research). SIMCAR provides a situation in which people have equal opportunities to attain their goals—such equality does not exist in real social structures. Just as we cannot expect that all Mexican children will attain the positions in real life they achieved while playing SIMCAR, so we should not expect all the United States adolescents to attain their desired life-styles.

Utility

Predictive validity provides some assurance that an instrument measures with reasonable accuracy what it purports to measure. To test predictive validity, we compare our findings with those of other investigations that employ different measures. But no researcher constructs an instrument to measure a phenomenon that could have been measured as easily or effectively in another way. It is reassuring that we can corroborate some of our findings with survey and census data in both Mexico and the United States, but we do not believe that we could have accomplished this research with surveys or the analyses of census data. We sought to build an instrument that would allow us to observe the strategies used by families in different cultures to deal with a social structure. We also needed to observe intrafamilial interaction in the process of making decisions and choosing alternative strategies. Moreover, we needed to control the success and failure outcomes in the families' efforts to achieve their goals as well as introduce some equivalent of social change in assessing the child's abilities to adapt problem-solving strategies. Finally, our technique had to be applicable to peasant villages as well as blue- and white-collar families in the United States and Mexico; that is, it had to be culturally appropriate to each of the communities while maintaining conceptual equivalence across communities and societies.

The cultural appropriateness of the game is exemplified by its face validity. It is not likely that participants would have experienced such a strong sense of reality if the stimuli with which they were confronted did not reflect the world in which they lived. The extent to which SIMCAR provided conceptual equivalence is reflected in the comparisons we were able to make. Our measures of comparative values, the strategies of the different participants, indications of sexual differences in power, indications of sex-linked role preferences, and all of the comparisons reported in Chapters 5 and 6 relate to the game's conceptual equivalences. The data yielded commonalities as well as differences between communities and societies, lending further support to the thesis that we were able to measure similar phenomenon in both cultures.

In a real sense, this book provides the data for assessing SIMCAR's utility. We have provided the evidence, it is for the reader to make the judgment.

SOCIALIZATION AND SOCIAL CHANGE IN MEXICO AND IN THE UNITED STATES

Even if we accept the validity of these data, there remains the question of how much they contribute to understanding the course of social change. Throughout this study our concern with social change has been twofold: We have sought to explain how people are socialized to adapt to social changes and how socialization contributes to the types of changes that take place. Underlying this latter concern is the question of the role the individual plays in affecting changes at the societal level. This question has two parts: (*a*) do societal changes require changes in individual actions? (*b*) do individual actions, albeit aggregated over large numbers of people, affect the course of social change?

The answer to the first part of the question is inherent in the concept. Social change is about changes in human relations. Marx's concepts of the interactions between social classes, Töennies principles of gemeinschaft and gesellschaft, Durkheim's notion of mechanical and organic solidarity, Maine's concept of status and contract are all examples of social changes interpreted in terms of alterations of relationships between human actors (see Naegele, 1961, pp. 1216–1218, for a discussion of social change and social relations).

The question of whether or how individual actions produce social changes is more complex and, consequently, the source of greater controversy. For example, consider the evidence that Mexican peasant and blue-collar adolescents have the motivational and behavioral flexibility to seek the best job opportunities wherever they are, to commit themselves to the training necessary for such jobs, and to be willing to defer gratification until they obtain the top positions. These are all behaviors usually associated with upward social mobility. Assume that these data are an accurate representation of this group of Mexicans. Would we then predict that this generation of Mexicans will be upwardly mobile? Clearly, such a prediction would be unwarranted. More than individual motivation, values, and skill are necessary to produce social mobility in a country. These individual attributes are meaningless in the absence of job opportunities which are created by natural resources, investment capital, training facilities, markets, and so forth. But should not such orientations and behaviors contribute to greater worker productivity, producing surpluses that can be reinvested, the net effect being improved job opportunities? The answer would be yes only if we stipulate *other things being equal*. Of course, other things are never equal. In addition to a willing and trained work force, productivity depends on plant efficiency, proper equipment, worker morale, and a variety of hidden costs, such as those associated with payoffs and bribery. As we have seen throughout this book, individual actions are constrained and channeled by conditions in the social structure. The distribution of key resources, access to appropriate information, and the formal and informal interaction networks affect how and with whom individuals will act in any institution or organization.

Does this mean that individual actions are meaningless? Let us return to our hypothetical example. Suppose there is a production system that is efficient and rationalized, with reward systems that are perceived as fair. What would happen to the productivity of such a system if it did not have a willing, committed, and competent work force? Clearly, productivity would be low. The basic fact is that no system, however powerful, can induce change without the passive or active compliance of a large majority of its people (see Tallman, 1976, pp. 194–197).

In brief, it appears that the values, orientations, and behavior patterns of the people who make up a social system are not sufficient in themselves to produce social changes; but, on the other hand, social change will not occur if such values, orientations, and behaviors do not also change.

In sum, the aggregated roles, values, orientations, life goals, and cognitive styles of a population provide a necessary, but not sufficient, set of conditions for explaining the course of social change. It should follow that theories of socialization, designed to predict the identities people seek and the strategies they will use to obtain those identities, can contribute to an explanation of social change.

Our data suggest that Mexico has available to it a generation of people who are ambitious, committed to upward mobility and hard work, willing to exercise control on family size, ready to give up immediate rewards for long term gain and to go wherever there is work. Such a work force seems ideally suited for a country committed to industrial development. As we have seen, Mexico has continued to develop rapidly. Interestingly, nowhere in our reading has this growth been attributed to the industriousness of the Mexican worker.

The problem for Mexico, then, is not its work force, but maintaining a

level of industrial growth that can provide enough jobs. This will be a formidable task. The decline in the birth rate which began in the late 1960s
will not begin to show up in the labor force until the late 1980s, (Cornelius,
1981). Moreover, this decline may be partially offset by the larger number
of adult women who will be seeking employment. Our findings support
such a prediction. As we saw in Chapter 6, the Mexicans were more inclined than the North Americans to emphasize career opportunities for
girls and to place less emphasis on the role of housewife. Thus, even considering a predicted gross national product growth rate of over 8% in the
1980s (Clement & Green, 1978), the discovery and development of large oil
and gas reserves, the migration of millions of Mexicans to the United
States, and the 1–3 million Mexicans who work at least part-time in the
United States, Mexico would still continue to have a backlog of 10 million
unemployed or underemployed workers (Cornelius, 1981). It is estimated
that 31–33 million jobs would have to be created to meet the demand for
new jobs in the next 20 years, but even if this could be accomplished, it
would not affect this backlog. The major developmental plans in Mexico
seem to center on the industrial rather than on the agricultural sector, suggesting continuing migration to urban areas with an increase in the number
and size of shantytowns and the gradual reorganization of Mexican community life.

What will happen to the optimism, ambition, and willingness to defer
gratification under conditions of chronic unemployment? Will the current
generation socialize their children in the belief that they can "better themselves," or will there be greater disaffection and disillusionment? The answers to these questions lie in economic forces, many of them beyond Mexico's control. The world economy, the willingness of the United States to
absorb some of Mexico's surplus labor, and Mexico's own continued rate of
growth all contribute to the availability of more jobs.

This much seems clear. Mexicans have rising expectations that this generation of workers will have a better material life than their parents. It is
more likely than not that for millions these expectations will be frustrated.
If, as Horowitz (1966) claims, "The main fact about the mental set of developing man is that he uniformly blames his shortcomings, his failings, and
his condition on society rather than on himself as in former times [p. 291],"
failure to meet these expectations could result in increased political turmoil. Even if this is not the case, a growing disillusionment and sense of
alienation among the work force in Mexico could contribute to a declining
rate of productivity.

The next 20 years appear to be critical. Economists think that if the Mexican birth rate continues to decline and if the growth of the economy can be
sustained at 6.6–8% per annum, then it will be possible for Mexico to ap-

proximate a full-employment economy. Our theory suggests that should this occur, and the odds are that it will not, the life goals of Mexicans will change, new identities will be sought, new social problems will emerge, and new pressures will be brought to bear on the social system to solve those problems.

The United States is an example. In the winter of 1971–1972, the North Americans represented in this study were fully employed and living under economic conditions that would be described as affluent by most world standards. It was the latter stages of an era in which people thought and talked openly of a postscarcity society. One group of intellectuals, following the theme of the economist Robert Theobold, declared in 1964 that, "The economy of abundance can sustain all citizens in comfort and economic security whether or not they engage in what is commonly reckoned as work (The Ad Hoc Committee on the Triple Revolution, quoted in Bell, 1976, p. 462)."

The economy, then, was not perceived as a problem for the United States families we studied and the "Protestant work ethic" seemed anachronistic. Daniel Bell (1976) attributed this decline of the work ethic to the success of capitalism. "Through mass production and mass consumption, it (capitalism) destroyed the protestant ethic by zealously promoting a hedonistic style of life. By the middle of the twentieth century, capitalism sought to justify itself not by work or property, but by the status badges of material possessions and by the promotion of pleasure (p. 477)." But the promotion of pleasure is ephemeral, especially pleasure that derives from interpersonal relations. Obtaining pleasure through interpersonal relations is particularly difficult in modern industrial urban societies (see Bronfenbrenner, 1972, p. 121).

This seemed to be the problem faced by the United States families we studied. Living in affluence in a bureaucratic and impersonal society, they sought ways to maintain interpersonal closeness. However, rather than seeking new social forms or institutions, they turned to the oldest of social institutions, the family. The family provided a place where interpersonal relations were of primary importance. The emphasis was on the personal rather than the social aspects of identity. Work, though necessary, should provide more than remuneration or status; it should be intrinsically satisfying. The United States family data, in both the interviews and in SIMCAR performance, reflect a wish for gemeinschaft, a return to the closeness and informality of the small community. If these data reflect attitudes of the larger population, they suggest a basis for the growing criticism of bureaucracy, the desire to curb the power of the central government, the growth of suburbs accompanied by the readiness to let the larger central cities decay, and the mounting criticism of "paternalism" in a welfare state. The "culture of narcissism" seemed to be tinged with a sense of nostalgia for a simpler time.

Part of the desire for a simpler world may be the result of information overload. As we noted in Chapters 2 and 3, when people are faced with more information than they can process, they are likely to try to simplify the amount and diversity of information with which they are confronted (Schroder *et al.*, 1967). The postindustrial society, according to Daniel Bell (1976), is an information society. He points out that, "(W)ith the 'exponential' growth of knowledge and the multiplication of fields and interests, the knowledge that any single individual can retain about the variety of events or the span of knowledge inevitably diminishes (p. 468)." A world with so much unprocessed information can make the individual feel as if things are out of his or her control and, consequently, can foster a desire for relationships in a more manageable environment.

Our data suggest that, despite the psychology of abundance, socialization in the United States was less likely to stress an optimistic future than was socialization in Mexico. As we have seen, the United States families emphasized psychological factors and the development of the unique and distinguishing aspects of the child, taking the child's personality and desires seriously. The emphasis among Mexicans was primarily social, concerned with assisting the child to adequately prepare for exigencies extant in the social structure. The greater individualization among North Americans may be partially accounted for by the greater diversity in their social structure. It seemed that United States families and adolescents saw the social structure as being capable of adapting and absorbing any special interests and skills the child might manifest.

Such structural flexibility may have existed under periods of rapid economic expansions, but it does not exist today. In fact, in 1982, as the children we studied are entering the labor market, the psychology of abundance seems to be part of an illusory past. Most Americans today are not poor. They are, however, confronting the consequences of limited economic growth and a constricting job market. Inflation has eroded the real income of the average worker. The basic component of the American dream, a home of one's own, is no longer possible for the average wage earner. The scarcity and increased cost of all types of energy, the pollution of the atmosphere, land, and water and the costs of rectifying such problems, the degenerating quality of life in the major cities of the country, and the growing competition for United States and world markets from foreign industries, have all contributed to a necessary reassessment of opportunity in American society. It is a cliché of the early 1980s that Americans are faced with "hard choices."

At this juncture it is not clear what direction United States society will take, though there is no shortage of advice and predictions. There are those who advocate restricting growth and development (Daly, 1973; Illich, 1971; Mathews, 1972). These analysts claim that continued economic growth not only benefits only the most advantaged, but also it is rapidly depleting irreplaceable natural resources. Some argue that we have already overshot the earth's capacity and are now stealing from the future (Catton, 1980). Implicit in this perspective is the advocacy of a simpler life-style in which specialization, professionalization, and bureaucratization of society are curtailed in favor of establishing local decision making and control (Illich, 1971; Lasch, 1979). "Citizens will have to take the solution of their problems into their own hands. They will have to create their own 'communities of competence.' Only then will the productive capacities of modern capitalism, together with the scientific knowledge that now serves it, come to serve the interests of humanity instead [Lasch, p. 396]."

Others see progress continuing. The current problems of scarcity are temporary and will be overcome now, as in the past, through improved technology.

> Materials can be recycled. New sources of energy (e.g., solar energy) can be tapped. We do not yet have a full inventory of the mineral and metal resources of the earth (in the oceans, in Siberia, the Amazon basin, etc.). Resources are properly measured in economic, not physical, terms, and on the basis of relative costs new investments are made which can irrigate arid land, drain swampy land, clear forests, explore for new resources, or stimulate the process of extraction and transmutation (Bell, 1976, p. 494).

The future for Daniel Bell is almost diametrically opposed to the one advocated by Daly, Mathews, Illich, and Catton. Life in the postindustrial society will grow increasingly more complex; there will be greater specialization, more emphasis on professionalism, and above all, a continuing and increasing production of knowledge. The primary change is from an emphasis on the production of goods to an emphasis on the production of knowledge. Information will be produced and processed technologically. Social organization and bureaucracy will not be lessened but changed, since the management problems will be different. The human being, in Bell's conception, has completed the mastery over nature. Thus, the postindustrial society becomes a "game between persons."

These are the visions of intellectuals. The political processes and the policies implemented through these processes often show little resemblance to such visions. At this writing, United States policy ignores both the question of limiting industrial growth and the development of a scientifically oriented meritocracy in favor of implementing an economic model advocating accelerated industrial growth. The antibureaucratic sentiments of the population are interpreted in policies that would remove regulatory constraints and provide financial incentives to business, thereby encouraging increased resource and industrial development. Huge cuts in government spending are expected to cut taxes, decelerate rising inflation, and "get government off people's backs."

In broad outline, three models of social change seem to be vying for predominance in the United States.[5] A "reduced scale" model which argues for placing constraints on continuing economic development, a "postindustrial" model which predicts a society of continued technological development focusing on the generation of more sophisticated information and information processing, and an "industrial growth" model which seeks an ever increasing expansion of the gross national product. A relevant question to us is how the data collected on the socialization of adolescents in 1971–1972 illuminates our knowledge of the course of events in 1981–1982 and beyond. It is of some interest that none of the critics or theorists mentioned earlier examine socialization processes or outcomes as a component in their explanations of social change. Lasch discusses socialization as part of his critique of current American society, but he does not examine the issue of how current socialization processes might affect the future.

In considering the implications of our data for each of the three models of change discussed above, the reader is reminded that these data are not representative of United States society. Given the heterogeneity of the United States, we cannot reasonably consider the national implications of these findings. Rather, we shall limit ourselves to the question: How would families such as the ones we studied be affected by and affect the changes implied by each of these models?

Theories advocating simplifying society by limiting industrial growth, increasing environmental protection, limiting the size and power of bureaucracies, and emphasizing local control, seem in accord with the gemeinschaft orientation of the Twin Cities families in this study. This reduced scale model is also consonant with the unwillingness of the United States families to commit themselves to geographic mobility or changes in lifestyle, simply for material gain. Even the lack of an optimistic outlook is appropriate for the changes sought in this model. For example, William Catton (1980) proposes that "the less hopeful we assume human prospects to

---

[5] Our choice of perspectives is highly selective and designed primarily to provide contrast. We have avoided using the classic critiques of society emanating from the right or left, since the arguments are generally well known and do not specifically pertain to recent changes in Mexico and the United States, except as they represent specific cases of more general principles.

be, the more likely we are to act in ways that will minimize the hardships ahead for our species (p. 262)."

The degree of individualization and the focus on the personal aspects of identity in the socialization process suggest, however, that the adolescents in the study would find it difficult to adapt to the more limiting and restricting life-styles implicit in the reduced scale model of society. The evidence of psychological flexibility in the families suggests the capacity to adapt to changes that are in accord with life-style goals. Interestingly, if our theory of socialization is correct, a reversion to simpler social structures would eventually result in a gradual loss of psychological flexibility.

The postindustrial society depicted by Daniel Bell clearly does not fit the gemeinschaft orientation of the families we studied. It is a society that continues to grow in complexity, specialization, and bureaucratization. It is first and foremost a meritocracy where familism and interpersonal satisfaction are not as highly regarded as social goals. At the same time the emphasis on interpersonal skills and on psychological understanding of people would prepare the participants in this study to perform in a society that involves "games" between people. The emphasis on specialization is also compatible with a socialization process that allows for the development of a child's unique qualities. Although such a society would not offer opportunities for the adolescents we studied to realize the types of identities they seek, it may be that they would still have learned the performance skills necessary to function effectively.

The model of continued economic growth appears to be least appropriate to the socialization outcomes we observed. Ironically, it seems ideal for the Mexicans. The opportunity structure in this model is determined by market forces rather than by governmental planning.

In this sense it requires the kind of flexibility that SIMCAR called for—a willingness to alter the direction of one's efforts in the face of market information. The trade-off is between doing what one wants to do and doing what will provide the most material benefit. We have seen that the adolescents in the United States sample were reluctant to give up what they wanted to do for material advancement. The emphasis on efficiency in this model suggests that the gemeinschaft values would not be implemented even though these values are often alluded to by the politicians advocating the model.

It is possible that in the 10 years since the data were collected, the changing economy may have so increased people's anxiety about material survival that greater stress would be placed on material achievement as a life goal. Even if this were so, the socialization process for the adolescents we studied was so well underway that it would be unlikely that some aspects of their life strategies would change appreciably. We doubt, for example, that these young people would place work above family or material well-being above personal satisfaction. They evidence sufficient flexibility to react to the realities of changing economic conditions, but their life goals would not change. They may have to work to live, but they do not live to work.

The work ethic may not be as important in a capital intensive economy as it is in a labor intensive one, but productivity in any free economy depends upon a work force that is motivated, future oriented, and ready to defer immediate gratification. The Americans we studied, blue- and white-collar alike, do not meet these requirements.

We began this research anticipating that Mexico and the United States would be changing rapidly and that the social structure faced by the adolescents in this study when they became young adults would be different from the one in which they were being socialized. We began also with the belief that the ways in which people were socialized would have something to do with the course of social change. As we conclude this work, it is apparent that change has been rapid in both countries although the components and rates of these changes were quite different. The changes in Mexico were essentially linear and cumulative. The course was set and the effort consistent. Improve the rate of productivity, and thereby establish the country's political and economic independence. The problems for Mexico in achieving these goals are formidable, perhaps overwhelming, but generally knowable.

Is Mexico succeeding? A study of socialization for social change cannot provide the answer. This research does suggest, however, that one of the problems facing Mexico may be the rising expectations of its poor population. It also suggests that understanding the contribution of socialization to social change requires taking into account the time lag between when socialization occurs and when it begins to influence social change. For example, it may take 20 or 30 years for the full impact of changing orientations to family size to have an effect on the Mexican labor market. Such delays are not easy for the individual to understand or accept. The commitment to work and limit family size is based on self-interest. Failure to attain personal goals despite hard work, deferring immediate gratifications, and generally following the "rules" for advancement, can lead to political unrest. If this occurs the rate of progress is likely to be further delayed.

Unlike Mexico, the changes taking place in the United States do not lend themselves to easy categorization. They are multifaceted, affecting morality, interpersonal relations, social statuses, politics, and economics. The 1970s provided a hiatus in the civil conflict which dominated the late 1960s, but it remained a period of public analysis and self-criticism. "The age of exuberance," to use William Catton's phrase, was over. There was serious debate over the wisdom of the American life-style and a variety of solutions were proposed.

The United States adolescents in our study were being raised to give high priority to their own happiness and satisfactions. Their families were flexible, tolerant, empathic, and understanding. The emphasis was on interpersonal relationships and the importance of the family. In the midst of affluence, material benefits were considered to be less important than enhancing human relationships. These socialization practices could lead to self-indulgence or narcissistic hedonism. They could also lead to a soberly realistic view of the future; a view that was able to recognize the limits to the satisfaction attainable from material goods and the importance of human beings exercising responsibility and concern for one another. Such an outlook could accept the limits of material growth and might view human well-being as more important than political or economic hegemony.

Appendix 1

PRE-EXPERIMENTAL INTERVIEW SCHEDULE

United States Version

We are from the Family Study Center of the University of Minnesota. We appreciate your willingness to give us this time. As we stated in our letter, we are trying to find out how families go about making decisions. Eventually we hope to find ways to help families deal with their everyday problems. Some of the solutions lie within the family, others outside the family. This is a beginning effort.

This interview is preliminary to the main research we plan to do. We want to find out what you think about a number of issues. Most of the questions we will ask are concerned with the things you believe in. There are no right or wrong answers to these questions since people have different opinions.

You should also know that your answers will be completely confidential. Your name is on a card in this folder. After we select the families for the second part of the study we will destroy the cards of everyone but those selected; after we visit the families selected again, we will destroy those cards. Then all we will use are numbers. We will be concerned only with statistics and not with individual families. We want to make this as anonymous as possible in the hope that you will be free to answer the questions as honestly as you can. In order to make this go more quickly we would like to talk with each of you separately.

I.   To start with, I would like to talk about your background.

1. Where were you born?_____
    (Indicate the city and the state.)

2. What year were you born?_____

3. How many children do you have?_____·_____

4. What are the ages of all your children? (Interviewer: Start from
    the oldest child and go to the youngest child. Then indicate
    whether each of the children is a boy or a girl by checking B or
    G in the boxes below the ages. Circle child to be used in the
    game.)

Oldest   Youngest

B	G	B	G	B	G	B	G	B	G	B	G	B	G	B	G	B	G	B	G	B	G	B	G	B	G	B	G

5. Are there other relatives or persons living in the household be-
    sides the immediate family?

    Yes_____   No_____

    If yes, what is their relationship?

    _____

6. How far did you go in school?

    1. Some grade school
    2. Completed grade school
    3. Some high school
    4. Completed high school
    5. Completed high school and also had other training, but not
        college (e.g., technical training, business school)
    6. Some college
    7. Completed college
    8. Some graduate work
    9. Graduate degree, M.D., M.A., Ph.D., etc.

7a. (Give card to respondent)
    Would you circle the number that comes closest to showing your
    total family income from last year.
    (Put card in envelope)

7b. (Give card to respondent)
    Would you please circle the number that comes closest to showing
    the individual contributions of the husband, the wife, and the
    children, to the total family income.
    (Put card in envelope)

8. For the most part, where was your childhood and adolescence spent?

   1. Farm
   2. Fringe area -- lived in country but father employed in town
   3. Small town -- up to 2499
   4. Small town -- 2500 - 24,999
   5. Large town -- 25,000 - 100,000
   6. Urban community in metropolitan area of 100,000
   7. Suburban community in a metropolitan area of 100,000 or more

9. What is your religious preference?_____

10. Where were your parents born?

    Father_____

    Mother_____

11. Where were your grandparents born?

	Mother's Side	Father's Side
Grandfather		
Grandmother		

12. Would you tell me what your usual occupation is? (For wife ask her occupation)

    _____

    _____

    (Write in sufficient detail. If necessary ask respondent to describe what he does.)

13. Do you work?

    1. Part-time?   4. No (check housewives)
    2. Full time?   5. Unemployed?
    3. Seasonally or occasionally?   6. Work in family business
                                              without pay?

14. How good a chance do you think you have of getting ahead in your present job?

    1. A good chance
    2. A fairly good chance
    3. Not much chance

15. What is the best position you ever expect to have?

    _____(one phrase)

16a. Is there another job you would rather have than the one you have now?

1. Yes   2. No

16b. If yes, what kind of job?

_____(one phrase)

17. If you were to choose a different kind of work, which of the following would be most important to you?

a. _____More money

b. _____An interesting job

c. _____A job in another location

d. _____A job that you are better trained for

(Interviewer: Mark 1 for most important and then reread remaining 3 items asking which would be next most important. Mark 2 before that item and reread again for positions 3 and 4.)

18. (Interviewer note: Have wife answer for herself, not for husband.)

We would like to know the kinds of things that might interfere with you (or your husband's) taking a better job. Suppose you (or your husband) were offered a much better job. Would you tell us if any of the following situations might stop you from making the change, be a serious consideration but not stop you, or would not matter at all. (Note: Have wife respond for herself.)

		1-Might stop	2-Serious but not stop	3-Would not matter
a.	Endanger your health	1	2	3
b.	Leave your family for some time	1	2	3
c.	Move around the country a lot	1	2	3
d.	Leave your community	1	2	3
e.	Leave your friends	1	2	3
f.	Give up leisure time	1	2	3
g.	Keep quiet about political views	1	2	3
h.	Keep quiet about religious views	1	2	3
i.	Learn a new routine	1	2	3
j.	Work harder than you are now	1	2	3
k.	Take on more responsibility	1	2	3

19. Have you ever felt that somehow you have allowed opportunities for success to slip through your fingers? (Wife responds for herself.)

1. Never

2. Seldom

3. Often

4. Do not know

5. Never had opportunity for success

II. In every family somebody decides such things as where the family should live and so on. Many families talk things over first, but the <u>final</u> decision often has to be made by the husband or wife or some other relative. Could you tell us who you believe SHOULD (emphasize should) make the final decision in the following situations? (Mention alternatives after every item.)

1. What job the husband should take

2. How you are going to spend your time together

3. How the children are raised

4. Which friends you see the most

5. The best place for the family to live

6. About the wife working outside the home

7. How the money is used

8. About the number of children wanted

		Husband always	Husband more than wife	Husband and wife exactly. the same	Wife more than husband	Wife always
1.	Husband's job	1	2	3	4	5
2.	Time together	1	2	3	4	5
3.	Raising children	1	2	3	4	5
4.	Friends seen	1	2	3	4	5
5.	Family home	1	2	3	4	5
6.	Wife's work	1	2	3	4	5
7.	Money	1	2	3	4	5
8.	Children	1	2	3	4	5

		Relative (specify)	N.A.
1.	Husband's job	6 _____	7
2.	Time together	6 _____	7
3.	Raising children	6 _____	7
4.	Friends seen	6 _____	7
5.	Family home	6 _____	7
6.	Wife's work	6 _____	7
7.	Money	6 _____	7
8.	Children wanted	6 _____	7

III. Now I would like to read you three sets of statements. I want you to tell me which you believe is most important to you. Even though you think they are all important please choose one that is <u>most</u> important, then the statement that is next most important.

    A. These are the statements - which is most important to you?

        1. Making certain that the community I live in is safe

        2. Controlling my own behavior

        3. Making certain my children learn to behave properly and responsibly

    Which is most important?_____(write in number)

    (Reread remaining statements)

    Which is next most important?_____(write in number)

    B. I will now read you three more statements.

        1. Getting along well with my family

        2. Getting along well with my neighbors

        3. Feeling good about myself

    Which is most important?_____(write in number)

    (Reread remaining statements)

    Which is next most important?_____(write in number)

    C. Here are three more statements.

        1. Making a lot of money for myself and my family

        2. Making certain my parents are well cared for

        3. Helping to make everyone in my community well-off

    Which is most important?_____(write in number)

(Reread remaining statements)

Which is next most important?_____(write in number)

D. This is the last set of statements.

  1. My own happiness
  2. The happiness of my family
  3. A happy and friendly community to live in

Which is most important?_____(write in number)

(Reread remaining statements)

Which is next most important?_____(write in number)

IV. Here are a number of different situations: Each requires that a choice be made.

  1. Two boys, aged 15 and 12, are helping their father fix the roof of the house. The father tells them he will take the one who does the best work to town. He is only able to take one child. Both boys want to go badly and work very hard. The father cannot decide who did the best work. Who should he take to town?

The older	The younger	Neither
1	2	3

  1a. Why?_____
         (one sentence only)

  2. A husband and a wife have an argument as to how to spend some extra money for fixing the house. As the argument goes on, the husband realizes his wife is right but if he gives in to her he feels he will lose respect. What should he do?

Give in to his wife	Maintain his own opinion
1	2

  2a. Why should he do this?_____

  3. An uncle wants one of two sons in a family to go to work for him. It is a job which pays well and both boys want to go. The younger boy has had experience in this kind of work. The older boy has no experience and has not shown an interest in this type of work before but needs the money badly. Who should go?

The younger	The older
1	2

  3a. Why?_____
         (one sentence only)

4. There is money in a town to send one student to college. Two of the best students apply. One is the son of the mayor and if he gets the scholarship, he will probably be very influential in the town. The other comes from a family which is poor and not respected in the town. Who should get to go?

The mayor's son   The poor boy
       1   2

4a. Why do you think _____should get to go?_____
    _____(one sentence only)

5. (United States) A church is giving a festival. The wealthy members of the congregation give a great deal of money. The poor members have donated hours of time and hard work. The congregation usually gives an award to the person who has contributed most to the success of the festival. Should the award go to the person who has contributed the most money or the person who has worked the hardest?

Contributed most money   Worked the hardest
         1   2

5a. Why?_____
         (one sentence only)

5b. Which contribution do you think was most valuable?

Most money   Worked hardest
     1   2

6. Two people are working in the same factory. One has worked there for many years – the other came only recently but gets more work done. Who should get more pay?

The one who has worked in the   The man who gets more work
plant longer   done
         1   2

6a. Why?_____
         (one sentence only)

7. Imagine you own a farm and you want to hire one person to help you. Two people who are equally good workers apply. One is a relative who is not very poor. The other is a stranger who is very poor. To whom would you give the job?

The relative   The poor stranger
     1   2

7a. Why?_____
         (one sentence only)

8. Two rural communities apply for government funds to improve farm production. One community has shown it can do very well on limited resources and has a higher level of production than the other community which is extremely poor. Which community should get the funds?

The one with a high level of
production _____   The poor community
              1   2

8a. Why would you give the funds to _____community?

_____
(one sentence only)

9. Suppose you were responsible for hiring a new worker in a plant. Two people apply, both unmarried and both equally qualified. One is a woman, the other a man. If you were forced to choose which would you hire?

Woman   Man
  1   2

9a. Why do you think you would make this choice?_____
_____(one sentence only)

10. Two men are arguing about politics. One is older, the other is highly educated. Which man do you think you would be more inclined to agree with?

Older man   Educated Man
    1   2

10a. Why?_____
          (one sentence only)

11. Imagine you have a daughter, age 20, and a son, age 17, and both of them need money to stay in college. You have only enough money for one of them. Who would you give the money to?

The daughter   The son
     1   2

11a. Why?_____
          (one sentence only)

12. Suppose you own a business and two people come to you for a job. One is your brother's daughter, the other is a man who is a stranger. Both are equally qualified. Who would you give the job to?

Your brother's daughter   The man who is a stranger
           1   2

12a. Why?_____
          (one sentence only)

V.   The following questions have to do with your view of the ideal marriage. For each question, would you tell us whether you think it is: Essential; usually desirable; makes no difference; usually not desirable; not desirable.

		Essential	Usually desirable	No differece	Usually not desirable	Definitely not desirable
1.	That the husband should be the social equal of his wife?	1	2	3	4	5
2.	That the wife should be the social equal of her husband?	1	2	3	4	5
3.	That the husband should be at least equal to his wife in intelligence?	1	2	3	4	5
4.	That the husband and wife should have similar interests, such as TV, movies, books, etc.? (Interviewer: give examples)	1	2	3	4	5
5.	That husband and wife should each respect the other's religious, political, or ethical convictions and not try to change them?	1	2	3	4	5
6.	Importance of the wife's devoting the major part of her interests and energies to her home and family.	1	2	3	4	5
7.	Importance of the home being a place where family members and their friends can relax and enjoy themselves at all times.	1	2	3	4	5
8.	Importance of having children in the family.	1	2	3	4	5
9.	Importance of the children being good and well-behaved at all times.	1	2	3	4	5
0.	Importance of the children growing up in a home atmosphere in which their ideas and feelings are considered and talked over in making family decisions.	1	2	3	4	5
1.	Importance of family members taking part in many recreational activities together.	1	2	3	4	5

B. Who do you think (the husband or the wife) should have greater
   influence in each of the following areas? (Then interviewer
   goes to...)

		Husband much more	Husband somewhat more	About the same	Wife somewhat more	Wife much more
1.	Relationship with relatives	1	2	3	4	5
2.	Choice of friends	1	2	3	4	5
3.	Recreation and social activities	1	2	3	4	5
4.	Running the household	1	2	3	4	5

VI. 1. (If daughter in the family)
        Which do you think is more important for your daughter(s)?
        (Interviewer note: Mark 1 for most important and reread remaining
        3 items asking which would be next most important. Mark 2 before
        that item and reread again for positions 3 and 4.)

    a._____A good job

    b._____A college education

    c._____A good marriage

    d._____A religious vocation devoting one's life
                            to God

   2. (If son in the family) How far would you like your son(s) to go
       in school?

       1. Some high school?_____

       2. High school graduation?_____

       3. Some college or job training?_____

       4. Graduate from college?_____

       5. Do not know?_____

   3. (If a daughter in the family) How far would you like your daughter
       to go in school?

       1. Some high school?_____

       2. High school graduation?_____

       3. Business or trade school?_____

       4. Some college?_____

       5. Graduated from college?_____

       6. Other?_____

       7. Do not know?_____

VII. A. I now want to show you a series of 10 pictures depicting occupations. Suppose we lived in a perfect world and your son (daughter)
could have any job he or she wanted, would you pick the picture
that represents the job you would <u>most</u> like him or her to have.
Then the job you would like him or her to have next and so on until you have only one picture left.
(Interviewee must choose between son and daughter.

1. _____		6. _____	
2. _____		7. _____	
3. _____		8. _____	
4. _____		9. _____	
5. _____		10. _____	

B. I will show you each of the pictures again and I would like you to
tell me whether you think your son's or daughter's chances of getting such a job are (good, so/so, poor), under present conditions
assuming your child wants the job very much and will work hard to
get it.

Card #	good	so/so	poor
1. _____	1	2	3
2. _____	1	2	3
3. _____	1	2	3
4. _____	1	2	3
5. _____	1	2	3
6. _____	1	2	3
7. _____	1	2	3
8. _____	1	2	3
9. _____	1	2	3
10. _____	1	2	3

C. Finally, would you take the pictures one more time and pick out
the job that you think your son or daughter is <u>most likely</u> to
have when he or she grows up. Then the job he or she is next
<u>most likely</u> to have all the way down to the job he or she is
least likely to have.

1. _____
2. _____
3. _____
4. _____
5. _____
6. _____
7. _____

      8. _____

      9. _____

    10. _____

VII. Now I would like to talk with you about different beliefs people have.

    1. <u>Child Training</u>

        Some people were talking about the way children should be brought up. Here are three different ideas.

        1. Some people say that children should be taught well the traditions of the past (the ways of the old people). They
(Past) believe the old ways are best, and that it is when children do not follow them too much that things go wrong.

        2. Some people say that children should be taught some of the old traditions (ways of the old people), but it is wrong to insist that they stick to these ways. These people believe
(Pres) that it is necessary for children always to learn about and take on whatever of the new ways will best help them to get along in the world today.

        3. Some people do not believe children should be taught much about past traditions (the ways of the old people) at all except as an interesting story of what has gone on before.
(Fut) These people believe that the world goes along best when children are taught the things that will make them want to find out for themselves new ways of doing things to replace the old.

      Which of these people had the best idea about how children should be taught?_____

      Considering again all three ideas, which would most other persons in _____ say had the better idea?_____

    2. <u>Expectations about Change</u>

        Three older people were talking about what they thought their children would have when they were grown. Here is what each one said:

        3. One said: I really expect my children to have more than I
(Fut) have had if they work hard and plan right. There are always good chances for people who try.

        2. The second one said: I do not know whether my children will be better off, worse off, or just the same. Things always
(Pres) go up and down even if one works hard, so we cannot really tell.

1. The third one said: I expect my children to have just about
   the same as I have had or bring things back as they once
(Past) were. It is their job to work hard and find ways to keep
   things going as they have been in the past.

Which of these people do you think had the best idea?_____

Which of these three people would most other _____your age think
had the best idea?_____

3. Ceremonial Innovation

Some people in a community like your own say that the religious
ceremonies (the church services) were changing from what they
used to be.

3. Some people were really pleased because of the changes in
   religious ceremonies. They felt that new ways are usually
(Fut) better than old ones, and they like to keep everything--
   even ceremonies--moving ahead.

1. Some people were unhappy because of the change. They felt
   that religious ceremonies should be kept exactly--in every
(Past) way--as they had been in the past.

2. Some people felt that the old ways for religious ceremonies
   were best but you just cannot hang on to them. It makes
(Pres) life easier just to accept some changes as they come along.

Which of these three said most nearly what you would believe is
right?_____

Which of the three would most other _____say was most right?

4. Water Allocation

The government is going to help a community like yours to get
more water by redrilling and cleaning out a community well. The
government officials suggest that the community should have a
plan for dividing the extra water, but do not say what kind of
plan. Since the amount of extra water that may come in is not
known, people feel differently about planning.

1. Some say that whatever water comes in should be divided just
(Past) about like water was always divided in the past.

3. Others want to work out a really good plan ahead of time for
(Fut) dividing whatever water comes in.

2. Still others want to just wait until the water comes in be-
(Pres) fore deciding on how it will be divided.

Which of these ways do you think is usually best in cases like this?

Which of the three ways do you think most other persons in _____
would think best?_____

IX.   PEOPLE HAVE DIFFERENT OPINIONS ABOUT THE STATEMENTS IN THIS LIST.

WOULD YOU TELL US IF YOU DISAGREE OR AGREE WITH THEM? MARK THE "1"
IF YOU DISAGREE, THE "2" IF YOU ARE NOT SURE, AND THE "3" IF YOU
AGREE.

		DISAGREE	NOT SURE	AGREE
1.	If a teenager can get a good job, he is foolish to finish high school.	1	2	3
2.	If a fellow can get a good job when he graduates from high school, he is foolish to go to college.	1	2	3
3.	It makes good sense to take a job with good prospects for the future even if it would pay much less than the other jobs available.	1	2	3
4.	People should be willing to do without some of the things they feel they need in order to save up money.	1	2	3
5.	The money you save gives you at least as good a feeling as things you buy.	1	2	3
6.	Money is made to spend, not save.	1	2	3

7. From what you have experienced, who would you say usually wins
    in settling arguments?
    1. The tough and strong   2. The smart and tactful

8. When you get angry at a person, do you generally prefer:
    1. To let your temper quiet down before you try to settle
        the argument
    2. To settle matters right away

9. Teenagers have to be careful about the behavior of the crowd
    they go with.
    1. Yes   2. No

10. I think the ideal age for a boy to marry is:
    1. 16 or less   4. 19   7. 23 or 24
    2. 17   5. 20   8. 25 or 26
    3. 18   6. 21 or 22   9. 27 or older

11. I think the ideal age for a girl to marry is:
    1. 16 or less   4. 19   7. 23 or 24
    2. 17   5. 20   8. 25 or 26
    3. 18   6. 21 or 22   9. 27 or older

12. If you won a big prize, say $2000 dollars, what would you do?
    1. Spend most of it right away on things you and your family want
    2. Save most of it for education or for a business

X. Does your child (aged 12-15) play games - other than sports or other physical activities?

1. Yes_____   2. No _____

If yes, can you name some of them?

_____

XI. QUESTION TO BE ASKED AT THE END OF EVERYTHING.

As we explained to you in our letter, a number of families will be selected to participate in the second part of our study. At a later date, we will ask these families to participate in a game. This game will be played by the parents and the child in the lab where we will observe you playing the game. Families selected for this part of the study will receive up to $15 for participating. This session takes about an hour to complete. If your family is selected, would you be interested in participating?

_____ YES   _____ NO

INTRODUCCION

Mexican Version

EL INSTITUTO MEXICANO DE ESTUDIOS SOCIALES, A.C., está realizando un estudio de cómo las familias toman decisiones.

Este cuestionario tiene por objeto captar la realidad social y las opiniones de los mismos padres de familia, en vistas a la elaboración de planes de mejoramiento familiar.

La realización de este estudio no tiene ninguna relación con instituciones gubernamentales, comerciales, ni de otro tipo. Su carácter es exclusivamente científico y cultural.

Por todo ésto, no interesa la identidad del entrevistado sino la verdad de sus respuestas. Estas son una cooperación extraordinaria para el conocimiento y el mejoramiento de la familia mexicana.

Se agradece mucho la colaboración de todas las personas a quienes les hatocado, por sorteo al azar, el quedar incluídos en la muestra de esta encuesta social.

IDENTIFICACIÓN   1.01.- No. de Cuestionario_____

Nombre: _____

Dirección:

Calle:_____

Colonia:_____

FECHA_____

I.1.02.   Sexo.

   1. Masculino

   2. Femenino

1.03.   Localidad.

   1. Zacapu

   2. Tiríndaro

   3. Naranja de Tapia

   4. Tariácuri

   5. Tarejero

1.04.   ¿En qué año nació Ud.? _____

   Entonces ¿cuántos años tiene? _____

   1. Menos de 30 años

   2. de 30 a 34 años

   3. de 35 a 39 años

   4. de 40 a 44 años

   5. de 45 a 49 años

   6. de 50 a 54 años

   7. de 55 a 59 años

   8. de 60 y más años

¿En qué localidad y Estado nació?:

	Localidad	Municipio	Estado
1.05. Usted			
1.06. Su Papá			
1.07. Su Mamá			

1. Misma localidad.
2. Localidad rural en el mismo municipio.
3. Localidad urbana en el mismo municipio.
4. Localidad rural en otro municipio del mismo Estado.
5. Localidad urbana en otro municipio del mismo Estado.
6. Localidad rural en otro Estado.
7. Localidad urbana en otro Estado.
8. En el extranjero.
9. No sabe, sin información.

Ahora, ¿en qué localidad viven?

	Localidad	Municipio	Estado	Falleció
1.08. Su Papá				
1.09. Su Mamá				

1. Misma localidad en que nació.
2. Localidad rural en el mismo municipio.
3. Localidad urbana en el mismo municipio.
4. Localidad rural en otro municipio del mismo Estado.
5. Localidad urbana en otro municipio del mismo Estado.
6. Localidad rural en otro Estado.
7. Localidad urbana en otro Estado.
8. En el extranjero.
9. No sabe, sin información, no se aplica.

1.10. ¿En dónde pasó la mayor parte de su infancia?

      1. en el mismo lugar

      2. otro... ¿cuál _____

                      Localidad   Municipio   Estado

      (Nota: Si es divorciado o separado o viudo se termina la encuesta).

1.11. ¿Cuál es su estado civil actual?

      1. Casado Iglesia

      2. Casado Civil

      3. Casado Iglesia - Civil

      4. Unión Libre

      (Nota: Para mujeres solamente).

1.12. ¿Cuántos hijos vivos tiene Ud.?

      1. uno

      2. dos

      3. tres

      4. cuatro

      5. cinco

      6. seis

      7. siete

      8. ocho

      9. nueve y más

      (Nota: Para mujeres solamente).

1.13. ¿Qué edades tienen sus hijos? (años cumplidos)

El Mayor   El Menor

F	M	F	M	F	M	F	M	F	M	F	M	F	M	F	M	F	M	F	M	F	M	F	M

1.14. ¿Hasta qué año de estudios llegó Ud.? _____

    1. Ninguno

    2. Ninguno, pero sabe leer y escribir

    3. Primaria incompleta

    4. Primaria completa

    5. Secundaria incompleta

    6. Secundaria completa o equivalente

    7. Escuela técnica (Agropecuaria o Comercial, etc.)

    8. Normal

    9. Preparatoria incompleta

   10. Preparatoria completa

   11. Carrera profesional incompleta

   12. Carrera profesional completa

1.15. ¿Cuántas personas de la familia trabajan ahora?

    1. uno

    2. dos

    3. tres

    4. cuatro

    5. cinco

    6. seis

    7. siete

    8. ocho

    9. nueve y más

(Nota: Al campesino se le preguntará el número de cosechas que
obtuvo el año pasado y cuánto obtuvo en cada una, calculando y
dividiéndolo entre 12 meses).

1.16. ¿Cuánto gana cada una mensualmente?

Padre: _____

Madre: _____

Hijos: _____

_____

_____

Otros: _____

_____ Suma Total

(Sumar el ingreso mensual de cada miembro)

1. Menos de 100	11. de 4500 a 4999
2. de 100 a 490	12. de 5000 a 5499
3. de 500 a 999	13. de 5500 a 5999
4. de 1000 a 1499	14. de 6000 a 6499
5. de 1500 a 1999	15. de 6500 a 6999
6. de 2000 a 2499	16. de 7000 a 7499
7. de 2500 a 2999	17. de 7500 a 7999
8. de 3000 a 3499	18. de 8000 y más
9. de 3500 a 3999	19. No sabe
10. de 4000 a 4499	20. No quiere proporcionar el dato

(Entrevistador: Describa ampliamente.)

1.17. ¿Cuál es su ocupación actual?

_____

_____

_____

1.18. ¿Tiene algún otro trabajo?

    1. Si - -¿Cuál es? _____

    2. No.

> 1. No trabaja
>
> 2. Desempleado
>
> 3. Trabaja con esposo sin remuneración
>
> 4. Artesano
>
> 5. Campesino
>
> 6. Obrero no calificado
>
> 7. Obrero calificado
>
> 8. Empleado en servicios
>
> 9. Empleado en un Comercio (dependiente)
>
> 10. Empleado en una Oficina
>
> 11. Comerciante (dueño)
>
> 12. Profesionista

1.19. ¿Cuántas horas trabaja Ud. al día? _____ hrs.

Para Hombres

1. Desempleado	1. No trabaja (labores del hogar)
2. Por temporadas u ocasionalmente	2. Trabaja sin remuneración (mujeres que ayudan al marido)
3. Medio tiempo	3. Por temporadas u ocasionalmente (con remuneración)
4. Tiempo completo	4. Medio tiempo (con remuneración)
	5. Tiempo completo (con remuneración)

1.20. En el trabajo que hace actualmente, ¿qué oportunidades cree que tiene para progresar?

    1. Buenas

    2. Regulares

    3. Malas

1.21. ¿Cuál es el mejor puesto que podría Ud. alcanzar? _____

_____

1.22. ¿Hay algún otro trabajo que le gustaría tener en lugar del que tiene ahora?

1. Si – – – – – ¿Cuál es? (especifique)_____

_____

2. No

(Enumere los trabajos por orden de importancia del 1 a 4)

1.23. Si pudiera escoger otro trabajo, ¿cuál sería más importante para usted?

_____ Un trabajo en que ganara más dinero.

_____ Un trabajo que fuera más interesante.

_____ Un trabajo que estuviera en un lugar mejor.

_____ Un trabajo para el que estuviera preparado.

Si le ofrecieran a Ud. o a su esposo un trabajo mejor ¿qué haría usted en el caso de que

	Lo aceptaría sin reservas.	Lo aceptaría con reservas.	No lo aceptaría
1.24. Su salud peligrara.	1	2	3
1.25. Tuviera que dejar a su familia por algún tiempo.	1	2	3
1.26. Tuviera que viajar frecuentemente.	1	2	3
1.27. Tuviera que cambiarse a otro lugar.	1	2	3
1.28. Tuviera que dejar a sus amigos.	1	2	3
1.29. Tuviera menos tiempo para divertirse.	1	2	3
1.30. Tuviera que callar sus opiniones políticas.	1	2	3
1.31. Tuviera que callar sus opiniones religiosas.	1	2	3
1.32. Tuviera que cambiar a una nueva rutina.	1	2	3
1.33. Tuviera un trabajo más intenso que el que tiene ahora.	1	2	3
1.34. Tuviera más responsabilidades.	1	2	3

(Nota: La esposa debe responder por si misma.)

1.35. ¿Alguna vez ha sentido que ha dejado pasar buenas oportunidades?

    1. Nunca

    2. Pocas veces

    3. Muchas veces

    4. Siente que nunca ha tenido buenas oportunidades.

    5. No sabe

1.36. ¿Tiene Ud. alguna religión?

    1. Si – – – – – – ¿Cuál es? _____

    2. No – – – – – – Dice que es solo "Creyente"

    3. No – – – – – – Ninguna

II.   En todas las familias existen momentos y situaciones en los que se tienen que tomar decisiones, y éstas a veces son tomadas por la esposa y a veces por el esposo. ¿Me podría decir quién debería de tomar decisiones en su familia en los siguientes casos?

¿Quién debería de tomar la última decisión al:	El esposo	La esposa	Los dos juntos	Otra persona (especificar-quién)	No se aplica
2.01. Escoger su trabajo actual (esposo).	1	2	3	4	9
2.02. Pasar su tiempo juntos (por ejemplo el escoger a dónde ir de paseo).	1	2	3	4	9
2.03. Educar a los hijos en la casa.	1	2	3	4	9
2.04. Visitar a sus amistades.	1	2	3	4	9
2.05. Tener o no tener más hijos.	1	2	3	4	9
2.06. Decidir que la esposa trabaje o no, ahora fuera del hogar.	1	2	3	4	9
2.07. Gastar el dinero.	1	2	3	4	9
2.08. Escoger el lugar donde vivir.	1	2	3	4	9

III. (Para la siguiente serie de preguntas leer las 3 alternativas y anotar cuál es la más importante).

    3.01. ¿Qué le parece a Ud. más importante?

        1. Que haya tranquilidad en la localidad en donde vive, o

        2. Que Ud. se comporte bien ante los demás, o

        3. Que sus hijos se porten bien y cumplan con sus responsabilidades.

    3.02. ¿Qué le parece a Ud. más importante?

        1. Llevarse bien con su Familia, o

        2. Llevarse bien con sus vecinos, o

        3. Sentirse contento consigo mismo.

    3.03. ¿Qué le interesa más?

        1. Ganar mucho dinero para Ud. y sus hijos, o

        2. Asegurarse de que no les falte nada a sus padres, o

        3. Ayudar a que todos en su comunidad estén bien.

    3.04. Para Ud. ¿qué tiene mayor importancia?

        1. Su propia felicidad, o

        2. La felicidad de su familia, o

        3. La felicidad de la comunidad en donde vive.

IV. A continuación le voy a leer diferentes situaciones que requieren tomar una decisión.

4.01. Dos jóvenes de 15 y 12 años están ayudando a su papá a arreglar el techo de su casa. El papá les dice que llevará a pasear al que trabaje mejor de los dos. Sólo puede llevar a uno de sus hijos. Como los dos tienen muchas ganas de ir, trabajan mucho. El papá no sabe a cuál llevar. ¿A quién cree Ud. que deberá llevar a pasear?

El Mayor	El Menor	Ninguno
1	2	3

¿Por qué? _____

_____

4.02. Un matrimonio tiene una discusión acerca de cómo gastar un poco de dinero que les sobró. En un momento de la discusión el marido se da cuenta de que su mujer tiene la razón, pero siente que si se la da, perderá respeto. ¿Ud. qué cree que debe hacer el marido?

Darle la razón a su esposa	Sostener su propia opinión
1	2

¿Por qué piensa así? _____

_____

4.03. Un carpintero quiere que uno de sus sobrinos se vaya a trabajar con él. Como se trata de un trabajo que paga bien, ambos jóvenes quieren ir. El menor de los dos ya ha tenido experiencia en este tipo de trabajo. El mayor no ha tenido experiencia ni había mostrado interés en este tipo de trabajo, pero necesita el dinero. ¿A quién cree Ud. que se le deba dar el trabajo?

Al Menor	Al Mayor
1	2

¿Por qué? _____

_____

4.04. Una comunidad tiene dinero para mandar solamente a estudiar a una persona a la Universidad. Dos de los mejores estudiantes del pueblo quieren ir. Uno de ellos es hijo del Presidente Municipal y si le dan la beca, probablemente llegue a ser muy influyente en la comunidad. El otro estudiante viene de una familia pobre del pueblo. ¿A quién cree Ud. que se le deba dar el dinero para que se vaya a estudiar?

Al hijo del Presidente Municipal   Al hijo de la familia pobre

        1   2

¿Por qué? _____

_____

4.05. Un pueblo celebra cada año la festividad de su santo patrón. Los ricos contribuyen con dinero y los pobres con su tiempo y trabajo. ¿Qué contribución cree Ud. que sea la más valiosa?

Dinero   Trabajo

    1   2

¿Por qué? _____

_____

4.06. Dos personas están trabajando en la misma fábrica. Uno lleva trabajando ahí muchos años. El otro acaba de entrar pero produce más. ¿Quién cree Ud. que deba de recibir un mejor salario?

El que lleva más años en la fábrica   El que produce más

         1   2

¿Por qué? _____

_____

4.07. Imagínese que Ud. es dueño de un rancho y quiere emplear a un trabajador para que le ayude. Dos personas están dispuestas a trabajar. Una de ellas es pariente suyo que no es muy pobre y la otra persona es un extraño que sí está muy pobre. ¿A quién le daría Ud. el trabajo?

Al pariente   Al extraño pobre

    1   2

¿Por qué? _____

_____

4.08. Dos comunidades solicitan la ayuda del gobierno para mejorar su producción de maíz. Una comunidad ha demostrado ya, que puede producir más maíz con pocos recursos mientras que la otra comunidad produce menos y es mucho más pobre. ¿A qué comunidad cree Ud. que le debería ayudar el gobierno?

A la que produce más maíz   A la comunidad pobre

           1   2

¿Por qué? _____

_____

4.09. Supongamos que Ud. fuera el encargado de emplear a un trabajador en una tienda y que tiene que escoger entre dos personas que quieren el trabajo. Las dos son solteras e igualmente calificadas. Una de ellas es una mujer y la otra es un hombre. ¿A quién emplearía Ud.?

Mujer   Hombre

  1   2

¿Por qué? _____

_____

4.10. Dos hombres están discutiendo de política. Uno de ellos es más viejo y el otro ha tenido una buena educación. ¿Con quién estaría Ud. más de acuerdo?

Con el hombre más viejo   Con el hombre con educación

       1   2

¿Por qué? _____

_____

4.11. Imagínese que Ud. tiene una hija de 20 años y un hijo de 17 con la misma inteligencia. Los dos necesitan dinero para seguir estudiando. Sin embargo, Ud. sólo tiene dinero para enviar a la escuela a uno de ellos. ¿A quién le daría Ud. el dinero?

A la hija   Al hijo

  1   2

¿Por qué? _____

_____

4.12. Suponga que Ud. es dueño de un negocio y que dos personas solicitan trabajo. Una de estas personas es su sobrina y la otra es
un hombre desconocido. Los dos están igualmente calificados para el puesto. ¿A quién se lo daría Ud.?

A la hija de su hermano   Al hombre desconocido

         1   2

¿Por qué? _____

_____

V.

5.01. Ahora le quiero enseñar una serie de fotografías de distintas
ocupaciones. Suponga que vive en un mundo perfecto en el cual
su hijo-a podrá conseguir el trabajo que desee. Sería Ud. tan
amable en escoger la fotografía que represente el trabajo que a
Ud. más le gustaría que tuviera. Después, el trabajo que le gustaría en segundo lugar y así, sucesivamente, hasta que quede so-
lo una fotografía.

Fotografía:

1º _____

2º _____

3º _____

4º _____

5º _____

6º _____

7º _____

8º _____

9º _____

10º _____

5.02. Ahora pensando en sus actuales condiciones de vida, quisiera saber qué oportunidades cree Ud. que tendrá su hijo-a de conseguir ese trabajo.

Fotografía:	Buenas oportunidades	Regulares oportunidades	Malas oportunidades
1º	1	2	3
2º	1	2	3
3º	1	2	3
4º	1	2	3
5º	1	2	3
6º	1	2	3
7º	1	2	3
8º	1	2	3
9º	1	2	3
10º	1	2	3

5.03. Por último, quisiera que revise las fotografías una vez más para que escoja el trabajo que Ud. cree que su hijo (a) en verdad va a tener cuando sea grande. Después, escoja el trabajo que estaría en 2º lugar, y así, sucesivamente, hasta escoger aquel trabajo que Ud. menos cree que el o ella desempeñará.

Fotografía:

1º _____

2º _____

3º _____

4º _____

5º _____

7º _____

8º _____

9º _____

10º _____

VI.

A. Las siguientes preguntas tratan de su opinión sobre el matrimonio
ideal. Nos gustaría saber qué piensa Ud. acerca de:

Piensa Ud. que ésto:	Es muy importante	Es poco importante	No es nada importante
6.01. ¿Qué el marido tenga por lo menos la misma inteligencia que su esposa?	1	2	3
6.02. ¿Qué tanto el marido como la esposa tengan gustos parecidos? (ejem.: ver el mismo programa de T.V.)	1	2	3
6.03. ¿Qué tanto el marido como la esposa respetan lo que el otro piensa sin que trate de cambiarlo?	1	2	3
6.04. ¿Qué la esposa dedique la mayor parte de su tiempo a su hogar y familia?	1	2	3
6.05. ¿Qué el hogar sea un lugar en donde los miembros de la familia y sus amigos estén a gusto en todo momento?	1	2	3
6.06. ¿Qué tengan hijos en la familia?	1	2	3
6.07. ¿Qué los hijos sean buenos y se porten bien en todo momento.	1	2	3
6.08. ¿Qué en las decisiones familiares se tome en cuenta las ideas y opiniones de los hijos?	1	2	3
6.09. ¿Qué el marido, la esposa y los hijos se diviertan juntos?	1	2	3

B.   ¿quién piensa Ud. que debería tener mayor influencia:

	El marido la mayoría de las veces	Tanto el esposo como la esposa por igual	La esposa la mayoría de las veces
6.10. En las relaciones con los parientes?	1	2	3
6.11. En la elección de amistades?	1	2	3
6.12. En las diversiones?	1	2	3
6.13. En la supervisión del hogar?			

VII.

7.01. ¿Hasta qué año le gustaría que sus <u>hijos</u> fueran a la escuela?

1. Que terminara la primaria
2. Que terminara la secundaria
3. Que terminara la preparatoria
4. Que terminara una carrera técnica o comercial
5. Que empezara una carrera universitaria
6. Que terminara una carrera universitaria
7. Otro (especifique) _____
8. No sabe

7.02. ¿Hasta qué año le gustaría que sus <u>hijas</u> fueran a la escuela?

1. Que terminara la primaria
2. Que terminara la secundaria
3. Que terminara la preparatoria
4. Que terminara una carrera técnica, comercial o de enfermería
5. Que empezara una carrera universitaria
6. Que terminara una carrera universitaria
7. Otro (especifique) _____
8. No sabe

7.03. ¿Qué cree Ud. que sea lo más importante para sus <u>hijas</u>? (Jerarquizar, en orden de importancia, del 1 al 4.)

_____ Un buen matrimonio.

_____ Un buen trabajo.

_____ Una carrera universitaria.

_____ Una vocación religiosa.

VIII.   Ahora quisiera charlar con Ud. acerca de las diferentes ideas que tienen las personas. Le voy a presentar una serie de tres alternativas para que Ud. escoja aquélla con la que esté más de acuerdo.

8.01.   Educación de los Hijos

Aquí hay tres diferentes opiniones sobre la manera de enseñar a los niños. ¿Cuál de estas tres maneras de enseñar a los niños le parece mejor?

1. Algunas personas creen que a los niños se les debe enseñar con mucho cuidado las costumbres del pasado. Esta gente cree que <u>las viejas costumbres son siempre las mejores</u>, y dicen que cuando los niños no las siguen les va mal.

2. Utras personas creen que los niños deben conocer las costumbres pero no se debe insistir en que se sigan estas costumbres al pie de la letra. Dicen que los hijos necesitan <u>aprender y aceptar muchas cosas nuevas para vivir mejor</u>.

3. Algunas personas más creen que a los hijos no se les debe de enseñar mucho de las viejas costumbres, sino sólo como una historia interesante de lo que sucedió en el pasado. Estas personas dicen que la vida es mejor para todos cuando <u>los hijos aprenden a buscar por sí solos nuevos modos de hacer las cosas</u>.

8.02.   Expectativas sobre el Cambio

Tres señores platicaban sobre lo que ellos quisieran que sus hijos tuvieran cuando fueran grandes. Cada uno pensaba de distinta manera.

1. Uno dijo: Yo en verdad <u>espero que mis hijos tengan más de lo que yo tuve</u> si trabajan duro y planean bien las cosas. Siempre hay buenas oportunidades para aquellos que trabajan.

2. El segundo dijo: <u>Yo no se si mis hijos estarán mejor, igual o peor que yo</u>. La vida sube y baja aún cuando la gente trabaja duro. Así es la vida!

3. El tercer señor dijo: <u>Yo espero que mis hijos tengan más o menos lo mismo que yo he tenido</u>. Ellos deben trabajar duro y encontrar la forma de mantener las cosas como estaban en el pasado.

¿Cuál de estas personas cree Ud. que tenía la mejor idea?

8.03. Cambios Religiosos

Algunas personas en un lugar como éste dicen que las costumbres y fiestas religiosas han cambiado comparándolas con lo que eran antes.

1. Algunas personas están realmente contentas por los cambios en las costumbres y fiestas religiosas. Ellas sienten que los cambios son buenos y les gusta que todo, aún las costumbres y fiestas religiosas, cambien.

2. Otras personas no estaban muy contentas con los cambios. Ellas pensaban que las costumbres y fiestas religiosas deberían ser exactamente como en el pasado.

3. Algunas otras personas más, pensaban que las costumbres y fiestas religiosas del pasado eran mejores, pero que no era posible conservarlas igual. Estas gentes creen que la vida es más fácil si se aceptan los cambios que vienen con el tiempo.

8.04. Pozo de Agua

El Gobierno va a ayudar a un Pueblo a obtener más agua por medio de la limpieza y perforación de un pozo. Las autoridades municipales piensan que se debería hacer un plan para distribuir el agua extra que van a tener. No saben la cantidad de agua extra que va a haber, así que todos piensan en forma diferente sobre la elaboración del plan.

1. Algunos dicen que no importa la cantidad de agua extra que pueda haber. Esta deberá repartirse como siempre se ha hecho en el pasado.

2. Otros quieren elaborar un plan realmente bueno antes de saber cuánta agua van a tener.

3. Y otros piensan que es mejor esperar a ver cuánta agua va a haber antes de decidirse en cómo repartirla.

IX.   Todas las personas por lo general tienen diferentes formas de pensar. ¿Nos podría decir si está de acuerdo o en desacuerdo con las siguientes ideas?

	De acuerdo	No está seguro	En desacuerdo
9.01. Si un (a) muchacho (a) puede conseguir un buen trabajo sería un tonto (a) si continúa estudiando.	1	2	3
9.02. Aceptaría Ud. un trabajo con futuro aunque ahí ahora le pagaran menos que en otros trabajos disponibles.	1	2	3
9.03. Las personas no deberían comprar algunas cosas que piensen que son necesarias para poder ahorrar algún dinero.	1	2	3
9.04. El dinero que ahorra le da igual o mayor satisfacción que si Ud. comprara algo.			
9.05. El dinero es para gastarse y no para ahorrarse.	1	2	3

9.06. Pensando en sus propias experiencias, ¿quién cree Ud. que gane por lo general, las discusiones?

1. Los fuertes e impulsivos, o

2. Los inteligentes y prudentes.

9.07. Cuando Ud. se enoja con alguien por lo general prefiere:

1. Dejar que el genio se le baje antes de tratar de seguir con la discusión, o

2. Arreglar las cosas inmediatamente.

9.08. La juventud debería cuidarse del comportamiento de la gente con quien anda.

1. Si   2. No

9.09. En su opinión, ¿Cuál es la edad ideal para que un hombre (o mujer) se case? _____ años.

9.10. Si se ganara Ud. un premio grande ¿que haría Ud. con ese dinero?
1. Gastaría la mayor parte en cosas que deseara su familia y Ud, o
2. Ahorraría la mayor parte para la educación de sus hijos o lo invertiría en algún negocio.

X.   Un número de familias serán seleccionadas para participar en la segunda parte de este estudio. Se necesitará la participación de los padres y de uno de sus hijos (as) de 12 a 14 años. Las familias seleccionadas recibirán una cantidad de dinero hasta de 50 (Cincuenta pesos) por participar. Este juego durará entre una hora y media y dos horas. Quisiéramos saber si Ud. estaría dispuesto a participar, si su familia fuera seleccionada.

        1. Si   2. No

Lugar de Residencia

Calle _____ No. _____
Colonia _____ Teléfono_____
Poblado _____
Otras señas _____
_____

¿Cuándo podrían participar en el juego?
Día _____ Hora _____

MUCHAS GRACIAS POR SU COOPERACION.

EVALUACION DEL ENTREVISTADOR

1. Tiempo de la entrevista:

    _____ Hrs.

    _____ Min.

2. Actitud de la persona entrevistada en términos de aceptación:

    1. Voluntaria

    2. Indiferente

    3. Temerosa

    4. Forzada

3. Grado de cooperación:

    1. Excelente

    2. Buena

    3. Regular

    4. Mala

4. ¿Sabía la persona que el estudio se estaba llevando a cabo en la zona?

    1. Si

    2. No

5. ¿Qué problemas (si los hubo) tuvo la persona entrevistada durante la entrevista?

    1. Ninguno

    2. Sí hubo problemas (especifique) _____

    _____

    _____

    _____

    _____

6. Otros comentarios, por parte del entrevistador, que podrían contri-
    buir o ser de interés para los propósitos de este estudio.

    _____

    _____

    _____

    _____

    _____

    _____

    _____

    _____

    _____

    _____

    _____

    _____

    Entrevistador: _____
    Supervisor: _____

Appendix 2

JOB REQUIREMENTS

OFFICE:

  Executive: 1. College diploma with 2 years experience.

  Administrative: 1. College diploma, no experience necessary, OR
                  2. High school diploma with 4 years experience.

  Skilled: 1. High school diploma, no experience necessary.

  Unskilled: 1. No school, no experience necessary.

  Part-time: $1.50/hour,   maximum 10 hours/week.

AGRICULTURAL WORK AND HOME ECONOMICS:

  Ag Eng or Nutritionist: 1. Agricultural and Home Economics school
                            diploma with 4 years experience.

  Skilled: 1. Agricultural and Home Economics school diploma, 2 years
           experience necessary, OR
           2. High school diploma with 4 years experience.

  Semi-skilled: 1. High school diploma no experience necessary.

  Unskilled: 1. No school, no experience necessary.

  Part-time: same as above part-time.

TOOL AND MACHINE WORK AND CLOTHING CONSTRUCTION:

  Supervisor or Chief designer: 1. Trade school diploma with 4 years
                                experience.

  Skilled: 1. Trade school diploma, 2 years experience necessary, OR
           2. High school diploma with 4 years experience.

  Semi-skilled: 1. High school diploma, no experience necessary.

  Unskilled: 1. No school, no experience necessary.

  Part-time: same as above part-time.

Appendix 3

FAMILY UNPLANNED EVENT CARDS (Mexico)

ROUND	ZACAPU WHITE COLLAR	ZACAPU BLUE COLLAR	VILLAGES
SUCCESS			
1	--	--	--
2	Gain 5 points (pres. of class)	Gain 5 points (pres. of class)	Gain 5 points (pres. of class)
3	Social mobility (scholarship or gain $250) (pay $200)	Social mobility (scholarship or gain $125) (pay $100)	Social mobility (scholarship or gain $25) (pay $20 or $40)
4	Won raffle--$100	Won raffle--$50	Won raffle--$10
FAILURE			
1	--	--	--
2	Failed school year (may or may not repeat)	Failed school year (may or may not repeat)	Failed school year (may or may not repeat)
3	Social mobility (scholarship or gain $250) (pay $200)	Social mobility (scholarship or gain $125) (pay $100)	Social mobility (scholarship or gain $25) (pay $40?)
4	Repair roof--$100	Repair roof--$50	Repair roof--$10
NEUTRAL			
1	--	--	--
2	Gain 5 points (pres. of class)	Gain 5 points (pres. of class)	Gain 5 points (pres. of class)
3	Social mobility (scholarship or gain $250) (pay $200)	Social mobility (scholarship or gain $125) (pay $100)	Social mobility (scholarship or gain $25) (pay $40?)
4	Sick Mother (5 hours housework)	Sick Mother (5 hours housework)	Sick Mother (5 hours housework)

UNPLANNED EVENT CARDS: SUCCESS (United States)

1. Nothing unplanned will happen this year.

2. If you went to high school you were elected president of your class. You will receive 5 points.

3. If you have a full-time job, you will receive a bonus $25 this coming year. If you are in college, you will receive a scholarship for this coming year.

4. You have a chance for a job in another town which will always pay $25 more than you can earn where you are. If you are in school you can go to school in this town free. You must pay $40 to travel to this town. You may choose whether you wish to move or not.

5. If you participated in sports you have been elected captain of your team. You will receive 5 points more.

6. You have won $10 in a raffle.

7. Nothing unplanned will happen this year.

UNPLANNED EVENT CARDS: FAILURE

1. Nothing unplanned will happen this year.

2. If you went to school, you did not have good relations with your teacher. You flunked last year.

3. Your father has had a serious operation. Your income has been reduced $20.

4. You have a chance for a job in another town which will always pay $25 more than you can earn where you are. If you are in school, you can go to school in this other town free. You must pay $40 to travel to this town. You may choose whether you wish to move or not.

5. If you worked full time, you lost your job. Next year, you will receive $50 because of your insurance.

6. The roof on your house needs to be fixed next year and will cost you $10.

7. Nothing unplanned will happen this year.

UNPLANNED EVENT CARDS: NEUTRAL

1. Nothing unplanned will happen this year.

2. If you went to high school, you were elected president of your class, and you will receive 5 points.

3. The roof of your house needs to be fixed this year and will cost you $1█

4. You have a chance for a job in another town which will always pay $25 more than you can earn where you are. You must pay $40 to travel to this town. You may choose whether you wish to move or not.

5. Nothing unplanned will happen this year.

6. If you participated in sports, you have been elected captain on your team. You will receive 10 points more.

7. Your mother is sick and you have dedicated to work 5 hours more in housework.

Appendix 4

CHILD'S UNPLANNED EVENT CARDS: HIGH SCHOOL, OFFICE (United States)

1. Nothing unplanned happened this year.

2. If you participated in athletics you have been elected captain of your team. You receive 10 bonus points.

3. If you are in high school and you have studied sufficiently to pass, you get a scholarship to college or the trade school of your choice.

4. The country has job problems now, and they may get worse. There are too many people trying for too few jobs in office work. Because there are already too many people in these jobs, all the executive and administrative positions are filled. No more people will be allowed to have these positions.

5. There are not enough people in high level jobs in agricultural work and the food industry, or in tool and machine work and clothing construction. A new school has been started to train people for these jobs. The school takes 2 years of study and costs $30/year. It counts as much as graduating from college or trade school. Time spent in this school will also count as work experience. <u>You may enter this school anytime you wish</u>.

6. Job problems continue in office work. If you have a skilled or higher position there, you are demoted one level.

7. If you hold a job in tool and machine work and clothing construction, you receive a $30 raise. This is because there is still a shortage of people in these jobs.

8. Too many people have jobs in office work. If you have a skilled or higher position in this type of work, you have to take a special on-the-job course at half-salary for 1 year.

9. You have a chance for a job in another town which will always pay $25 more than you can earn where you are. If you are in school you can go to school in this other town free. You must pay $20 to travel to this town. You may choose whether you wish to move or not.

10. Nothing unplanned happened this year.

11. If you are married, you have a child.

CHILD'S UNPLANNED EVENT CARDS: TRADE-AGRICULTURAL SCHOOL

1. Nothing unplanned happened this year.

2. If you participated in athletics, you have been elected captain of your team. You receive 10 bonus points.

3. If you are in high school and you have studied sufficiently to pass, you get a scholarship to college or the trade school of your choice.

4. The country has job problems now, and they may get worse. There are too many people with trade school diplomas trying for too few jobs in agricultural work and the food industry. Because there are already too many people in these jobs, all the agricultural engineer and chief dietician positions are filled. No more people will be allowed to have these positions.

5. There are not enough people in high level jobs in tool and machine work and clothing construction, or in office work. A new school has been started to train people for these jobs. The school takes 2 years of study and costs $30/year. It counts as much as graduating from college or trade school. Time spent in this school will also count as work experience. <u>You may enter this school anytime you wish</u>.

6. Job problems continue in agricultural work and the food industry. If you have a skilled or higher position there, you are demoted one level.

7. If you hold a job in tool and machine work or in clothing construction, you receive a $30 raise. This is because there is still a shortage of people in these jobs.

8. Too many people have jobs in agricultural work and the food industry. If you have a skilled or higher position in this type of work, you have to take a special on-the-job course at half-salary for 1 year.

9. You have a chance for a job in another town which will always pays $25 more than you can earn where you are. If you are in school, you can go to school in this other town free. You must pay $20 to travel to this town. You must choose now whether you wish to move or not.

10. Nothing unplanned happened this year.

11. If you are married, you have a child.

CHILD'S UNPLANNED EVENT CARDS: TRADE SCHOOL

1. Nothing unplanned happened this year.

2. If you participated in athletics you have been elected captain of your team. You receive 10 bonus points.

3. If you are in high school and you have studied sufficiently to pass, you get a scholarship to college or the trade school of your choice.

4. The country has job problems now, and they may get worse. There are too many people with trade school diplomas trying for too few jobs in tool and machine work and clothing construction. Because there are already to many people in these jobs, all the supervisor and chief designer positions are filled. No more people will be allowed to have these positions.

5. There are not enough people in high level jobs in agricultural work and the food industry, or in office work. A new school has been started to train people for these jobs. The school takes 2 years of study and costs $30/year. It counts as much as graduating from college or trade school. Time spent in this school will also count as work experience. You may enter this school anytime you wish.

6. Job problems continue in tool and machine work and clothing construction. If you have a skilled or higher position there, you are demoted one level.

7. If you hold a job in office work, or in agricultural work and the food industry, you receive a $30 raise. This is because there is still a shortage of people in these jobs.

8. Too many people have jobs in tool and machine work and clothing construction. If you have a skilled or higher position in this type of work, you have to take a special on-the-job course at half-salary for 1 year.

9. You have a chance for a job in another town which will always pay $25 more than you can earn where you are. If you are in school you can go to school in this other town free. You must pay $20 to travel to this town. You may choose whether you wish to move or not.

10. Nothing unplanned happened this year.

11. If you are married, you have a child.

CHILD'S UNPLANNED EVENT CARDS: HIGH SCHOOL, AGRICULTURE

1. Nothing unplanned happened this year.

2. If you participated in athletics, you have been elected captain of your team. You receive 10 bonus points.

3. If you are in high school, and you have studied sufficiently to pass, you get a scholarship to college or the trade school of your choice.

4. The country has job problems now, and they may get worse. There are too many people trying for too few jobs in agricultural work and the food industry. Because there are already too many people in these jobs, all the agricultural engineer, chief dietician, and skilled positions are filled. No more people will be allowed to have these positions.

5. There are not enough people in high level jobs in tool and machine work and clothing construction, or in office work. A new school has been started to train people for these jobs. The school takes 2 years of study and costs $30/year. It counts as much as graduating from college or trade school. Time spent in this school will also count as work experience. You may enter this school anytime you wish.

6. Job problems continue in agricultural work and the food industry. If you have a skilled or higher position there, you are demoted one level.

7. If you hold a job in tool and machine work or in clothing construction, you receive a $30 raise. This is because there still is a shortage of people in these jobs.

8. Too many people have jobs in agricultural work and the food industry. If you have a semiskilled or higher position in this type of work, you have to take a special on-the-job course at half-salary for 1 year.

9. You have a chance for a job in another town which will always pay $25 more than you can earn where you are. If you are in school you can go to school in this other town free. You must pay $20 to travel to this town. You may choose whether you wish to move or not.

CHILD'S UNPLANNED EVENT CARDS: HIGH SCHOOL, MACHINE

1. Nothing unplanned happened this year.

2. If you participated in athletics you have been elected captain of your team. You receive 10 bonus points.

3. If you are in high school and you have studied sufficiently to pass, you get a scholarship to college or the trade school of your choice.

4. The country has job problems now, and they may get worse. There are too many people trying for too few jobs in tool and machine work and clothing construction. Because there are already too many people in these jobs, all the supervisor, chief designer, and skilled positions are filled. No more people will be allowed to have these positions.

5. There are not enough people in high level jobs in agricultural work and the food industry, or in office work. A new school has been started to train people for these jobs. The school takes 2 years of study and costs $30/year. It counts as much as graduating from college or trade school. Time spent in this school will also count as work experience. You may enter this school anytime you wish.

6. Job problems continue in tool and machine work and clothing construction. If you have a skilled or higher position there, you are demoted one level.

7. If you hold a job in office work, or in agricultural work and the food industry, you receive a $30 raise. This is because there is still a shortage of people in these jobs.

8. Too many people have jobs in tool and machine work and clothing construction. If you have a semiskilled or higher position in this type of work, you have to take a special on-the-job course at half-salary for 1 year.

9. You have a chance for a job in another town which will always pay $25 more than you can earn where you are. If you are in school you can go to school in this other town free. You must pay $20 to travel to this town. You may choose whether you wish to move or not.

10. Nothing unplanned happened this year.

11. If you are married, you have a child.

CHILD'S UNPLANNED EVENT CARDS: OFFICE, COLLEGE

1. Nothing unplanned happened this year.

2. If you participated in athletics, you have been elected captain of your team. You receive 10 bonus points.

3. If you are in high school and you have studied sufficiently to pass, you get a scholarship to the college or the trade school of your choice.

4. The country has job problems now, and they may get worse. There are too many people with college diplomas trying for too few jobs in office work. Because there are already too many people in these jobs, all the executive positions are filled. No more people will be allowed to have these positions.

5. There are not enough people in high level jobs in agricultural work and the food industry, or in tool and machine work and clothing construction. A new school has been started to train people for these jobs. The school takes 2 years of study and costs $30/year. It counts as much as graduating from college or trade school. Time spent in this school will also count as work experience. <u>You may enter this school anytime you wish.</u>

6. Job problems continue in office work. If you have a skilled or higher position there, you are demoted one level.

7. There is still a shortage of people in tool and machine work and clothing construction. From now on, all of these jobs will pay $30 a week more.

8. Too many people have jobs in office work. If you have an administrative or higher position in this type of work, you have to take a special on-the-job course at half-salary for 1 year.

9. You have a chance for a job in another town which will always pay $25 more than you can earn where you are. If you are in school, you can go to school in this other town free. You must pay $20 to travel to this town. You may choose whether you wish to move or not.

10. Nothing unplanned happened this year.

11. If you are married, you have a child.

Appendix 5

GAME INSTRUCTIONS AND RULES:

MEXICAN VERSION

Este ejercicio en el que van a participar nos revela como un niño (muchacho) de catorce años va a pasar su vida durante los próximos doce años. Cada ronda (puntaje en la table), representará un año en su vida. Como familia del niño ustedes van a decidir el tipo de actividades en la que él deberá participar durante dicho tiempo.

El dinero y las horas que vamos a usar son las que ustedes tendrán cada semana del año. Aunque cada ronda represente un año, nosotros solamente usaremos la cantidad de dinero y el número de horas de una semana para representar ese año completo. Esto es para ahorrar tiempo y computación.

REGLAS

El propósito del ejercicio es el de obtener el máximo número de puntuaciones que les sea posible. Ustedes obtienen puntuaciones por medio de las actividades en que participan tales como ver la tele, o casarse. Uds. también obtienen puntos por cualquier artículo que compren. Según la importancia de la actividad, o más grande sea el artículo que se ha seleccionado, Uds. recibirán más puntos por ellos.

Por cada punto que Uds. reciban, recibirán un centavo (en efectivo), cuando acabe el ejercicio.

El total de puntos que Uds. reciben en el ejercicio depende de la manera que Uds. usen su tiempo y dinero, acompañado de un poco de suerte.

Estas fichas representan las horas en una semana. Para cada ronda, Uds. tendrán 80 fichas por las 80 horas que tienen a su disposición.

El dinero representa la entrada de su familia. Para cada ronda, además de las fichas, Uds. recibirán 100 pesos.

El 80% de esto deberá ir al presupuesto domestico para pagar por casa, comida ropa y cosas por el estilo. Uds. pueden gastar el resto en educación, en compras, en los niños, o lo puede ahorrar. Si desean, pueden ahorrar de ronda a ronda y gastar los ahorros más tarde.

Los números verdes en la tabla muestran el número de horas que van a necesitar si deciden tomar parte en tal actividad. Por ejemplo, si el niño va a estudiar bachillerato o ir a la universidad, Uds. tendrán que usar por lo menos 40 horas por semana en clases. Si el cuadrado no tiene números verdes, por ejemplo, para estudios o quehaceres domésticos, el número de horas que van a usar depende de, Uds.

Los números azules indican el costo de un artículo o una actividad en la que desee participar. Por ejemplo, el costo de estudiar bachillerato es de 10 por semana, 5 por semana por su primer hijo, 1 por cada hora que pasen en deportes o 10 para comprar artículos de deporte.

Para Empezar el Ejercicio

La mejor manera de aprender este ejercicio es mediante su participación Para empezar, Uds. cobran la entrada de la familia y las fichas por las 80 horas.

Entregar el dinero (100).

Ahora, Uds. pondrán el 80% del dinero ú 80 pesos en el cuadrado para el presupuesto de la familia por casa, comida y ropa.

Luego, Uds. decidirán que es lo que su hijo de 14 años va a hacer este año -- ir la escuela buscar trabajo, casarse, tener hijos -- o lo que sea. Uds. colocarán las fichas de horas en sus respectivo cuadrados. Si compran algo o si la actividad cuesta dinero pongan el dinero junto a la actividad o en el artículo en la tienda respectiva. Yo los recogeré al término de cada "ronda." Uds. notan que para obtener casi todos los trabajos es necesario un cierto tipo de educación y años de experiencia Uds. deben de tener la educación y/o la experiencia que necesiten para realizar cada trabajo. Cuanto mejor sea su educación, el niño podrá empezar con un mejor trabajo y su promoción será más rápida, y al terminar el ejercicio el niño puede tener un mejor trabajo.

También recuerden que para ir a la universidad, deben de poseer el bachillerato. Si el niño atiende clases es importante saber que el resultado que obtiene depende del tiempo que dedique a sus estudios. Si sus estudios no son suficientes el niño obtendrá notas bajas y consecuentemente puntos bajos.

Ahora Uds. pueden empezar a decidir que es lo que este niño hará este año y colocarán las fichas de horas en la tabla.

Ahora, Uds. van a coger una tarjeta de acontecimiento que no está planeado. Como en la vida real, algunos acontecimientos, buenos y malos, nos ocurren sin haberlos planeado. Esto es lo que la tarjeta representa. Si la tarjeta les conviene a Uds. sigan las instrucciones. Quédense con ella para recordarles lo que tienen que hacer en la próxima ronda.

Puntuación

Ahora, les voy a preguntar cuanto tiempo han usado en las diferentes actividades. De esto, dependerán sus puntuaciones y los marcaré en los cuadrados en la tabla de puntuaciones para el primer año. (Edad catorce años.)

1. Fue a la escuela. Si fué así, cuanto tiempo estudió

   Horario completo

Menos de 5..........F.....0	(si F es la nota, y quiere
de 6 a 10...........D.....2	continuar en la escuela,
de 11 a 15..........G.....5	el próximo año debe de
16 y más............A....10	participar en la ronda de
	nuevo)

   (si F es la nota, y quiere continuar en la escuela, el próximo año debe de participar en la ronda de nuevo)

   Horario parcial

   Menos de 2..........F.....0
   de 3 a 5............D.....2
   de 6 a 10...........C.....5
   de 11 a 15..........A....10

   Se graduó y recibió su diploma

   Bachillerato..............15
   Escuela vocacional........15
   Universidad...............15

2. Consiguió un trabajo.

   Si fue así, ¿fué su primer trabajo por horas? _____ 10

   o: fué su primer trabajo por horario completo?_____ 20

   ¿Recibió un ascenso este año?   25

3. Se casó este año?

   Si fue así.   50

   ¿Tuvo un hijo?

   Si fue así.   50

   ¿Participó en quehaceres domésticos?

4. Ahora, les preguntaré acerca de actividades en su tiempo libre.

   ¿Participó en una de las siguientes actividades?

   Deportes........2 por cada hora

   Asociaciones....2 por cada hora

   Vió la televisión y escuchó y la radio..........1 por cada hora

   Visitó a amigos y familiares........2 por cada hora

5. ¿Participó en actividades religiosas?

   ¿Si fue así fué a misa? _____2 por cada hora

   ¿Fué a la catequesi?   _____2 por cada hora

6. ¿Compró algún artículo en la tienda?

   Dígame que compró.

Automóvil...............30	Ropa nueva..................5
Artículos deportivos....70	Mejora miento de casa........40
Muebles.................20	Vacación....................10
Luna de miel............25	(por una semana-soltero(a)-o
	20 por una semana casados)
	Lancha......................25

7. ¿Ahorró dinero?

   Si fué así por cada dólar (no es acumulativo)

Puntuación total

Sumar a las ganancias hasta ahora.

   Recuerden que _____ahora tiene un año más _____.

El tiene ahora años. Uds. deciden ahora lo que él va a hacer este año.

Avísenme cuando terminen de colocar las fichas.

(Regresen a recoger el dinero)

Appendix 6

GAME INSTRUCTIONS AND RULES:

UNITED STATES VERSION

Preface

<u>Experimenter reads</u>:

First of all, I want to thank you for participating in this study. This experiment is being conducted by the family problem-solving research center. We are primarily concerned with how families go about doing certain tasks. This game should take about 1 hour to play so please try not to take any longer than that.

For research purposes we will be taping the game by tape recorder and camera. These tapes will be coded by our researchers and then erased (If applicable, add: So that they will not interfere, they are observing the game in a different room.)

We will use a tape recorder to help us in playing the game. First the tape will tell something about the game, and they will give you the instructions for playing it. We will have a practice round without the tape, to help you get acquainted with the game. For the rest of the rounds, the tape recorder will be used. If you have questions at any time, I will stop the tape.

Introduction

<u>Experimenter turns on tape</u>

The game we are about to play is a way for you to describe how a 16-year-old child might go through life over the next 10 years. Each round (point to scoreboard), then, represents 2 years of his life. As a family you will be deciding what sorts of things he should do during this time.

The money and hours we will use are what you have to work with each week of the year. Although each round represents 2 years, we only use the amount of money and the number of hours in 1 week to represent those 2 years. This is to save time and figuring.

Rules

The object of the game is to get as many points as you can. You get points for things you do, like watching television or getting married. You also get points for any item you buy. The more important the activity or the bigger the item, the more points you receive for it.

For each point that you collect, you will be paid $.01 (in real money) at the end of the game.

The number of points you get in the game depends on how you spend your time and money, and some luck.

oints: The chips represent hours in a week. For each round you will have 60 chips for the 60 hours that you have to spend.

oints: The money represents your family income. For each round you will get $100. Eighty percent of this must go into the household budget to pay for food, clothing, housing, and the like. The remainder you can spend on education, things at the store, children, or save. You can keep savings from round to round to spend later if you want.

oints: The red numbers on the playing board tell you how many hours you have to spend if you take part in that activity. For example, if you go to high school or college you must spend at least 30 hours/week in class. If there are no red numbers in a box, for example, for study or housework, the number of hours you spend is up to you.

oints: The blue numbers tell you how much money an activity or a thing at the store costs. For example, it costs $10/week to go to high school, $15/week for your first child, $1 for each hour you spend on athletics, or $10 to buy sporting equipment.

Starting the Game

The best way to learn about the game is to start playing it. To play, you start by collecting your family's income and 60 hour chips from the assistant.

Experimenter puts $100 on Board

Now, you put 80% of the money or $80 in the box for the family budget to pay for food, clothing, and similar expenses.

Next, you decide what this 16-year-old child will do this year--go to school, get a job, get married, have a child, or whatever. You will place the hour chips in the proper boxes. If you buy something or if the activity costs money, put the money next to the activity or on the item in the store. The assistant will collect it at the end of the round.

E points: Note that to get most jobs a certain type of education and
years of experience are needed. You must have the necessary education and/or experience to get each job. The better your education,
the better the job you can start at, the faster you will advance,
and the better the job you can get before the game ends. Also,
remember, to go to college or any of the trade schools, you must
have a high school diploma. If you go to school it is important to
know that how well you do in school depends partly on how much time

E points: you study. If you do not study enough, you will get low grades and
few points.

UNPLANNED EVENT CARD

E points: Before each round, you will receive an unplanned event card.
Just as in real life, some events, both good and bad, happen to us
when we do not plan for them. This is what the card represents.
If the card applies to you, do what it says. Keep it to remind you
what to do in the next round.

          Now you can start deciding what this child will do this year
and you can place your hour chips on the playing board.
****

Experimenter turns off tape, and says:

          "Before starting this practice round, I'll read the Unplanned
Event card for this round."

Experimenter reads card and gives it to subjects.
****

          (After one-half hour during practice round the family is not
near completion of the round, the Experimenter says; "Since this
game should take about 1 hour to play, please try to hurry along.")

Re: Average Family

          Upon completion of the practice round, the Experimenter marks
off points on the scoreboard. After giving the "Total for your
Family," the Experimenter says; "These scores to the right of your
totals are the average scores of families who have already played
this game, so you can compare how you're doing with how well they
did."
****

The Experimenter then goes back to gameboard: Collects money, chips go back, gives new money, and explains "Old" and "New" money; the Experimenter says; "Remember that you can keep savings from round to round to spend later if you want. You must, however, keep your savings from the current round separate from those of past rounds because only the new savings count towards points for that round."

The Experimenter points out the "Old" from the "New" on the gameboard.

****

SECOND ROUND

The Experimenter says; "For the remainder of the game we will use the tape to help us. If you have questions at any time, I will turn off the tape. However, try to make your decisions in the time alloted by the tape."

The Experimenter then reads Unplanned Event Card, gives it to subjects, and turns on tape.

****

Procedure for Remaining Rounds

At signal for end of round, turn off tape; tally up scoreboard: cite "Average Family" with appropriate S, F, N, comments; collect money; chips go back; give new money; read Unplanned Event card; turn on tape.

<u>United States Scoring</u>

Now I will ask you how much time he spent doing different things. From this, I will score your points and write them in the boxes on the scoreboard for the <u>first</u> <u>year</u> (<u>age</u> <u>14</u>).

I.   Did he go to school?

If so, how much time did he study?

<u>Full time</u>

Less than 5.....F.....0	(if F is grade, and want to
6 to 10.........D.....2	stay in school following year,
11 to 15........C.....5	has to replay the round)
16 and over.....A....10	

<u>Part-time</u>

Less than 2.....F.....0
3 to 5..........D.....2
6 to 10.........C.....5
11 to 15........A....10

Did he graduate and get a diploma?

High School....15
Vocational.....15
College........15

II.   Did he get a job?

If so, was it _____first part-time job?	10
was it _____first full-time job?	20
Did you get a promotion this year?	25

III. Did he get married this year?

If so, 50.

Did he have a child?

If so, 50.

Did he do any housework?

If so, 1 for each hour.

IV. Now I will ask about leisure activities. Did he do any of the
     following?

     Athletics.........................2 for each hour
     Clubs.............................2 for each hour
     Watch television and listen to
         radio.........................1 for each hour
     Spend time with friends and
         relatives.....................2 for each hour

V.   Did he participate in religious activities?

     If so,...2 for each hour

VI. Did he buy anything at the store? Tell me what you bought.

     Car.............30   New clothes.......10
     Sporting goods......10   Improvements......40
     New furniture.......20   Vacation..........10 for one week (not
     Honeymoon..........25   married)
                              ....20 for 1 week (married)
                              Boat..............25

VII. Did you save any money?

     If so, 1 for each dollar. (not cumulative)

TOTAL SCORE

ADD TO "EARNINGS SO FAR"

     Remember, _____ is now 1 year older -- he is now _____.
You can now decide what he will do this year. When you have finished
placing the chips, tell me.

     (Return to COLLECT MONEY.)

Appendix 7

OBSERVATIONS OF POWER AND SUPPORT

1. Each observer will record all pertinent actions of all family members, including both the originating and recipient actor.

2. All pertinent actions are all POWER and SUPPORT actions, as defined below.

    POWER

    1. <u>Definition</u>: Actions intended to control, initiate, change, or modify the behavior of another member of the family.

    2. Scoring procedure: Any suggestions made as to how to play the game are counted as power acts. The first step is to record the symbol of the originating person, then the symbol of the person who is the recipient, and then the symbol describing the act, that is:

        P+ Power-plus (order or suggestion accepted or followed)
        P- Power-minus (order or suggestion specifically rejected.
             "No, that won't work," etc.)
        P+- (order or suggestion ignored)

        Thus, a total act might be as follows:

        H W P+ Father's suggestion to mother accepted and carried out
                 by her
        S W P+- Son's suggestion to mother ignored by her
        W H P- Mother's suggestion to father refused by him

    3. Suggestions made to the whole family must be specified: H W S P+ or -.

    SUPPORT

    1. <u>Definition</u>: Actions intended to establish, maintain, or restore, as an end in itself, a positive affective relationship with another family member, and the opposite: Actions intended to punish or devalue another member of the family, or an action of his or hers.

    2. Support is Bipolar. That is, we will record the acts which are hostile, rejective, or aggressive in nature.

    3. Scoring procedure: This is exactly parallel to the scoring procedure for power. The individual initiating the act, and the individual toward whom it is directed are recorded in that order, followed by the symbol indicating that the support was positive or negative.

    4. Types of acts to be scored + or - might be as follows:

<table>
<tr><td>Score + for:</td><td>Score − for:</td></tr>
</table>

Score + for:	Score − for:
Praise	Criticisms
Helps, cooperates	Hinders, refuses to cooperate
Terms of endearment or liking	Terms of disparagement, name calling
Encouragement, nurturance	Physical demonstrations of dislike
Physical demonstration of affection (hugs, kisses)	or disapproval (pushes away, shoving)
Requests for help or affection	Cursing
General expressions of positive emotion or enjoyment	Rejection of requests for help or sympathy
	General expression of negative affect, including dislike of the game

5. Support acts (both + and −) can be directed towards oneself. Be sure to record these.

6. Remember to score all acts as originated. However, a request for help which is rejected is also counted as a negative support act originated by the person(s) rejecting the request for help.

Appendix 8

SCORE BOARD

AGE	EDUCATION			JOB			FAMILY			LEISURE						CH.	STORE	SAVE	TOTAL
	GRADE	POINTS	DIPLOMA	1st PART-TIME	1st FULL-TIME	PROMOTION	MARRIAGE	CHILD	HOUSEWORK	ATHLETICS	CLUBS	TV and RADIO	RELATIVES	FRIENDS and DATES	TIME BY YOURSELF	CHURCH			
16																			
17																			
18																			
19																			
20																			
21																			
22																			
23																			
24																			
25																			
26																			
TOTAL																			

I.D. _____

DATE _____

SCOREBOARD SUPPLEMENT: ALLOCATION OF HOURS: WHAT IS ATTAINED (Child Game)

	EDUCATION			JOB		STORE
AGE	WHAT SCHOOL	NEW SCHOOL	HOURS	WHAT IS JOB	WHAT IS BOUGHT	SOCIAL MOBILITY
18						
19						
20						
21						
22						
23						
24						
25						
26						
TOTAL						

I.D. _____

Date _____

Family _____   Child _____

SCOREBOARD SUPPLEMENT: ALLOCATION OF HOURS: WHAT IS ATTAINED (Family Game)

| AGE | EDUCATION | | JOB | | STORE |
	WHAT SCHOOL	HOURS	WHAT IS JOB	SOCIAL MOBILITY	WHAT IS BOUGHT
16-17					
18-19					
20-21					
22-23					
24-25					
26-27					
TOTAL					

I.D. _____

Date _____

Family _____ Child _____

Appendix 9

POST-EXPERIMENTAL INTERVIEW

Now that you have finished playing the game we would like to ask you about some of your impressions of the game.

1. First of all, did you enjoy playing this game?

2. Was there anything that you did not understand about the game?

3. Why did you choose to send your son or daughter to _____ school? (high school, college, etc.)

4. Did your child get the job you wanted him or her most to have during the game?

    If not, why do you think he did not?

    Why did you want him or her to have this job?

5. Did you feel that the unplanned event cards helped or hindered you?

    Why? Which ones?

6. I noticed you saved (<u>did not save</u>) money throughout (at the end of) the game.

    Do you think this helped or hurt how well you did?

7. Why did you have your son or daughter <u>get married</u> when you did? or not get married?

8. Why did you spend as much time/no time as you did in religious activiti

9. What about the time spent with <u>friends</u>--was that important?

10. Why did you have the child spend _____ hours with friends?

11. Did you feel the time you had the child spend with relatives was valuable?

    Why?

12. I noticed you spent _____ at the store. Why did you buy these things? Were there other things you wanted to buy and were not able to?

13. When you were playing the game, were you trying only to get the most number of points, or were you making choices that you would in real life?

14. All in all, compared to other families, how successful do you think you were?

15. If you were to play the game again, would you do anything different?

References

Aberle, D. F., & K. D. Naegele
    1952   "Middle-class fathers' occupational role and attitudes toward children." *American Journal of Orthopsychiatry* 22: 366–378.

Aldous, J.
    1971   "A framework for the analysis of family problem solving." Pp. 265–281 in J. Aldous, T. Condon, R. Hill, M. Straus, & I. Tallman (eds.), *Family Problem Solving: A Symposium on Theoretical, Methodological and Substantive Concerns.* Hinsdale, Ill.: The Dryden Press.

Apter, D. E.
    1971   *Choice and the Politics of Allocation.* New Haven: Yale University Press.

Armer, M.
    1973   "Methodological problems and possibilities in comparative research." Pp. 44–79 in M. Armer & A. Grimshaw (eds.), *Comparative Social Research: Methodological Problems and Strategies.* New York: John Wiley.

Armer, M., & L. Isaac
    1978   "Consequences of psychological modernity." *American Sociological Review* 43 (3, June): 316–334.

Armer, M., & A. Schnaiberg
    1975   "Individual modernity, alienation and socioeconomic status: A replication in Costa Rica." *Studies in Comparative International Development* 10: 35–47.

Aronfreed, J.
    1969   "The concept of internalization." Pp. 263–323 in D. A. Goslin (ed.), *Handbook of Socialization Theory and Research.* Chicago: Rand McNally.

Aronson, E., & J. M. Carlsmith
    1962   "Performance expectancy as a determinant of actual performance." *Journal of Abnormal and Social Psychology* 65: 178–182.

297

Ashby, L., & B. Stave, eds.
  1972   *The Discontented Society: Interpretations of Twentieth-Century American Protest.* Chicago: Rand McNally.
Bachrach, P., & M. S. Baratz
  1970   *Power and Poverty: Theory and Practice.* New York: Oxford University Press.
Bandura, A.
  1969   "Social-learning theory of identificatory processes." Pp. 213–262 in D. A. Goslin (ed.), *Handbook of Socialization Theory and Research.* Chicago: Rand McNally.
  1971   "Vicarious and self-reinforcement processes." Pp. 228–278 in R. Glaser (ed.), *The Nature of Reinforcement.* New York: Academic Press.
  1977a   *Social Learning Theory.* Englewood Cliffs, N. J.: Prentice–Hall, Inc.
  1977b   "Self efficacy: Toward a unifying theory of behavioral change." *Psychological Review* 84 (2): 191–215.
Barry, H. III, I. L. Child, & M. Bacon
  1957   "Relation of child training to subsistence economy." *American Anthropologist* 61: 51–63.
Becker, H. S., B. Geer, E. C. Hughes, & A. Strauss
  1961   *Boys in White.* Chicago: University of Chicago Press.
Bee, H. L.
  1971   "Socialization for problem solving." Pp. 186–211 in J. Aldous, T. Condon, R. Hill, M. Straus, & I. Tallman (eds.), *Family Problem Solving.* Hinsdale, Ill.: The Dryden Press.
Bell, D.
  1968   "The measurement of knowledge and technology." Pp. 145–246 in E. Sheldon & W. E. Moore (eds.), *Indicators of Social Change.* New York: Russell Sage Foundation.
  1976   *The Coming of Post-Industrial Society.* New York: Basic Books.
Bell, R.
  1965   "Lower class Negro mothers' aspirations for their children." *Social Forces* 42 (May): 493–500.
Bell, W.
  1958   "Social choice, life styles, and suburban residence." *American Journal of Sociology* 62 (January): 391–398.
Bensman, J., & B. Rosenberg
  1976   *Mass, Class and Bureaucracy: An Introduction to Sociology.* New York: Praeger.
Bernstein, B.
  1960   "Language and social class." *British Journal of Sociology* 11 (3): 271–276.
  1961   "Social class and linguistic development: A theory of social learning." Pp. 288–314 in A. H. Halsey, J. Flood, & C. A. Anderson (eds.), *Education, Economy, and Society.* Glencoe, Ill.: The Free Press.
Blau, P. M.
  1974   "Parameters of social structure." *American Sociological Review* 39: 615–635.
Blau, P. M., & O. D. Duncan
  1967   *The American Occupational Structure.* New York: John Wiley and Sons.
Blau, P. M., & W. R. Scott
  1962   *Formal Organizations: A Comparative Approach.* San Francisco: Chandler.
Blood, B., & M. Blood
  1978   *Marriage.* Third ed. New York: The Free Press.

Blood, R. O., & R. Hill
    1970   "Comparative analysis of family power structure: Problems of measurement and interpretation." Pp. 525–535 in R. Hill & R. Konig (eds.), *Families in East and West Paris*. The Hague: Mouton.

Blood, R. O., Jr., & D. M. Wolfe
    1960   *Husbands and Wives: The Dynamics of Married Living*. New York: Macmillan.

Blumer, H.
    1939   *An Appraisal of Thomas and Znaniecki's The Polish Peasant in Europe and America*. New York: Social Science Research Council.

Boocock, S.
    1968   "An experimental study of the learning effects of two games with simulated environments." In S. Boocock & E. O. Schild (eds.), *Simulation Games in Learning*. Beverly Hills, California: Sage Publications.
    1972   "Validity-testing of an intergeneration relations game." *Simulations and Games* 3 (March): 29–40.

Bossard, J., & E. S. Boll
    1960   *The Sociology of Child Development*. New York: Harper.

Bossen, L.
    1975   "Women in modernizing societies." *American Ethnologist* 3 (November): 587–601.

Brittain, C. V.
    1963   "Adolescent choices and parent-peer cross pressures." *American Sociological Review* 28 (3, June): 385–391.

Bronfenbrenner, U.
    1961   "Some familial antecedents of responsibility and leadership in adolescents." Pp. 239–272 in L. Petrullo & B. L. Bass (eds.), *Leadership and Interpersonal Behavior*. New York: Holt, Rinehart, and Winston.
    1970   *Two Worlds of Childhood U.S. and U.S.S.R.* New York: Russell Sage Foundation.
    1979   *The Ecology of Human Development*. Cambridge: Harvard University Press.

Bureau of Census
    1977   Department of Commerce. *The U.S. Fact Book*. New York: Grossett & Dunlap.

Camilleri, S. F., & J. Berger
    1967   "Decision making and social influence: A model and an experimental test." *Sociometry* 30: 365–378.

Campbell, A.
    1981a   *The Sense of Well-Being in America: Recent Patterns and Trends*. New York: McGraw–Hill.
    1981b   "The Paradox of Well-Being." *I.S.R. Newsletter* (Spring): 4–5.

Campbell, A., P. E. Converse, & W. L. Rodgers
    1976   *The Quality of American Life: Perceptions, Evaluations, and Satisfactions*. New York: Russell Sage.

Campbell, E. Q.
    1969   "Adolescent socialization." Pp. 821–859 in David A. Goslin (ed.), *Handbook of Socialization*. Chicago: Rand McNally.

Cartwright, D., & A. Zander
    1968   *Group Dynamics: Research and Theory*. Third ed. New York: Harper and Row.

Catton, W. R., Jr.
    1980   *Overshoot*. Urbana: The University of Illinois Press.

Chase–Dunn, C.
    1975   "The effects of international economic dependence on development and in-
            equality: A cross-national study." *American Sociological Review* 40: 720–738.
Clausen, J. A.
    1969   "A historical and comparative view of socialization theory and research." Pp.
            20–72 in J. A. Clausen (ed.), *Socialization and Society*. Boston: Little Brown and
            Co.
Clement, N. C., & L. C. Green
    1978   "The political economy of devaluation in Mexico." *Inter-American Economic
            Affairs* (Winter) 32, 3: 47–75.
Cohen, B. P.
    1980   "The conditional nature of scientific knowledge." Pp. 71–110 in Lee Freese
            (ed.), *Theoretical Methods in Sociology: Seven Essays*. Pittsburgh: University of
            Pittsburgh Press.
Cohen, R. L.
    1974   "Social class differences in the problem solving process: An integration of social
            organization, language and nonverbal communication." Unpublished doctoral
            dissertation, University of Minnesota, Minneapolis.
Coleman, J.
    1970   "Games as vehicles for social theory." *American Behavioral Scientist* 12: 2–6.
    1971   "Conflicting theories of societal change." *American Behavioral Scientist* 14:
            633–650.
Cone, C. A.
    1976   "Field and factories: Dynamics of migration in Mexico." Unpublished doctoral
            dissertation, University of Minnesota, Minneapolis.
Cooley, C. H.
    1909   *Social Organization*. New York: Schocken Books.
Cornelius, W. A.
    1981   "Immigration, Mexican Development Policy and The Future of U.S.–Mexican
            Relations." Pp. 7–16 in R. H. McBride (ed.), *Mexico and the United States: Pro-
            ceedings of the Binational American Assembly on Mexican American Relations*,
            Oct.-30-Nov. 2, 1980. Englewood Cliffs, N. J: Prentice-Hall, 1981.
Daly, H. E.
    1973   *Toward a Steady-State Economy*. San Francisco: W. H. Freeman.
D'Andrade, R. G.
    1966   "Sex differences and cultural institutions." Pp. 173–204 in E. Maccoby (ed.),
            The Development of Sex Differences. Palo Alto: Stanford University Press.
Della Fave, L.
    1974   "Success values: Are they universal or class-differential?" *American Journal of
            Sociology* 80 (July): 153–169.
Devereux, E. C., Jr., U. Bronfenbrenner, & G. J. Suci
    1962   "Patterns of parent behavior in the United States of America and the Federal
            Republic of Germany: A cross-national comparison." *International Social
            Science Journal* 14 (3): 488–506.
Diaz, M. N.
    1967   "Opposition and alliance in a Mexican town." Pp. 168–173 in J. Potter, M.
            Diaz, & G. Foster (eds.), *Peasant Society: A Reader*. Boston: Little, Brown and
            Co.
Diaz, M. N., & J. M. Potter
    1967   "The social life of peasants." Pp. 154–167 in J. Potter, M. Diaz, & G. Foster
            (eds.), *Peasant Society: A Reader*. Boston: Little, Brown and Co.

Di Renzo, G. J.
    1977   "Socialization, personality, and social systems." *Annual Review of Sociology* 3: 261-295.
Doob, L. W.
    1969   "Testing theories concerning a subculture of peasantry." Pp. 142-152 in C. Wharton (ed.), *Subsistence Agriculture and Economic Development.* Chicago: Aldine.
Douvan, E., & J. Adelson
    1966   *The Adolescent Experience.* New York: John Wiley and Sons.
Draper, P.
    1975   "Cultural pressure on sex differences." *American Ethnologist* 2: 602-616.
Dunnette, M. D., J. Campbell, & K. Jaastad
    1963   "The effect of group participation on brainstorming effectiveness for two industrial samples." *Journal of Applied Psychology* 47: 30-37.
Eisenstadt, S. N.
    1966   *Modernization: Protest and Change.* Englewood Cliffs, N. J.: Prentice-Hall.
Ekeh, P.
    1974   *Social Exchange Theory.* Cambridge: Harvard University Press.
Elder, G. H., Jr.
    1968   *Adolescent Socialization and Personality Development.* Chicago: Rand McNally and Co.
    1974   *Children of the Great Depression.* Chicago: University of Chicago Press.
Elu de Leñero, M. C.
    1969   *Hacia Donde va la Mujer Mexicana?* Mexico City: Instituto Mexicano de Estudio Sociales.
Emerson, R. M.
    1962   "Power-dependence relations." *American Sociological Review* 27: 31-41.
    1972   "Exchange theory, parts I and II." Pp. 38-87 in J. Berger, M. Zelditch, Jr., & B. Anderson (eds.), *Sociological Theories in Progress.* Boston: Houghton and Mifflin.
    1976   "Social exchange theory." Pp. 335-362 in A. Inkeles (ed.), *Annual Review of Sociology.* Palo Alto: Annual Reviews.
Erasmus, C.
    1961   *Man Takes Control.* Minneapolis: University of Minnesota Press.
Erikson, E. H.
    1950   *Childhood and Society.* New York: Norton.
    1958   *Young Man Luther.* New York: Norton.
    1959   "Identity and the life cycle." *Psychological Issues* 1.
    1962   "Youth: Fidelity and Diversity." *Daedalus* 91: 5-27.
    1968   "Identity and identity diffusion." Pp. 197-205 in C. Gordon & K. J. Gergen (eds.), *The Self in Social Interaction.* New York: Wiley.
Fagen, R., & W. Toughy
    1972   *Politics and Privilege in a Mexican City.* Stanford: Stanford University Press.
Feldman, A. S., & C. Hurn
    1966   "The experience of modernization." *Sociometry* 29: 378-395.
Firth, R.
    1969   "Social structure and peasant economy." Pp. 23-37 in C. Wharton (ed.), *Subsistence Agriculture and Economic Development.* Chicago: Aldine.
Flavell, J. H.
    1963   *The Developmental Psychology of Jean Piaget.* New York: Van Nostrand.

Foster, G. M.
1967   *Tzintzuntzan: Mexican Peasants in a Changing World.* Boston: Little, Brown and Co.

Freedman, J. L., & D. L. Sears
1965   "Selective exposure." Pp. 58–97 in L. Berkowitz (ed.), *Advances in Experimental Social Psychology (Vol. 2).* New York: Academic Press.

Frey, F. W.
1970   "Cross-cultural survey research in political science." Pp. 175–294 in R. T. Holt & J. E. Turner (eds.), *The Methodology of Comparative Research.* New York: The Free Press.

Gallegos, A., J. G. Peña, J. A. Solis, & A. Keller
1977   "Recent trends in contraceptive use in Mexico." *Studies in Family Planning* 8 (8, August).

Gecas, V.
1980   "Family and social structural influences on the career orientations of rural Mexican–American youth." *Rural Sociology* 45: 272–889.
1981   "Contexts of socialization." Pp. 165–199 in M. Rosenberg & R. Turner (eds.), *Sociological Perspectives in Social Psychology.* New York: Basic Books.

Gewirtz, J. L.
1969   "Mechanisms of social learning: Some roles of stimulation and behavior in early human development." Pp. 57–212 in D. Goslin (ed.), *Handbook of Socialization Theory and Research.* Chicago: Rand McNally.

Goffman, E.
1959   *The Presentation of Self in Everyday Life.* Garden City, New York: Doubleday Anchor Books.
1963   *Stigma.* Englewood Cliffs, N. J.: Prentice–Hall.

Goldsen, R. K., M. Rosenberg, E. A. Suchman, & R. M. Williams, Jr.
1960   *What College Students Think.* New York: Van Nostrand.

Gonzales–Casanova, P.
1968   "Dynamics of the class structure." Pp. 64–82 in J. A. Kahl (ed.), *Comparative Perspectives on Stratification: Mexico, Great Britain, Japan.* Boston: Little, Brown and Co.

Goode, W. J.
1963   *World Revolution and Family Patterns.* New York: The Free Press.

Gordon, C.
1968   "Self-conceptions: Configurations of content." Pp. 115–136 in C. Gordon & K. J. Gergen (eds.). *The Self in Social Interaction.* New York: John Wiley and Sons.

Gottlieb, D., & C. Ramsey
1964   *The American Adolescent.* Homewood, Ill.: The Dorsey Press.

Gross, E.
1968   "Plus ça change . . ? The sexual structure of occupations over time." *Social Problems* 16: 198–208.

Gurin, G., J. Veroff, & S. Feld
1960   *Americans View Their Mental Health: A Nationwide Interview Survey.* New York: Basic Books.

Gurr, T.
1970   *Why Men Rebel.* Princeton: Princeton University Press.

Gusfield, J.
1967   "Tradition and modernity: Misplaced polarities in the study of social change." *American Journal of Sociology* 72: 351–362.
Gwartney, J. D.
1977   *Microeconomies: Private and Public Choice.* New York: Academic Press.
Haavio–Mannila, E.
1971   "Convergences between East and West: Tradition and modernity in sex roles in Sweden, Finland, and the Soviet Union." *Acta Sociologica* 14: 144–225.
Hagen, E. E.
1961   *On The Theory of Social Change.* Homewood, Ill.: The Dorsey Press.
Haller, A. O., & I. W. Miller
1963   *The Occupational Aspirational Scale: Theory Structure and Correlates.* East Lansing: Michigan State University Agricultural Experiment Station.
Hannerz, U.
1969   *Soulside: Inquiries into Ghetto Culture and Community.* New York: Columbia University Press.
Hareven, T. K.
1976   "The family and gender roles in historical perspective." Pp. 97–118 in L. Carter, A. F. Scott, & W. Martqua (eds.), *Women and Men: Changing Roles, Relationships and Perceptions.* Aspen: Aspen Institute for Humanistic Studies.
Harter, S.
1978   "Effective motivation reconsidered: Toward a developmental model." *Human Development* 21: 34–64.
Hawley, A. H.
1960   *Human Ecology.* New York: Ronald Press.
Heath, A.
1976   *Rational Choice and Social Exchange.* Cambridge: Cambridge University Press.
Hermann, C. F.
1967   "Validation problems in games and simulation with special reference to international problems." *Behavioral Science* 12: 216–231.
Hess, R. O., & V. Shipman
1965   "Early blocks to children's learning." *Children* 12: 189–194.
Hill, R.
1970   *Family Development in Three Generations.* Cambridge: Shenkman Publishing Co.
Hill, R., & J. Aldous
1969   "Socialization for marriage and parenthood." Pp. 885–950 in D. A. Goslin (ed.), *Handbook of Socialization Theory and Research.* Chicago: Rand McNally.
Hoffman, L. R.
1965   "Group problem solving." Pp. 97–132 in L. Berkowitz (ed.), *Advances in Experimental Psychology.* New York: Academic Press.
Hoffman, L. R., & N. R. F. Maier
1961   "Quality and acceptance of problem solutions by member of homogeneous and heterogeneous groups." *Journal of Abnormal and Social Psychology* 64: 206–214.
Hoffman, L. W., & M. L. Hoffman
1973   "The value of children to parents." Pp. 7–300 in J. T. Fawcett (ed.), *Psychological Perspectives on Population.* New York: Basic Books.
Hole, J., & E. Levine
1971   *Rebirth of Feminism.* New York: Quadrangle.

Hollingshead, A. B.
   1957   *Two factor index of social position.* New Haven, Conn. (Mimeographed.)
Homans, G.
   1961   *Social Behavior: Its Elementary Forms.* New York: Harcourt, Brace and Jovanovich.
   1964   "Bringing men back in." *American Sociological Review* 29: 809–818.
Horner, M. S.
   1972   "Toward an understanding of achievement related conflicts in women." *Journal of Social Issues* 28 (2): 157–175.
Horowitz, I. L.
   1966   *Three Worlds of Development: The Theory and Practice of International Stratification.* New York: Oxford University Press.
Hoselitz, B. F.
   1960   *Sociological Aspects of Economic Growth.* Glencoe, Ill.: The Free Press.
Hoyenga, K. B., & K. T. Hoyenga
   1979   *The Question of Sex Differences.* Boston: Little, Brown and Co.
Hyman, H. H.
   1953   "The value systems of different classes." Pp. 426–442 in R. Bendix & S. M. Lipset (eds.), *Class, Status and Power: A Reader in Social Stratification.* Glencoe, Ill.: The Free Press.
Ihinger, M.
   1975   "The referee role and norms of equity: A contribution toward a theory of sibling conflict." *Journal of Marriage and The Family* 37 (3): 514–524.
Illich, I.
   1971   *De-schooling Society.* New York: Harper and Row.
Inhelder, B., & J. Piaget
   1958   *The Growth of Logical Thinking.* New York: Basic Books.
Inkeles, A.
   1966   "The modernization of man." Pp. 138–150 in M. Weiner (ed.), *Modernization: The Dynamics of Growth.* New York: Basic Books.
   1968   "Society, social structure, and child socialization." Pp. 75–129 in J. A. Clausen (ed.), *Socialization and Society.* Boston: Little, Brown and Co.
   1969   "Making men modern: On the causes and consequences of individual change in sex developing countries." *The American Journal of Sociology* 75: 208–225.
Janis, I. L., & L. Mann
   1977   *Decision Making: A Psychological Analysis of Conflict, Choice, and Commitment.* New York: The Free Press.
Johnson, C. L.
   1975   "Authority and power in Japanese–American marriage." Pp. 182–196 in R. Cromwell & D. Olson. (eds.). *Power in Families.* New York: John Wiley & Sons.
Kahl, J.
   1968   *The Measurement of Modernism: A Study of Values in Brazil and Mexico.* Austin: University of Texas Press.
Kelley, H. H., & J. W. Thibaut
   1969   "Group problem solving." Pp. 1–101 in G. Lindzey & E. Aronson (eds.), *Handbook of Social Psychology* (Vol 4). Second ed. Reading, Mass: Addison–Wesley.
Kerckhoff, A. C.
   1972   *Socialization and Social Class.* Englewood Cliffs, N. J.: Prentice–Hall.

Klein, D. M., & R. Hill
    1979   "Determinants of family problem solving effectiveness." Pp. 493–548 in W. R. Burr, R. Hill, F. Nye, & I. Reiss (eds.), *Contemporary Theories about the Family.* New York: The Free Press.
Kluckhohn, F., & F. Strodtbeck
    1961   *Variations in Value Orientations.* Evanston, Ill.: Row, Peterson.
Kohn, M.
    1969   *Class and Conformity.* Homewood, Ill.: The Dorsey Press.
Kohn, M., & C. Schooler
    1973   "Occupational experience and psychological functioning: An assessment of reciprocal effects." *American Sociological Review* 38: 97–118.
    1978   "The reciprocal effects of the substantive complexity of work and intellectual flexibility: A longitudinal assessment." *American Journal of Sociology* 84 (July): 24–52.
Komarovsky, M.
    1967   *Blue-Collar Marriage.* New York: Vintage Books.
Kuhn, A.
    1974   *The Logic of Social Systems.* San Francisco: Jossey–Bass.
Lasch, C.
    1979   *The Culture of Narcissism.* New York: Warner Books.
Lee, G. R.
    1977   *Family Structure and Interaction.* Philadelphia: Lippincott.
Leik, R. K. & I. Tallman
    1977   "Chronic imminence: For some people it is more rational to wait." Paper presented at the Pacific Sociological Meeting, San Diego.
Leñero Otero, L.
    1968   *Investigacion de la Familia en Mexico.* Mexico City: Instituto Mexicano de Estudios Sociales.
Lerner, D.
    1958   *The Passing of Traditional Society: Modernizing the Middle East.* New York: The Free Press.
Levy, M. J., Jr.
    1966   *Modernization and the Structure of Societies: A Setting for International Affairs.* Princeton: University Press.
Lewin, K.
    1953   "The field theory approach to adolescence." Pp. 32–60 in J. M. Seidman (ed.), *The Adolescent.* New York: The Dryden Press.
Lewis, O.
    1959   *Five Families.* New York: Basic Books.
    1961   *The Children of Sanchez.* New York: Random House.
Liebow, E.
    1967   *Tally's Corner.* Boston: Little, Brown and Co.
Lomnitz, L. A.
    1977   *Networks and Marginality: Life in a Mexican Shantytown.* New York: Academic Press.
Luria, A. R.
    1976   *Cognitive Development: Its Cultural and Social Foundations.* Cambridge: Harvard University Press.
Luten, D. B.
    1978   "The limits to growth controversy." Pp. 163–180 in K. A. Hammond, G.

Macenko, & W. B. Fairchild (eds.), *Sourcebook on the Environment.* Chicago: University of Chicago Press.

McClelland, D. C.
1961   *The Achieving Society.* Princeton: Van Nostrand Co.

McClelland, D. C., J. W. Atkinson, R. A. Clark, & F. L. Lowell
1953   *The Achievement Motive.* New York: Appleton-Century-Crofts.

McCloskey, H. M., & J. H. Schaar
1965   "Psychological dimensions of anomy." *American Sociological Review* 30 (February): 14–40.

Maccoby, M.
1967   "Love and authority: A study of Mexican villagers." Pp. 336–345 in J. Potter, M. Diaz, & B. Foster (eds.), *Peasant Society: A Reader.* Boston: Little, Brown and Co.

McGinn, N.
1966   "Marriage and family in middle-class Mexico." *Journal of Marriage and The Family* 28 (3): 305–313.

McKinley, D. G.
1964   *Social Class and Family Life.* New York: The Free Press of Glencoe.

Maier, N. R. F.
1970   *Problem Solving and Creativity in Individuals and Groups* (Basic Concepts in Psychology Series). Belmont, Calif.: Brooks–Cole.

Maier, N. R. F., & A. R. Solem
1952   "The contribution of a discussion leader to the quality of group thinking." *Human Relations* 5: 277–288.

Marotz, R.
1976   "Sex differentiation and equality: A Mexican–United States comparison of parental aspirations for daughters." *Journal of Comparative Family Studies* 7 (Spring): 41–53.

Marotz–Baden, R., & I. Tallman
1978   "Parental aspirations and expectations for daughters and sons: A comparative analysis." *Adolescence* 3 (59): 251–268.

Marriott, M.
1964   "Social change in an Indian village." Pp. 324–333 in A. Etzioni & E. Etzioni (eds.), *Social Change: Sources, Patterns, and Consequences.* New York: Basic Books.

Marsh, R. M.
1967   *Comparative Sociology.* New York: Harcourt, Brace and Co.

Marshall, H.
1979   "White movement to the suburbs." *American Sociological Review* 44 (December): 975–994.

Martin, W.
1956   "The Structuring of Social Relationships Engendered by Suburban Residence." *American Sociological Review* 21 (August): 446–452.

Mead, G. H.
1934   *Mind, Self and Society.* Chicago: University of Chicago Press.

Merton, R. K.
1957   *Social Theory and Social Structure.* New York: The Free Press of Glencoe.

Miller, D. R., & G. Swanson
1960   *The Changing of American Parents: A Study in the Detroit Area.* New York: Holt, Rinehart and Winston.

Miller, F. C.
    1973   *Old Villages and a New Town: Industrialization in Mexico.* Menlo Park, Calif.: Cummings Publishing Co.

Miller, J., K. M. Slomczynski, & R. V. Schoenberg
    1981   "Assessing comparability of measurement in cross-national research: Authoritarian-conservatism in different sociocultural settings." *Social Psychological Quarterly* 44: 178–191.

Miller, S. M., & F. Riessman
    1964   "The Working-Class Sub-Culture. A new view." Pp. 24–36 in A. B. Shostak & William Comberg (eds.), *Blue Collar World.* Englewood Cliffs, N. J.: Prentice Hall.

Mortimer, J. T.
    1976   "Social Class work and family: Some implications of the fathers occupation for family relationships and sons' career decisions." *Journal of Marriage and the Family* 38 (May): 241–54.

Mortimer, J. T., & R. G. Simmons
    1978   "Adult socialization." *Annual Review of Sociology* 4: 421–454.

Mowrer, E. R.
    1958   "The family in suburbia." Pp. 147–164 in W. M. Dobriner (ed.), *The Suburban Community.* New York: Putnam's.

Naegele, K. D.
    1961   "Social Change: Introduction." Pp. 1207–1222 in T. Parsons, E. Shils, K. D. Naegele, & J. R. Pitts (eds.), *Theories of Society.* New York: The Free Press.

Nagel, J. S.
    1978   "Mexico's population policy turnaround." *Population Bulletin* Publication of Population Reference Bureau: 33 (5) (December).

Nash, M.
    1967   "The social context of economic choice." Pp. 524–538 in G. Dalton (ed.), *Tribal and Peasant Economies.* New York: The Natural History Press.

Nelson, C.
    1971   *The Waiting Village: Social Change in Rural Mexico.* Boston: Little, Brown and Co.

Newell, A., & H. A. Simon
    1972   *Human Problem Solving.* Englewood Cliffs, N. J.: Prentice-Hall.

Nunnally, J. C.
    1967   *Psychometric Theory.* New York: McGraw-Hill.

Oakley, A.
    1974   *The Sociology of Housework.* New York: Pantheon Books.

Ogburn, W. F., & M. F. Nimkoff
    1965   *Technology and the Changing Family.* Boston: Houghton–Mifflin.

Olsen, M. E.
    1978   *The Process of Social Organization.* Second ed. New York: Holt, Rinehart and Winston.

Oosterbaan–Bulbulian, C.
    1975   "Causal attributions for success and failure performance outcomes received by self and others: An application of the attribution model of achievement behavior to group problem solving in mixed sex groups." Department of Sociology, University of Minnesota, Minneapolis.

Orne, M. T.
    1962   "On the social psychology of the psychological experiment." *American Psychologist* 17: 776–783.

Ornstein, M. D.
 1976   *Entry into the American Labor Force*. New York: Academic Press.
Parnes, H. S., R. C. Miljus, R. S. Spitz, & Associates
 1970   *Career Thresholds: A Longitudinal Study of the Educational and Labor Market Experience of Male Youth* (Vol. 1). Columbus: The Ohio State University Center for Human Resource Research. Washington, D.C.: U.S. Department of Labor.
Parsons, T., & R. F. Bales
 1955   *Family, Socialization and Interaction Process*. Glencoe, Ill.: The Free Press.
Paz, O.
 1961   *The Labyrinth of Solitude: Life and Thought in Mexico*. New York: Grove Press.
Pearlin, L. I.
 1971   *Class, Context and Family Relations*. Boston: Little, Brown & Co.
Pearlin, L. I., & M. L. Kohn
 1966   "Social class, occupation and parental values: A cross-national study." *American Sociological Review* 31: 466–479.
Piker, J.
 1968   *Entry into the Labor Force; A Survey of Literature on the Experiences of Negro and White Youths*. Ann Arbor: Institute of Labor and Industrial Relations.
Pi–Sunyer, O.
 1972   *ZAMORA: Change and Continuity in a Mexican Town*. New York: Holt, Rinehart and Winston.
Pitts, J. R.
 1961   "Introduction, Part III." Pp. 683–716 in T. Parsons, E. Shills, K. O. Naegele, & Jesse R. Pitts (eds.), *Theories of Society*. Glencoe, Ill.: The Free Press.
Popper, K. R.
 1959   *The Logic of Scientific Discovery*. New York: Basic Books.
Portes, A.
 1976   "On the sociology of national development: Theories and issues." *American Journal of Sociology* 82 (1, July): 55–85.
Portes, A., & J. Walton
 1976   *Urban Latin America*. Austin: University of Texas Press.
Poulantzas, N.
 1969   "The problem of the capitalist state." *New Left Review* 58: 67–78.
Przeworski, A., & H. Teune
 1970   *The Logic of Comparative Social Inquiry*. New York: John Wiley and Sons.
Rainwater, L.
 1966   "The crucible of identity." *Daedalus* 95: 172–216.
Rainwater, L., R. P. Coleman, & G. Handel
 1962   *Workingsman's Wife*. New York: McFadden–Bartell Corp.
Reiss, D.
 1971a   "Varieties of consensual experience I: A theory for relating family interaction to individual thinking." *Family Process* 10: 1–28.
 1971b   "Varieties of consensual experience II: Dimensions of a family's experience of its environment." *Family Process* 10: 28–35.
 1971c   "Varieties of consensual experience III: Contrasts between families of normals, delinquents, and schizophrenics." *Journal of Nervous and Mental Disease* 152: 73–95.
Reiss, I.
 1960   *Pre-Marital Sexual Standards in America*. New York: The Free Press.
 1980   *The Family System in America*. New York: Holt, Rinehart and Winston.

Reissman, L.
  1959   *Class in American Society.* New York: The Free Press of Glencoe.
Rheingold, H. L.
  1969   "The social and socializing infant." Pp. 779–790 in D. A. Goslin (ed.), *Handbook of Socialization Theory.* Chicago: Rand McNally.
Robinson, J. P., P. E. Converse, & A. Szalai
  1972   "Everyday life in twelve countries." In A. Szalai (ed.), *The Use of Time.* The Hague: Mouton.
Rodman, H.
  1963   "The lower class value stretch." *Social Forces* 42 (December): 205–215.
Rodman, H., & P. Voyandoff
  1969   "Social class and parents' aspirations for their children." *REINOV* 69 (8): 18.
Rogers, E. M.
  1969a   "Motivations, values, and attitudes of subsistence farmers: Toward a subculture of peasantry." Pp. 111–135 in E. Warton (ed.), *Subsistence Agriculture and Economic Development.* Chicago: Aldine Publishing Co.
  1969b   *Modernization among Peasants: The Impact of Communication.* New York: Holt, Rinehart and Winston.
Rogers, S. C.
  1975   "Female forms of power and the myth of male dominance: A model of female/male interaction in peasant society." *American Ethnologist* 2 (November): 727–756.
Rokeach, M.
  1973   *The Nature of Human Values.* New York: The Free Press.
Romanucci–Ross, L.
  1973   *Conflict, Violence, and Morality in a Mexican Village.* Palo Alto: Mayfield Publishing Co.
Ronen, S.
  1978   "Personal values: A basis for work motivation set and work attitude." *Organizational Behavior and Human Performance* 21 (1): 80–107.
Rosen, B. C.
  1959   "Race, ethnicity and the achievement syndrome." *American Sociological Review* 24: 47–60.
  1962   "Socialization and achievement motivation in Brazil." *American Sociological Review* 27: 612–624.
Rosenberg, M., & L. I. Pearlin
  1978   "Social class and self-esteem among children and adults." *American Journal of Sociology* 84: 53–77.
Rosenberg, M., & R. G. Simmons
  1972   *Black and White Self-Esteem: The Urban School Child.* Arnold and Caroline Rose Monograph Series, American Sociological Association.
Rosenfeld, H. L.
  1958   "Process of structural change within the Arab village extended family." *American Anthropologist* 60: 1127–1139.
Rosenthal, R.
  1966   *Experimenter effects in behavioral research.* New York: Appleton-Century-Crofts.
Sarnoff, I.
  1966   *Society with Fears.* New York: The Citadel Press.

Schatzman, L., & A. Strauss
    1955   "Social class and modes of communication." *American Journal of Sociology* 60: 329–338.
Schooler, C.
    1972   "Social antecedents of adult psychological functioning." *American Journal of Sociology* 78: 299–322.
Schroder, H. M., M. L. Driver, & S. Streufert
    1967   *Human Information Processing.* New York: Holt, Rinehart and Winston.
Schvaneveldt, J. D., & M. Ihinger
    1979   "Sibling relations within the family." Pp. 453–467 in W. Burr, R. Hill, F. I. Nye, & I. L. Reiss (eds.), *Contemporary Theories about the Family* (Vol. 1). New York: The Free Press.
Scott, J. F.
    1971   *Internalization of Norms.* Englewood Cliffs, N. J.: Prentice–Hall.
Scudder, D. F.
    1982   "Social change and the rationality of emergent social structures." Unpublished doctoral dissertation, Washington State University, Pullman.
Simmons, R. G., S. D. Klein, & R. L. Simmons
    1977   *Gift of Life: The Social and Psychological Impact of Organ Transplantation.* New York: John Wiley & Sons.
Simmons, R. G., F. Rosenberg, & M. Rosenberg
    1973   "Disturbance in the self-image at adolescence." *American Sociological Review* 38: 553–568.
Simon, H. A.
    1976   *Administrative Behavior: A Study of Decision-making Process in Administrative Organization.* New York: The Free Press.
Smelser, N. J.
    1964   "Toward a theory of modernization." Pp. 258–274 in A. Etzioni & E. Etzioni, (eds.), *Social Change.* New York: Basic Books.
    1966   "The modernization of social relationships." Pp. 110–121 in M. Weiner (ed.), *Modernization: The Dynamics of Growth.* New York: Basic Books.
    1968   *Essays in Sociological Explanation.* Englewood Cliffs, N. J.: Prentice–Hall.
Smith, D., & A. Inkeles
    1966   "The OM Scale: A comparative socio-psychological measure of individual modernity." *Sociometry* 29: 353–377.
Smith, M. B.
    1968   "Competence and socialization." Pp. 270–320 in J. A. Clausen (ed.), *Socialization and Society.* Boston: Little, Brown and Co.
Steiner, I. D.
    1972   *Group Process and Productivity.* New York: Academic Press.
Stern, C., & J. A. Kahl
    1968   "Stratification since the revolution." Pp. 5–30 in J. A. Kahl (ed.), *Comparative Perspectives on Stratification: Mexico, Great Britain, Japan.* Boston: Little, Brown and Co.
Stone, G. P.
    1962   "Appearance and the self." Pp. 86–118 in A. M. Rose (ed.) *Human Behavior and Social Processes.* Boston: Houghton Mifflin Co.
Strauss, A.
    1978   *Negotiations: Varieties, Contexts, Processes and Social Order.* San Francisco: Jossey–Bass.

Straus, M.
    1968   "Communication, creativity and problem solving ability of middle and working class families in three societies." *American Journal of Sociology* 73: 417–420.
    1969   "Phenomenal identity and conceptual equivalence of measurement in cross-national research." *Journal of Marriage and The Family* 31: 233–241.
    1972   "Family organization and problem solving ability in relation to societal modernization." *Journal of Comparative Family Studies* 3 (Spring): 70–83.

Straus, M., & I. Tallman
    1971   SIMFAM: A technique for observational measurement and experimental study of families." Pp. 381–433 in J. Aldous, T. Condon, R. Hill, M. Straus, & I. Tallman (eds.), *Family Problem Solving: A Symposium on Theoretical, Methodological, and Substantive Concerns.* Hinsdale, Ill.: The Dryden Press.

Strober, M. H.
    1976   "Women and men in the world of work: Present and future." Pp. 119–152 in L. Cater, A. Scott, & Mortyna (eds.), *Women and Men: Changing Roles.* New York: Aspen Institute of Humanistic Studies.

Strodtbeck, F. L.
    1958   "Family interaction, values, and achievement" Pp. 135–194 in D. C. McClelland, A. Baldwin, U. Bronfenbrenner, & F. L. Strodbeck (eds.), *Talent and Society.* New York: D. Van Nostrand Co. Inc.

Stryker, S.
    1979   "The profession: Comments from an interactionists perspective," *Sociological Focus* 12 (August): 175–186.
    1980   *Symbolic Interactionism.* Menlo Park, Calif.: The Benjamin/Cummings Publishing Co.

Stuckert, R. P.
    1963   "Occupational mobility and family relationships." *Social Forces* 41: 301–307.

Swanson, G.
    1974   "Family structure and the reflective intelligence of children." *Sociometry* 37 (December): 459–490.

Tallman, I.
    1967   "The balance principle and normative discrepancy." *Human Relations* 20: 341–355.
    1969   "Working class wives in suburbia: Fulfillment or crisis?" *Journal of Marriage and The Family* 33 (1): 65–72.
    1970   "The family as a small problem solving group." *Journal of Marriage and Family* 32 (1, February): 94–104.
    1971   "Family problem solving and social problems." Pp. 324–350 in J. Aldous, T. Condon, R. Hill, M. Straus, & I. Tallman (eds.), *Family Problem Solving.* Hinsdale, Ill.: Dryden.
    1972   "Social structure and socialization for change." Paper presented at theory workshop of National Council of Family Relations, Portland, Oregon.
    1976   *Passion, Action and Politics.* San Francisco: W. H. Freeman.

Tallman, I., & E. Brent
    1974   "A theory of family problem solving processes." Unpublished paper, University of Minnesota, Minneapolis.

Tallman, I., & M. Ihinger-Tallman
    1977   "A Theory of Socialization Processes." Paper presented at the Theory Workshop of the National Council on Family Relations Meetings. San Diego. (October).

1979   "Values, distributive justice and social change." *American Sociological Review* 44 (April): 216–235.

Tallman, I., D. Klein, R. Cohen, M. Ihinger, R. Marotz, P. Torsiello, & K. Troost
1974   A *Taxonomy of Group Problems: Implications for a Theory of Group Problem Solving.* Technical Report No. 73-1. Minnesota: Family Study Center Publication.

Tallman, I., & G. Miller
1974   "Class differences in family problem solving: The effects of verbal ability, hierarchical structure, and role expectations." *Sociometry* 37 (1): 13–37.

Tallman, I., & L. Wilson
1974   "Simulating social structures: The use of a simulation game in cross-national research." *Simulation and Games* 5 (June): 147–167.

Tallman, I., L. Wilson, & M. Straus
1974   "SIMCAR: A game simulation method for cross-national family research." *International Journal of Social Science Information* 13 (April): 121–144.

Taylor, D. W., P. C. Berry, & C. H. Block
1958   "Does group participation when using brainstorming facilitate or inhibit creative thinking?" *Administrative Science Quarterly* 3: 23–47.

TenHouten, W. D., T. J. Lei, F. Kendall, & C. W. Gordon
1971   "School ethnic composition, social contexts, and educational plans of Mexican–American and Anglo high school students." *American Journal of Sociology* 77 (July): 89–107.

Tharp, R. G.
1963   "Dimensions of marriage roles." *Marriage and Family Living* 25: 389–404.

Thomas, W. I., & F. Znaniecki
1918   *The Polish Peasant in Europe and America* (5 volumes). Boston: Houghton Mifflin.

Toffler, A.
1970   *Future Shock.* New York: Random House.

Turner, R. H.
1964   *The Social Context of Ambition.* San Francisco: Chandler.
1970   *Family Interaction.* New York: John Wiley and Sons.

Tversky, A., & D. Kahneman
1981   "The framing of decisions and the psychology of choice." *Science* 211: 453–458.

Vincent, C. E.
1966   "Family spongea: The adaptive function." *Journal of Marriage and The Family* 28: 29–36.

Wade, S., & W. Schramm
1969   "Mass media as sources of public affairs, science, and health knowledge." *Public Opinion Quarterly* 33: 197–209.

Walker, E. L., & R. W. Heyns
1962   *The Anatomy of Conformity.* Englewood Cliffs, N. J.: Prentice–Hall.

Wallerstein, I.
1974   *The Modern World-System—Capitalist Agriculture and the Origins of the European World Economy in the 16th Century.* New York: Academic Press.

Weber, M.
1976   [*The Protestant Edice and the Spirit of Capitalism*] (Talcott Parson, translator). Guildsford, Surrey: George Allen and Uncoin. Second Edition. (Originally published, 1930.)

Weick, K. E.
    1971   "Group processes, family processes and problem solving." Pp. 3–32 in J. Aldous, T. Condon, R. Hill, M. Straus, & I. Tallman (eds.), *Family Problem Solving: A Symposium on Theoretical, Methodological, and Substantive Concerns.* Hinsdale, Ill.: The Dryden Press.
Weiner, B., H. J. Heckhauser, W. Meyer, & R. Cook
    1972   "Causal assumptions and achievement behavior: A conceptual analysis of effort and reanalysis of focus of control." *Journal of Personality and Social Psychology* 21: 239–248.
Weiner, M.
    1966   "Introduction." Pp. 1–28 in M. Weiner (ed.), *Modernization: The Dynamics of Growth.* New York: Basic Books.
Wentworth, W. A.
    1980   *Context and Understanding: An Inquiry into Socialization Theory.* New York: Elsevier.
Whiting, B. B., & J. W. M. Whiting
    1971   "Task assignment and personality: A consideration of the effect of herding on personality." Pp. 33–44 in W. W. Lambert & R. Weisbrod (eds.), *Comparative Perspectives on Social Psychology.* Boston: Little, Brown and Co.
Whyte, W. H.
    1957   *The Organization Man.* New York: Anchor Books.
Willensky, H.
    1964   "Mass society and mass culture: Interdependence and independence." *American Sociological Review* 29: 173–197.
Winch, R. F., & R. L. Blumberg
    1968   "Societal complexity and familial organization." Pp. 70–92 in R. F. Winch & L. W. Goodman (eds.), *Selected Studies in Marriage and the Family.* New York: Holt, Rinehart and Winston.
Wood, R. C.
    1958   *Suburbia.* Boston: Houghton Mifflin Co.
Wrong, D.
    1961   "The oversocialized conception of man in modern sociology." *American Sociological Review* 26 (February): 183–193.
Young, F. W., & R. C. Young
    1966   "Individual commitment to industrialization in rural Mexico." *American Journal of Sociology* 71: 373–383.
Young, M., & P. Wilmott
    1973   *The Symmetrical Family.* New York: Patheon Books.
Zamarono, I.
    1981   "Se alcanzaron las metas en domografia: VLP." *Excelsior* 17 (March). (Published in Mexico City.)
Zigler, E., & I. L. Child
    1973   *Socialization and Personality Development.* Reading, Mass.: Addison–Wesley Publishing Co.

Author Index

A

Aberle, D. F., 68, *297*
Adelson, J., 28, *301*
Aldous, J., 54, 57, *297*, *303*
Apter, D. E., 47, 48, 107, 131, 135, 205, *297*
Armer, M., 8, 10, 86, *297*
Aronfreed, J., 27, 44, *297*
Aronson, E., 61, *297*
Ashby, L., 2, *298*
Atkinson, J. W., 177, *306*

B

Bachrach, P., 34, *298*
Bacon, M., 50, 175, *298*
Bales, R. F., 22, *308*
Bandura, A., 12, 13, 27, 28, 29, 30, 31, 44, 189, *298*
Baratz, M. S., 34, *298*
Barry, H., III, 50, 175, *298*
Becker, H. S., 25, *298*
Bee, H. L., 43, *298*
Bell, D., 2, 10, 77, 211, 212, 213, *298*
Bell, R., 64, *298*
Bell, W., 206, *298*

Bensman, J., 46, 49, *298*
Berger, J., 34, *299*
Bernstein, B., 43, 68, *298*
Berry, P. C., 43, *312*
Blau, P. M., 29, 45, 46, 47, 193, *298*
Block, C. H., 43, *312*
Blood, M., 40, *298*
Blood, R. O., Jr., 40, 87, 167, 168, 170, 174, *298*, *299*
Blumberg, R. L., 63, *313*
Blumer, H., 13, *299*
Boll, E. S., 54, *299*
Boocock, S., 92, 200, *299*
Bossard, J., 54, *299*
Bossen, L., 170, *299*
Brent, E., 32, *311*
Brittain, C. V., 27, *299*
Bronfenbrenner, U., 15, 26, 30, 177, 179, 198, 211, *299*, *300*

C

Camilleri, S. F., 34, *299*
Campbell, A., 206, *299*
Campbell, E. Q., 21, 22, 27, 30, *299*

Campbell, J., 43, *301*
Carlsmith, J. M., 61, 297
Cartwright, D., 24, 299
Catton, W. R., Jr., 2, 213, 215, 299
Chase-Dunn, C., 8, *300*
Child, I. L., 26, 50, 175, *298, 313*
Clark, R. A., 177, *306*
Clausen, J. A., 23, *300*
Clement, N. C., 210, *300*
Cohen, B. P., 54, 56, *300*
Cohen, R. L., 192, *300*
Coleman, J., 8, 90, *300*
Coleman, R. P., 167, 173, *308*
Cone, C. A., 75, 84, 116, 204, *300*
Converse, P. E., 171, 206, 299, *309*
Cook, R., 61, *313*
Cooley, C. H., 9, *300*
Cornelius, W. A., 205, 210, *300*

D
Daly, H. E., 2, 213, *300*
D'Andrade, R. G., 50, *300*
Della Fave, L., 64, *300*
Devereux, E. C., Jr., 15, 177, *300*
Diaz, M. N., 72, 155, *300*
DiRenzo, G. J., 23, *301*
Doob, L. W., 73, *301*
Douvan, E., 28, *301*
Draper, P., 175, *301*
Driver, M. L., 41, 42, 69, 212, *310*
Duncan, O. D., 45, 46, 47, *298*
Dunnette, M. D., 43, *301*

E
Eisenstadt, S. N., 75, *301*
Ekeh, P., 18, *301*
Elder, G. H., Jr., 11, 12, 14, 15, 21, 22, 27, 28, 55, 65, 189, 205, *301*
Elu de Lenero, M. C., 117, 154, *301*
Emerson, R. M., 25, 169, *301*
Erasmus, C., 154, *301*
Erikson, E. H. , 11, 14, 22, 27, 28, *301*

F
Fagen, R., 154, *301*
Feld, S., 31, *302*
Feldman, A. S., 10, *301*
Firth, R., 72, 73, *301*

Flavell, J. H., 12, *302*
Foster, G. M., 47, 73, 114, 135, 155, 174, 182, *302*
Freedman, J. L., 48, *302*
Frey, F. W., 86, 87, *302*

G
Gallegos, A., 204, *302*
Gecas, V., 11, 22, 23, 27, 43, 44, *302*
Geer, B., 25, *298*
Gewirtz, J. L., 44, *302*
Goffman, E., 24, 182, *302*
Goldsen, R. K., 206, *302*
Gonzales-Casanova, P., 1, *302*
Goode, W. J., 12, 63, 154, 155, 162, *302*
Gordon, C. W., 25, 39, 65, *302, 312*
Gottlieb, D., 28, *302*
Green, L. C., 210, *300*
Gross, E., 169, *302*
Gurin, G., 31, *302*
Gurr, T., 39, *302*
Gusfield, J., 10, *303*
Gwartney, J. D., 39, *303*

H
Haavio-Mannila, E., 171, *303*
Hagen, E. E., 7, *303*
Haller, A. O., 64, *303*
Handel, G., 167, 173, *308*
Hannerz, U., 173, 184, *303*
Hareven, T. K., 163, 164, 167, *303*
Harter, S., 177, 182, *303*
Hawley, A. H., 46, *303*
Heath, A., 25, *303*
Heckhauser, H. J., 61, *313*
Hermann, C. F., 200, *303*
Hess, R. O., 43, *303*
Heyns, R. W., 177, *312*
Hill, R., 27, 32, 43, 54, 87, 192, 299, 303, *305*
Hoffman, L. R., 43, *303*
Hoffman, L. W., 206, 207, *303*
Hoffman, M. L., 206, 207, *303*
Hole, J., 155, 170, *303*
Hollingshead, A. B., 105, *304*
Homans, G., 19, *304*
Horner, M. S., 177, *304*
Horowitz, I. L., 10, 210, *304*
Hoselitz, B. F., 7, *304*

Hoyenga, K. B., 177, *304*
Hoyenga, K. T., 177, *304*
Hughes, E. C., 25, *298*
Hurn, C., 10, *301*
Hyman, H. H., 64, *304*

I

Ihinger-Tallman, M., 9, 19, 54, *304, 310, 312*
Illich, I., 213, *304*
Inhelder, B., 40, *304*
Inkeles, A., 7, 10, 22, 23, 73, 131, *304, 310*
Isaac, L., 8, *297*

J

Jaastad, K., 43, *301*
Janis, I. L., 34, *304*
Johnson, C. L., 172, *304*

K

Kahl, J. A , 1, 7, 10, 40, 131, 154, *304, 310*
Kahneman, D., 34, *312*
Keller, A., 204, *302*
Kelley, H. H., 36, 43, 190, *304*
Kendall, F., 65, *312*
Kerckhoff, A. C., 64, *304*
Klein, D. M., 32, 43, 192, *305*
Klein, S. D., 34, *310*
Kluckhohn, F., 89, 121, *305*
Kohn, M. L., 40, 64, 68, 131, 192, *305, 308*
Komarovsky, M., 167, 173, *305*
Kuhn, A., 49, *305*

L

Lasch, C., 185, 198, 213, *305*
Lee, G. R., 15, 50, 63, 163, 175, *305*
Lei, T. J., 65, *312*
Leik, R. K., 34, 147, *305*
Leñero Otero, L., 117, 154, *305*
Lerner, D., 48, *305*
Levine, E., 155, 170, *303*
Levy, M. J., Jr., 11, *305*
Lewin, K., 21, *305*
Lewis, O., 154, *305*
Liebow, E., 116, 173, 184, *305*
Lomnitz, L. A., 121, 135, 192, 204, *305*
Lowell, F. L., 177, *306*
Luria, A. R., 131, 192, *305*
Luten, D. B., 2, *305*

M

McClelland, D. C., 7, 10, 14, 40, 177, *306*
McCloskey, H. M., 31, *306*
Maccoby, M., 12, *306*
McGinn, N., 154, *306*
McKinley, D. G., 68, 167, *306*
Maier, N. R. F., 36, 43, 191, *303, 306*
Mann, L., 34, *304*
Marotz-Baden, R., 64, 90, 167, *306*
Marriott, M., 75, *306*
Marsh, R. M., 107, *306*
Marshall, H., 206, *306*
Martin, W., 206, *306*
Mead, G. H., 9, 40, *306*
Merton, R. K., 203, *306*
Meyer, W., 61, *313*
Miljus, R. C., 47, *308*
Miller, D. R., 68, *306*
Miller, F. C., 73, 75, 115, 135, 192, 204, *307*
Miller, G., 10, 43, 192, *312*
Miller, I. W., 64, *303*
Miller, J., 87, *307*
Miller, S M., 192, *307*
Mortimer, J. T., 23, 68, *307*
Mowrer, E. R., 206, *307*

N

Naegele, K. D., 68, 208, 297, *307*
Nagel, J. S., 204, *307*
Nash, M., 114, *307*
Nelson, 73, *307*
Newell, A., 35, 38, *307*
Nimkoff, M. F., 13, *307*
Nunnally, J. C., 203, *307*

O

Oakley, A., 171, *307*
Ogburn, W. F., 13, *307*
Olsen, M. E., 46, *307*
Oosterbaan-Bulbulian, C., 61, *307*
Orne, M. T., 191, *307*
Ornstein, M. D., 38, 47, *308*

P

Parnes, H. S., 47, *308*
Parsons, T., 22, *308*
Paz, O., 154, *308*
Pearlin, L. I., 31, 68, 177, *308, 309*
Pena, J. G., 204, *302*

Piaget, J., 40, *304*
Piker, J., 48, *308*
Pi-Sunyer, O., 72, 75, 107, *308*
Pitts, J. R., 23, *308*
Popper, K. R., 19, *308*
Portes, A., 8, 10, 116, *308*
Potter, J. M., 72, *300*
Poulantzas, N., 18, *308*
Przeworski, A., 87, *308*

R

Rainwater, L., 68, 167, 173, *308*
Ramsey, C., 28, *302*
Rheingold, H. L., 26, *308*
Reiss, D., 58, *308*
Reiss, I., 49, 155, 206, 207, *309*
Reissman, L., 89, *309*
Riessman, F., 192, *307*
Robinson, J. P., 171, *309*
Rodgers, W. L., 206, *299*
Rodman, H., 64, 173, *309*
Rogers, E. M., 12, 40, 48, 73, 114, 135, *309*
Rogers, S. C., 163, 170, *309*
Rokeach, M., 39, 64, 205, *309*
Romanucci-Ross, L., 157, 162, 173, *309*
Ronen, S., 65, *309*
Rosen, B. C., 64, 65, *309*
Rosenberg, B., 46, 49, 206, *298, 302*
Rosenberg, F., 31, *310*
Rosenberg, M., 31, 64, *309, 310*
Rosenfeld, H. L., 73, *309*
Rosenthal, R., 191, *309*

S

Sarnoff, I., 65, *309*
Schaar, J. H., 31, *306*
Schatzman, L., 48, *310*
Schnaiberg, A., 10, *297*
Schoenberg, R. V., 87, *307*
Schooler, C., 40, 131, 192, *305, 310*
Schramm, W., 48, 135, *312*
Schroder, H. M., 41, 42, 69, 212, *310*
Schvaneveldt, J. D., 54, *310*
Scott, J. F., 27, *310*
Scott, W. R., 193, *298*
Scudder, D. F., 17, 18, *310*
Sears, D. L., 48, *302*
Shipman, V., 43, *303*

Simmons, R. G., 23, 31, 34, 64, *307, 309, 310*
Simmons, R. L., 34, *310*
Simon, H. A., 34, 35, 38, *307, 310*
Slomczynski, K. M., 87, *307*
Smelser, N. J., 7, 47, *310*
Smith, D., 10, 73, *310*
Smith, M. B., 12, 28, 61, *310*
Solem, A. R., 36, *306*
Solis, J. A., 204, *302*
Spitz, R. S., 47, *308*
Stave, B., 2, *298*
Steiner, I. D., 36, *310*
Stern, C., 1, *310*
Stone, G. P., 24, *310*
Straus, M., 10, 32, 35, 36, 37, 43, 68, 73, 86, 87, 90, 191, *311, 312*
Strauss, A., 25, 48, 61, *298, 310*
Streufert, S., 41, 42, 69, 212, *310*
Strober, M. H., 167, 169, 170, 171, *311*
Strodtbeck, F. L., 64, 65, 68, 89, 121, *305, 311*
Stryker, S., 22, 24, 29, 30, 39, 44, *311*
Stuckert, R. P., 40, *311*
Suchman, E. A., 206, *302*
Suci, G. J., 15, 177, *300*
Swanson, G., 24, 29, 40, 68, *306, 311*
Szalai, A., 171, *309*

T

Tallman, I., 9, 10, 19, 32, 34, 35, 36, 37, 39, 42, 43, 58, 64, 90, 147, 167, 191, 192, 193, 200, 209, *305, 306, 311, 312*
Taylor, D. W., 43, *312*
TenHouten, W. D., 65, *312*
Teune, H., 87, *308*
Tharp, R. G., 89, *312*
Thibaut, J. W., 36, 43, 190, *304*
Thomas, W. I., 13, *312*
Toffler, A., 42, *312*
Toughy, W., 154, *301*
Turner, R. H., 28, 64, *312*
Tversky, A., 34, *312*

V

Veroff, J., 31, *302*
Vincent, C. E., 50, *312*
Voyandoff, P., 64, *309*

W

Wade, S., 48, 135, *312*
Walker, E. L., 177, *312*
Wallerstein, I., 7, *312*
Walton, J., 116, *308*
Weber, M., 8, 185, *312*
Weick, K. E., 57, *313*
Weiner, B., 61, *313*
Weiner, M., 7, *313*
Wentworth, W. A., 9, 22, 23, *313*
Whiting, B. B., 175, *313*
Whiting, J. W. M., 175, *313*
Whyte, W. H., 206, *313*
Willensky, H., 135, *313*
Williams, R. M., Jr., 206, *302*
Wilmott, P., 155, 167, *313*
Wilson, L., 32, 35, 36, 37, 43, 90, 191, 200, *312*

Winch, R. F., 63, *313*
Wolfe, D. M., 87, 167, 168, 170, 174, *299*
Wood, R. C., 206, *313*
Wrong, D., 8, 23, *313*

Y

Young, F. W., 73, *313*
Young, M., 155, 167, *313*
Young, R. C., 73, *313*

Z

Zamarono, I., 204, *313*
Zander, A., 24, *299*
Zigler, E., 26, *313*
Znaniecki, F., 13, *312*

Subject Index

A

Achievement motivation, study of, 14–15, 189

Adolescents, *see also* Children's game performance
  career planning by, 35–37, 62
  problem solving by, 11–12
  self-image of, 31

Age segregation, 198

Ascribed structure, 45

Aspirations, *see* Goals; Parental goals; Success goals

B

Barriers, defined, 32

C

Career planning
  game simulation of, *see* Game simulation (SIMCAR)
  information search in, 34, 36, 42–43
  parental goals in, 65–68
  problem-solving process in, 32–38, 60–61

Childlessness, 207

Children
  decision to have, 134t, 136–137, 139(fig.), 204, 206–207
  and family power structure, 118

Children of the Great Depression (Elder), 15, 189

Children's game performance
  on goals and strategies, 132–138
  in problem solving, 140–147, 150–151
  sex differences in, 140, 175–182, 183–184, 193–194
  under success-failure condition, 138–140, 175–178, 193–194

Church membership, of sample families, 147–148

Community structures, 46–49
  affluence effects of, 195–196
  characterized, 46
  child's game performance and, 132–140, 145–147
  family structure and, 117–119
  industrial, 76–77
  life goals and, 111–117, 188
  modernizing, 74–76
  parental goals and, 186–187
  parent–child relations and, 120–131
  postindustrial, 77
  preindustrial village, 72–74
  role differentiation and, 47–48
  and socialization, 48–49, 72–77

Conceptual equivalence, 86, 87
Cross-national research, problems of, 86–87
Cultural appropriateness, 86–87
Culture of Narcissim, The (Lasch), 185

D
Depression, coping behavior in, 15, 189
Distributive justice beliefs, measure of, 89

E
Efficacy expectations, 31
Egalitarianism, family, and problem-solving
     behavior, 43, 127, 130–131, 144,
     192–193
Expectancy of success, 61–62
Expectations, *see* Parental goals
Extended family, 163

F
Face validity, 200–203
Family(s), *see also* Parental goals;
          Parent–child relations
   achievement goals of, 65–67, 79t
   consensus, 57–58
   division of labor in, 163–167
   internal structure of, 49–50
      power distribution and, 117–119,
          127–131, 144, 156–162
         dependency relations in, 169–174
      social structure and, 68–70
   life course of, 49
   problem solving, *see* Problem-solving
          behavior
Family planning goals, 134t, 136–137,
     139(fig.), 204, 206–207
Fathers, *see* Family(s); Parental goals;
          Parent-child relations
Front-stage behavior, 182

G
Game simulation (SIMCAR), 16; *see also*
          Children's game performance
   construction of, 91–92
   data collection for, 99–102
   described, 92–95
   instructions and rules, 97–99
      Mexican version, 292–296
      United States version, 298–303
   Mexican versus North American approach
          to, 190–191

postsimulation interview and debriefing,
     99
principles of, 90–91
research design of, 99–104
social change in, 96
success-failure condition in, 96, 138–140,
     175–178, 193–194
validity of, 207–208
   face, 200–203
   predictive, 203–207
Goals, *see also* Parental goals; Success goals
   in career planning, 33
   community structure and, 111–117
      in child's game performance, 132–138,
          188
   defined, 32
   formation of, 38–40
   motivation and, 56–58, 59
Great depression, coping behavior in, 15, 189

H
Housework, 171, 175

I
Identification process, 27–29
Identity
   formation of, 23–24, 28
      social structure in, 29–31
   social aspects of, 24–25
   temporal quality of, 25
Industrial society
   sex-role differences in, 162–164
   socialization in, 76–77
Infants, socializing influence of, 26
Information access and processing
   in problem solving, 34, 40–43, 59–61
   social structure and, 66, 68–70
   sources in, 36
Information society, 212, 213
Instituto Mexicano de Estudios Sociales
          (IMES), 82, 83, 89, 100, 102n
Instrumental goals, 33
Interview, survey, 87–90, 100–102

J
Job requirements, 278

K
Kluckhohn-Strodtbeck time orientation
          scale, 89, 121

L

Labor, division of, 163–167
Learning, identificatory, 28–29
Life chances, 45–46
    optimism about, 120–123, 188
Life goals, 65–66, 79t, 111–117, 188,
        205–206
Life-style goals, 38–40
Likert scales, 89

M

Machismo tradition, 154, 174
Marriage goals, 134t, 136
Means, defined, 32
Mexican families
    child's performance, 132–138, 145–147
    coping strategies of, 197, 199
    division of labor in, 164–168
    game approach of, 190–191
    life goals of, 112–117, 188
    optimism of, 120–123, 188
    power distribution in, 117, 118, 119,
        130–131, 154, 155–162, 170, 171,
        173–174, 182–184
    sampling procedures for, 85
    staff relations with, 104
Mexico
    consumer spending in, 205
    family planning in, 204
    income distribution in, 1
    presimulation interviews in, 100, 102
    research setting in, 102, 104
    rural-urban migration in, 204–205
    sample characteristics in, 105–107
    site selection in, 82–84
    social change in, 209–211, 216
    women in, 154
Michoacán, Mexico, site selection of, 83–84
Minneapolis (Minn.), *see* Twin Cities;
        Twin Cities families
Modernity, personal qualities for, 10
Modernizing societies, socialization in,
        74–76
Mothers, *see* Family(s); Parental goals;
        Parent–child relations

N

Need affiliation, 40
Normlessness, 198
Nuclear family, 49

O

Occupation ranking, in survey interviews,
        88–89
Occupation selection, *see* Career planning
Opportunity structure, 45–46, 64–66
Outcome expectations, in problem-solving
        behavior, 189–190

P

Parental goals, 65–66, 79t
    community structure and, 123–127,
        186–187
    rank ordering of, 88–89
    sex differences in, 123, 128t–129t,
        157–159, 172
        game performance and, 177, 179,
        183–184, 188
Parent–child relations
    community structure and, 120–131, 199
    critique of, 198–199
    identification process in, 27–29
    social structure in, 68–69
    teaching-learning roles in, 26–27
Peasant social structure
    modernizing, 74–76
    preindustrial, 72–74
Post-Experimental Interview, 314
Postindustrial societies, 2, 77, 212, 213,
        214, 215
Power and support, observations of,
        306–307
Predictive validity, 203–207
Pre-Experimental Interview Schedule
    Mexican version, 254–276
    United States version, 238–253
Preindustrial society
    sex roles in, 163
    socialization in, 72–74
Problem, defined, 32
Problem-solving behavior
    anticipatory success or failure in, 61–62
    in career planning, 32–38, 60–61
    in child's game performance, 140–147,
        150–151
    cognitive flexibility and, 191–193
    community structure and, 145–157,
        150–151
    evaluating process in, 43
    goal formation in, 38–40
    group, 57

Problem-solving behavior (*cont.*)
information search and processing in,
34, 36, 40–43, 59–61
model for, 71–72
motivating factors in, 188–190
problem, definition in, 31–32, 56–59
sex differences in, 178–182
socialization in, 10, 11–12
within social structure, 63–71, 79t
success-failure condition and, 138–140,
193–194
Protestant Ethic and the Spirit of Capitalism,
The (Weber), 185
Public behavior, 182–183

R
Research, functions of, 203
Resource theory, 169
Robo ritual, 155
Role differentiation, 47–48

S
St. Paul (Minn.), *see* Twin Cities; Twin
Cities families
Sample
characteristics, 105–107
church membership, 147–148
income distribution, 148
selection, 85–86
Savings and spending patterns, 134t,
135–137, 205
Score board, 310–312
Self-concept, identity bonds and, 28
Self-efficacy, 189n
Sex differences
data comparisons on, 153
in division of labor, 164–168
in industrial society, 162–164
in parental goals, 123, 128t–129t,
157–159, 172
game performance and, 177, 179,
183–184, 188
power-dependency relations and, 169–174
in problem-solving behavior, 178–182
social structures and, 155–174
similarities in, 174–178
under success–failure conditions, 140,
175–178, 193–194
working wives and, 167–168
SIMCAR (SIMulation of CAReer patterns),
see Game simulation (SIMCAR)

Simulation games, *see* Game simulation
(SIMCAR)
Site selection, 82–85
Social change, *see also* Socialization for
social change study
cultural idealism on, 18
defined, 6–7
in game simulation, 96
indicators of, 39
individual perspective on, 18–19
materialist perspective on, 17–18
preparation for, 2–4
rapid, 2
socialization and, 8–9, 208–209
in Mexico, 209–211, 216
in United States, 211–217
theory development for, 7–8
Socialization
for achievement, 14–15
defined, 6, 9, 22–24, 25
elements of, 22, 23–24
identification and, 27–29
indicators of, 13–14
problem-solving behavior and, 10,
11–12, 56–72
process of, 25–27
social change impact of, 208–209
social context for, 11, 29–31, 43–44,
72–80
theory of, 9–10
Socialization for social change study
basic themes of, 6–13
exchange perspective of, 5–6, 195
findings of, *see specific subject*
goals of, 4–5
methodology of, 13–17, 81–82; *see also*
Game simulation (SIMCAR)
for cross-national research, 86–87
survey interview in, 87–90, 100–102
model in, 55–56
premises of, 53–54
research staff of, 102n, 104
with retrospective data, 14–15
sample characteristics, 105–107
church membership, 147–148
income distribution, 148
sampling procedures in, 85–86
scope of, 54–55
site selection in, 82–85
socialization theory in, 9–10
theory evaluation in, 187–196

Social mobility goals, 134t, 139–140, 204–206
Social structure, 63–64
  ascribed and opportunity, 45–46
  career planning within, 36–37
  community, *see* Community structures
  coping strategy and, 197–199
  defined, 44–45
  family structure and, 68–70
  in identity formation, 29–31
  information access and, 66
  parental goals and, 64–68
  sex differences and, 155–174
    similarities in, 174–178
  in socialization, 43–44
Spending and savings patterns, 175
Structural functionalism, on socialization, 22–23
Success–failure condition, in game simulation, 96, 138–140, 175–178, 193–194
Success goals
  expectancy factors in, 61–62
  social strata and, 64
  value hierarchy for, 64–65
Survey interview, 87–90, 100–102
Symbolic interactionism, on socialization, 22

T
Terminal goals, 33
Twin Cities
  presimulation interviews in, 101–102
  research setting in, 102, 104
  sample characteristics in, 105–107
  site selection of, 82, 84–85
Twin Cities families
  child's performance, 132–138, 145–147

  coping strategies of, 197–199
  division of labor in, 164–168
  game approach of, 190, 191
  life goals of, 112–117
  optimism of, 120–123, 188
  power distribution in, 117–119, 130–131, 156–162, 182–184
    dependency relations and, 170–172, 174
  sampling procedures for, 85–86

U
United States
  family planning in, 206–207
  life-goal rankings in, 205–206
  research site in, *see* Twin Cities; Twin Cities families
  sex-role differences in, 154–155
  social change in, 2, 211–217
Unplanned event cards
  child, 284–289
  family, 280–282

V
Values, preferential orderings of, 39–40

W
Wives, *see also* Family(s)
  beating, 174, 182–183
  role diversification, 47–48
  working, 167–168, 169–170, 171
Work ethic, 150, 185–186, 211, 216
Working wives, 167–168, 169–170, 171

Z
Zacapu (Mexico), *see also* Mexican families
  site selection, 83–84

QUANTITATIVE STUDIES IN SOCIAL RELATIONS
(Continued from page ii)

Ronald C. Kessler and David F. Greenberg, LINEAR PANEL ANALYSIS: Models of Quantitative Change

Ivar Berg (Ed.), SOCIOLOGICAL PERSPECTIVES ON LABOR MARKETS

James Alan Fox (Ed.), METHODS IN QUANTITATIVE CRIMINOLOGY

James Alan Fox (Ed.), MODELS IN QUANTITATIVE CRIMINOLOGY

Philip K. Robins, Robert G. Spiegelman, Samuel Weiner, and Joseph G. Bell (Eds.), A GUARANTEED ANNUAL INCOME: Evidence from a Social Experiment

Zev Klein and Yohanan Eshel, INTEGRATING JERUSALEM SCHOOLS

Juan E. Mezzich and Herbert Solomon, TAXONOMY AND BEHAVIORAL SCIENCE

Walter Williams, GOVERNMENT BY AGENCY: Lessons from the Social Program Grants-in-Aid Experience

Peter H. Rossi, Richard A. Berk, and Kenneth J. Lenihan, MONEY, WORK, AND CRIME: Experimental Evidence

Robert M. Groves and Robert L. Kahn, SURVEYS BY TELEPHONE: A National Comparison with Personal Interviews

N. Krishnan Namboodiri (Ed.), SURVEY SAMPLING AND MEASUREMENT

Beverly Duncan and Otis Dudley Duncan, SEX TYPING AND SOCIAL ROLES: A Research Report

Donald J. Treiman, OCCUPATIONAL PRESTIGE IN COMPARATIVE PERSPECTIVE

Samuel Leinhardt (Ed.), SOCIAL NETWORKS: A Developing Paradigm

Richard A. Berk, Harold Brackman, and Selma Lesser, A MEASURE OF JUSTICE: An Empirical Study of Changes in the California Penal Code, 1955–1971

Richard F. Curtis and Elton F. Jackson, INEQUALITY IN AMERICAN COMMUNITIES

Eric Hanushek and John Jackson, STATISTICAL METHODS FOR SOCIAL SCIENTISTS

Edward O. Laumann and Franz U. Pappi, NETWORKS OF COLLECTIVE ACTION: A Perspective on Community Influence Systems

Walter Williams and Richard F. Elmore, SOCIAL PROGRAM IMPLEMENTATION

Roland J. Liebert, DISINTEGRATION AND POLITICAL ACTION: The Changing Functions of City Governments in America

James D. Wright, THE DISSENT OF THE GOVERNED: Alienation and Democracy in America

Seymour Sudman, APPLIED SAMPLING

QUANTITATIVE STUDIES IN SOCIAL RELATIONS

Michael D. Ornstein, ENTRY INTO THE AMERICAN LABOR FORCE

Carl A. Bennett and Arthur A. Lumsdaine (Eds.), EVALUATION AND EXPERIMENT: *Some Critical Issues in Assessing Social Programs*

H. M. Blalock, A. Aganbegian, F. M. Borodkin, Raymond Boudon, and Vittorio Capecchi (Eds.), QUANTITATIVE SOCIOLOGY: *International Perspectives on Mathematical and Statistical Modeling*

N. J. Demerath, III, Otto Larsen, and Karl F. Schuessler (Eds.), SOCIAL POLICY AND SOCIOLOGY

Henry W. Riecken and Robert F. Boruch (Eds.), SOCIAL EXPERIMENTATION: *A Method for Planning and Evaluating Social Intervention*

Arthur S. Goldberger and Otis Dudley Duncan (Eds.), STRUCTURAL EQUATION MODELS IN THE SOCIAL SCIENCES

Robert B. Tapp, RELIGION AMONG THE UNITARIAN UNIVERSALISTS: *Converts in the Stepfathers' House*

Kent S. Miller and Ralph Mason Dreger (Eds.), COMPARATIVE STUDIES OF BLACKS AND WHITES IN THE UNITED STATES

Douglas T. Hall and Benjamin Schneider, ORGANIZATIONAL CLIMATES AND CAREERS: *The Work Lives of Priests*

Robert L. Crain and Carol S. Weisman, DISCRIMINATION, PERSONALITY, AND ACHIEVEMENT: *A Survey of Northern Blacks*

Roger N. Shepard, A. Kimball Romney, and Sara Beth Nerlove (Eds.), MULTIDIMENSIONAL SCALING: *Theory and Applications in the Behavioral Sciences*, Volume I – Theory; Volume II – Applications

Peter H. Rossi and Walter Williams (Eds.), EVALUATING SOCIAL PROGRAMS: *Theory, Practice, and Politics*

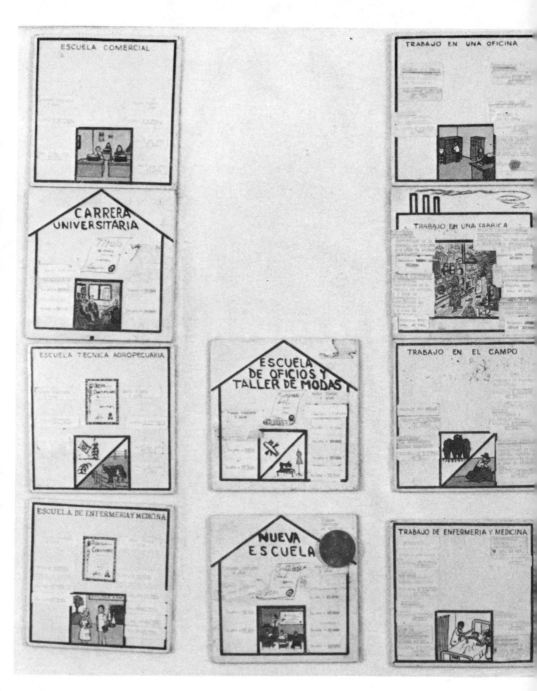

The Mexican Game Board.